"Call of the Pines" is well worth writing an old-fashioned book report on.... The story at times reads like a diary, making you feel privy with Henry and his thoughts.

Linda Blais, Lay Reader

This is well written – vivid... I was right there....
Scott. Ely, Professional Author

He (Reynolds) has his own unique way of reaching out to you from the pages of his penned words and touching all your emotions at one time.

J. Verner, Lay Reader

Reynolds continues his family saga in "CALL OF THE PINES," with adventures of his father's early years. This is the third in a wonderful series of full rich earthy stories of a South Georgia family. It reads like listening to your grandfather telling tales from a rocker on an old country porch.

Bill Jenkins, Professional Author & Bookseller

Books by William V. Reynolds

The Reynolds Family Saga:

River Pilot

Hard Times

Call of the Pines

For additional copies of *Call of the Pines* or other titles, please contact:

Double Eagle Enterprises, Inc.

735 Liberty Circle

Murphy, NC 28906

Phone: 828-494-BOOK

or visit our web site: www.doubleeagleenterprises.com

Copies may also be purchased through our distributor:

Book Masters, Inc.

2541 Ashland Road -- P.O. Box 2139

Mansfield, OH 44905

Sales: 800-247-6553

or visit www.atlasbooks.com

CALL OF THE PINES

CALL OF THE PINES

by

William V. Reynolds

Double Eagle Enterprises, Inc.

Murphy, NC

Author's Note

Although this book uses accounts given to the author about real people, it is a work of fiction. With the exception of the names of the immediate Reynolds family, Hester family, and certain public figures, all names are fictitious and should in no way be construed to be actual persons, living or dead.

* * *

Cover Painting by: Alice Mittelbach

Library of Congress Cataloging-in-Publication Data
ISBN: 0-9700320-2-1

Printed in the United States of America
Book Masters, Inc. Mansfield OH

Dedication

To my mother's memory with love.

Contents

.

I
The Farm and the Sawmill

"Henry!" George Reynolds called from the carriage loading zone of the sawmill.

Henry heard the call, but he didn't answer right away. He'd been assigned the job of firing the boiler. It was hot work, and Henry's clothes were soaked with sweat. He tossed the pine slab into the yawning mouth of the firebox before he answered his uncle.

"Comin', Uncle George," Henry called as he slammed the door of the firebox.

Henry was a tall, gangly lad of thirteen. He had reached most of his adult height, standing more than five and a half feet. He was so thin it looked as if his britches would fall off his hips at each step. His tall, thin looks would later earn him the nickname, "Slim," among his friends.

"Yes, sir. What you want?" Henry asked as he trotted up to George.

"I want you to take the truck and go get us another load of logs from the Wolf Pit."

"Yes, sir. You want me to go right now?"

George looked at the sun. It stood at its zenith, which indicated noon by sun time. "The time snuck up on me. Looks like it's dinner time. You can wait 'til after dinner, I reckon. But leave right after dinner. We'll need 'em by the middle of the evenin'."

George was referring to the noon meal. South Georgians ate breakfast, dinner, and supper. Daylight hours were broken into morning--before noon--and evening.

A hand signal caught the eye of the sawyer. George was calling a halt for the noon meal. Everybody usually went to the house for dinner except the boiler fireman. The boiler had to be kept hot to keep up a head of steam, so one person was elected to stay and fire the boiler until he was relieved for his meal. Alvin was the unfortunate fellow who had to wait for his food today.

"Alvin, you take first watch on the boiler. I'll send somebody to relieve you as soon as they finish eatin'," George ordered as the crew stopped work.

Alvin wasn't happy about the assignment, but he didn't say anything. His father had a way of giving an order that you simply did not question. "Okay, Pa," he complied.

Alvin watched as the rest of the crew made their way to the house. The crew consisted of family. Occasionally, neighbors were hired to help at the mill, but the family ran everything for the most part.

The house stood downhill from the sawmill slightly to the northeast. It had been built some seventeen years ago when George and Gussie married. They had thought it large enough when they had moved in, but they were wondering now that they had six children with one on the way. It consisted of a sitting room with adjoining bedrooms on the front. The kitchen had been built some thirty feet behind to avoid a kitchen fire setting the main part of the house on fire.

A thirty-foot, covered walk bridged the space between the two major parts of the structure. The well curb had been built so that you could stand on the walk and draw water with the rope and pulley. A wash bench beside the well held a couple of wash pans.

Annie Lee, Henry's cousin, who was just a year older than Henry, had drawn a bucket of water when he bounded up the steps onto the walk. She smiled at Henry before she said, "Hi, how's it goin'?"

Henry smiled back, "Just fine. How're you?"

Annie Lee was a tall, slender girl of fourteen. Her dark auburn hair fell well over her shoulders. Her brown eyes sparkled with mischief most of the time. She and Henry were fast friends in spite of the fact that Henry sometimes picked at her teasingly.

"You look hot and tired."

"I am. Can't wait to get some of that water."

"Here, take this," Annie Lee handed Henry the dipper with a fresh fill of water.

He took a long drink from it, handed the dipper back to her, and wiped his mouth on his shirt sleeve. There was a place near the elbow that wasn't wet with sweat. "Thanks," he grinned.

"Okay, boys, let's get a move on. I want to get back to work before the sun goes down!" George said with emphasis.

That was the signal to get moving. Everybody lined up at the two wash pans and soon their hands were peeling from the lye soap and cool water. When all had clean hands, they filed into the kitchen and took their places around the table.

Gussie, George's wife, who was great with child, stood near the table giving orders. She saw that everybody was seated before she spoke.

"Y'all bow your heads for the blessin'," she commanded. A quiet fell over the room like a wake. "Jack, would you like to say the blessing?"

Jack, who was only eight, said in his little boy's voice, "God is great. God is good. Let us thank him for our food. Ah-men."

Gussie looked over the table, "Y'all take out now. I hope there's enough for everybody. I declare it looks like I can't hardly fix enough vittles fer working men."

She really didn't have to worry. The table was spread with lots of farm fresh food. There were fresh black-eyed peas, fresh sliced tomatoes, corn on the cob, even some turnip greens. Two large platters of sweet smelling baked cornbread along with fried salt pork with a bit boiled in each of the vegetables for flavoring completed the meal.

Annie Lee and Sussie, her younger sister, had been busy most of the morning preparing the noon meal. Gussie had overseen it all. She wasn't able to do all the work--she was soon to deliver their seventh child--but she kept her finger on each and every chore that had to be done. As long as there was a child old enough to do it, it got done.

The food was passed around the table. Plates were heaped with generous portions. Everybody ate quietly. There wasn't much conversation. The objective was to get your stomach full as quickly as possible so you could rest a few minutes before you had to go back to work.

Henry was one of the first to finish. He pushed back his chair and said, "Excuse, me. I'll be goin' after that load of logs now, if it's okay."

George took the last bite of a piece of cornbread, "That's fine. Let me finish my drink, and I'll go with you just to check the truck. Need to be sure it's all right before you take off to the Wolf Pit."

Henry picked up his hat from the wash bench and waited for his uncle to catch up. George Reynolds stood more than six feet tall. He was a big man, but he wasn't fat. He carried his three hundred pounds as if it were much less. His shirts often split in the sleeves when his muscles bulged. Gussie was forever having to put splices in his shirts.

Henry's father had died seven years earlier. George had sort of taken Henry under his wing. Henry's mother, Eva, had her hands full with four young ones after Gus, Henry's daddy, died. George felt he could help Eva and be a father figure to Henry at the same time.

George and Henry walked step for step together to the shade tree where the Model-TT, two-ton truck sat. George checked the engine oil, the radiator, and kicked all the tires before he turned to Henry.

"Be sure you don't let this radiator run low on water. If the engine gets too hot, it'll burn it up. I can't afford to spend money on a new engine right now. You understand me?"

"Yes, sir. I'll be extra careful, Uncle George."

"See that you do. Climb up there and set the throttle. I'll give it a spin for you."

Henry climbed on the homemade seat of the truck. There was no cabin. The driver and his passengers were totally exposed to the elements. Ford built these trucks for custom use by their owners. That is, they built a chassis. The buyer built whatever body he wanted. This particular truck had been fitted with a wooden body about ten feet long. A wooden bench on the front served as a driver and passenger seat.

Directly over the rear single wheels of the truck, a bolster sat on a swivel that allowed it to swing some six to ten inches above the flat platform. A pole ran through the bolster to another bolster on a second set of wheels, forming a log trailer. Every thing was custom built. Each trucker had to design his own body and/or trailer. George had built this one for the express purpose of hauling logs.

George stepped to the front of the truck, inserted the crank, pulled it once, and stepped back. The engine spat, but refused to start. He repeated the operation. The engine spat, coughed, and skipped as it warmed up.

Electric starters were available at an added cost, but George didn't see the need for one. That was just another expense he could do without. George handed the crank to Henry.

"Stow it in the box under the seat."

Henry complied. The engine had begun to idle more smoothly now.

George waved Henry on, "Go ahead. Drive careful now. I'm countin' on you."

"I'll do it," Henry said as he engaged the clutch. The truck bucked a time or two before it smoothed out. Henry was on his way.

George stood and watched until Henry was out of sight across the branch. That boy was going to do all right. This was the first time he'd been off for a load by himself. That concerned George a little, but what the hell, he's got to learn sometime, George thought.

Henry drove in first gear for a while, then managed to shift to second. Soon he'd managed to get the truck in high gear. He could travel along pretty well as long as he could keep the wheels out of the sand beds. Most of the country roads were still three paths--one for the horse or mule, two for the wagon. There weren't any paved roads. The U. S. Highway Department, or whatever they called it, was grading the road about a mile away to pave it. At least that's what the mule drivers had told Henry earlier.

The truck bounced as Henry hit a hole in the road. There wasn't any water in the hole, but it pulled the front of the truck, and he almost lost control. He narrowly missed a pine sapling on the right. A yank on the wheel brought the vehicle back in line, but he'd over compensated. He had to correct his steering again. Finally, he was in control again.

It felt good to be on this errand alone. Ordinarily, he would have had either George or Alvin along. He wasn't quite sure why his Uncle George had picked him for the trip, but he was tickled pink to be going. It made him feel as if he was really becoming a man.

* * *

Henry pulled up to the entrance of the Wolf Pit. Earth had been hauled out to form the pit. It had been adapted as a logging brow. The logs were piled on the hillside so that they could be rolled onto the bed of a truck without using man or machine power. It was known as the Wolf Pit because it belonged to the

Wolf family.

Henry remembered one of the family, Bob, with some regret. Bob had taught school at Hamilton School. Henry was something of a slow learner--hardheaded--in Bob's words. Anyhow, Henry and Bob hadn't hit it off well. Bob had used his position as teacher to intimidate Henry, whipping him a number of times. Henry's rebellious spirit had rankled Bob so that the two became life long enemies. Henry was glad he didn't have to deal with Bob.

Henry had been here before, so he knew he would have to back the truck and trailer into the loading zone. There was one big problem. The pit lay on the other side of a small creek or branch as it was called locally. There was no way to pull the truck across the branch and turn it around. This made it necessary to back the rig some one hundred fifty feet.

Henry had done some backing, but he'd never had to back so far through such a small opening. Trees stood on each side of the road through the branch not more than nine feet apart. You didn't have much room for error with a seven-foot body to get through that opening.

Henry pulled the truck and trailer so that it was more or less in line with the road. He engaged the reverse gear and eased back toward his target. The first try backed the trailer into the tree on the left of the road. The Ford's four-cylinder engine died as the trailer came to rest against the tree.

Cursing under his breath, Henry jumped off the truck seat, retrieved the crank from under the seat, and waded through the gall-berry bushes to the front of the truck. He pushed the crank into its slot, gave it a pull, and stepped back. The warm engine rewarded him with a cough, then caught and began to idle.

Henry stowed the crank, mounted the seat, and tried again. Pulling forward, he managed to back again, but he hit the tree on the opposite side this time. However, he was able to keep from choking the engine down. He pulled forward again. What to do?

For some reason he couldn't get that damn trailer where it was supposed to go. He'd have to do something. Uncle George was expecting him back by the middle of the evening.

Henry studied his options. If he could see where he was going, it would be a lot easier to steer. That's what he needed--some way to see where he was going. There were no mirrors on a log truck. Mirrors were a luxury. Besides, they would have been knocked off easily, so why put them on?

While Henry was puzzling his dilemma, he had an idea. The firewall between the driver's seat and engine was flat--there was no windshield. What if he could sit on the firewall? Then, he could see where he was steering. But that led to another question. He could control the throttle--it was located on the steering column--but how could he engage the clutch? He considered the problem for a moment. Suddenly, he had an idea. If he could find a stick long enough to reach the clutch, he could release it with the stick.

Jumping off the truck seat, Henry ran into the branch. He ought to be able to find something here to meet his needs. There were usually broken pieces of wood of one kind or another in the branch. He found a small gum sapling about six feet long. It had been broken off for some time. Henry decided it wasn't too rotten to suit his purpose.

Climbing back aboard the truck, Henry mounted the firewall in front of the steering wheel, placed his stick on the clutch experimentally, and began trying his plan. Driving backward was a little awkward at first, but he soon had the hang of it. The trailer slipped through the opening leaving plenty of room on each side. Finally the truck was in position.

Now came the chore of loading the logs. Gravity did most of the work, but you had to be sure things were lined up right. Just one misstep could send a log off the opposite side of the trailer. Then you had to pull the log back up the hill. That required a cart and a team of either oxen or mules. The moral of the story--don't mess up.

Henry checked the stakes on the off side of the trailer. They seemed secure. He lowered the stakes on the loading side. Then the skids were positioned so that the logs rolled down them onto the trailer bed.

Retrieving the cant hook, a tool with a four-foot wooden handle and a curved hook, Henry went to the log pile. He sank the tooth of the cant hook into the butt of a log, exerted all his weight against it, and watched it roll onto the skids. The log rolled down the skids, bounced as it hit the trailer bolsters, and came to rest against the far side stakes.

That's good, Henry thought. Now if I can just get the rest to line up that good. He turned and rolled another log. The log loaded all right, but it was crooked against the first one. That would have to be straightened. It wouldn't do to let it lie like that. Henry went around the trailer, set his hook in the out-of-line end and twisted the log into place.

The loading took the better part of an hour. It had taken about an hour to make the trip--what with all the rough roads you couldn't average more than ten miles per hour. That gave him an hour or less to make the return trip. Henry began to worry. What would Uncle George say? Would he give him hell for taking so long?

Henry had no way of knowing, but George had allowed him plenty of time. George knew you learned best by experience. He wouldn't have been surprised if it had taken Henry all evening to do the job. He just wanted him to learn to handle responsibility.

When the load was on the truck, Henry pulled it out far enough to toss a chain across the logs. He then bound the load by pulling it together with a set of binders. This operation tightened the chain which fastened the logs to one another as well as the trailer.

Satisfied that his load was secure, Henry cranked the engine, mounted the truck, and proceeded to pull the load out of the pit.

The truck moved slowly under full throttle in first gear. The transmission and drive train made a grinding noise as the truck lumbered through the branch. The wheels cut deep ruts as they entered the soft sandy soil of the run. Water washed the wheels to near the hubs, but the open throttle gave the engine enough fuel to keep the truck moving.

The truck cleared the branch and moved on down the logging road. The ruts were so deep in some places that the differential housing scraped the soil and grass. The housing hit an occasional dirt bank plowing through it. Steam rose from the radiator. The engine was starting to heat up from the hard pull. Henry cut the throttle a little. He would try to keep it from overheating by cutting his speed slightly.

The truck continued to lumber along. Steam still rose from the radiator, but the pressure wasn't as high as it had been. Finally the logging road gave way to a better packed, more frequently traveled three path road. The ruts weren't so deep here. Henry thought he might be able to shift gears now. He tried it. The truck began to slow and almost choked down. That wouldn't do. He was going to have to give it more throttle.

There was a branch just ahead. Henry decided he'd better stop and refill the radiator. No telling how much water had boiled away in that long pull. Stopping the truck just short of the run of the branch, Henry jumped down with a coffee can in hand. He scooped up one can of water, then another, as he filled the radiator. There now, that ought to do it. He climbed back aboard, engaged the clutch, set the throttle, and eased the truck and trailer across the branch.

A truck driver has to become accustomed to his load. Every load pulls differently due to weight distribution or length. Your load is never neutral--it always pushes or holds you back. It, therefore, becomes the driver's task to learn each new load as he pulls it. Henry had soon gotten the feel of the load and was making good time.

As a young man of thirteen, Henry was beginning to mature physically. His voice had already changed, and his hormones were beginning to awaken his sexuality. Girls had become infinitely more interesting in the last year. His mind turned to them again as he drove along. He became so engrossed once that he almost hit a tree. Have to watch that, he thought.

But the thoughts wouldn't go away. He kept remembering that Saturday night at the dance. That Branch girl--what was her name? Sadie?--had let him feel her breast. Henry remembered thinking they were about the size of hen eggs. They felt kind of like soft-boiled eggs with the shells off, only they were warm. She let him have his way for a while, but she drew the line when he tried to feel her legs. He grinned. He could still feel the sting of her hand where she had slapped him across the face. Oh, well, there would be other girls and other times.

* * *

The hot summer days lingered. The crops had to be laid by. There was always mill work to be done. George had no lack of jobs. His neighbors knew they could depend on him. He delivered where so many others promised and failed. The result was a never-ending stream of orders for lumber or one kind of hauling job or another.

Henry was a beneficiary of this trust. He was kept busy plowing the fields behind one of George's mules, working at the sawmill, or hauling some load or other. It was good to have the work. He could make a few dollars to spend, and at the same time, send his mother something to help with expenses. He had five brothers and sisters now, and it seemed like there was never enough money to keep body and soul together.

Henry could have used some more schooling, but that was out of the question. School had been a nightmare for him. His teachers never seemed to understand that he had special learning problems. Even if they had, they had too many students to give him as much time as he needed. Miss Bessie was the only one who had been able to help him, but she had had to leave--to have a baby, he thought.

Anyway, he'd left school with a more or less third grade education. It was a handicap he would carry with him the rest of his life. It wasn't that he didn't have a good mind. He'd learned a great deal about mechanical things from his grandfather, Alonzo--better known to him as "Pappy."

Early on, Pappy had taught him to work on the farm implements. He remembered one time when he'd tried to fit a gear the wrong way. Pappy had smiled at him and said, "John,"--Pappy always called him, John--"that won't work."

Sure enough, no matter how he tried, he couldn't make the thing fit. Pappy had recognized his talent and helped him develop it. He was becoming more proficient with mechanics each day. It came in handy lots of times.

Henry often thought about his father. Gus had died in the spring of 1920. Henry hadn't been quite six years old. He had missed his father, although Gus hadn't been at home a lot. Gus worked the river piloting timber rafts. That kind of work kept him away from home, but he had spent as much time with his family as his work would allow. Henry remembered riding in the old Ford his father had bought. The way he remembered it, there was almost as much pushing as there was riding.

He wondered what life would have been like if his father had lived. His mother had married old man Liggit a couple of years after Gus died. Henry had never approved of the marriage, but nobody was interested in what he thought. The result had been a disaster as far as he could tell. His mother and the old man had fought over a number of things. They thought their fights were private for the most part, but Henry knew what was going on. He often thought things couldn't get any worse.

* * *

A year had passed since George first sent Henry off on his own to get the load of logs. Since that time, Henry had made several trips around the county hauling logs or farm commodities of one kind or another. George had come to rely on him as if he were a grown man, even though he was only fourteen.

The summer was upon them once more. Alvin and Henry had been sent to the fields to plow the crop. It would need one last cleaning before it began to pollinate. The two young men finished in a couple of days. Henry didn't mind plowing a mule, but he much preferred working at the mill or, even better, driving the truck.

George made his announcement that night. "Boys, get you a good night's rest. There'll be no juking t'night. We've got a big order for lumber. We're gonna need to saw and deliver thirty thousand board feet in the next two weeks."

Alvin and Henry had been planning to go to one of the nearby night spots, but George had put a cramp in that. No need to argue. Alvin, especially, was as scared of his father as if he'd been a rattlesnake. This fear might have been greatly responsible for the event that followed.

The next morning the family was up and busy before daylight. George sent Henry to start a fire in the mill boiler. Henry opened the firebox, stirred the coals that still glowed from the last fire, and tossed some kindling on the glowing coals. The fire started, and Henry fed the flames. Soon a roaring fire began to heat the water in the reservoir. Henry pumped water with the hand pump to fill the water tank.

As soon as the rest of the crew arrived, George gave orders. Everybody went to work. Alvin was assigned to the saw to begin. George had been training Henry to saw, but he was in a hurry to fill this order. He needed Alvin, who was more experienced, to do this job. The crew went to work.

A log was rolled on the carriage. The steam engine was engaged. Belts transferred the power to the saw and the carriage.

The carriage eased forward as the huge spinning saw ripped a bark slab from the log's side. A reversal of the carriage brought the log back to its starting position.

Alvin reached for his cant hook, gripped the log, and spun it ninety degrees positioning it to cut another slab. The saw tore through the log leaving a smooth cut. The pace was set. One by one, boards were sliced from the log. The stacker picked them up and carried them away.

The crew had been working steadily for about half the morning when a small problem developed. One of the belts had slipped. Alvin saw what was happening in time to disengage the saw.

George put the belt back in place, turned to Alvin, and said, "Start it up again."

Alvin complied. Just as the engine reached full power the belt flew off again. Have to cut the damn thing shorter, George thought to himself.

"Cut! Cut! Switch the damn thing off," George shouted at Alvin.

Alvin, who had started to make another cut, turned to look at his father. The noise was so loud he couldn't hear a word. As he turned, he lost his footing and fell. The spinning saw ripped into his left arm.

II
The Horse and his Rider

Blood spurted from the saw cut. The saw's teeth bit into the flesh sending pieces flying. Alvin was spattered by his own blood as the saw mangled his arm between the shoulder and elbow.

Everything seemed to be happening in slow motion. George saw Alvin fall. He couldn't believe his eyes. No one spoke. The huff of the steam engine and the sound of the ripping saw were the only audible sounds. Time stood still.

Suddenly, Alvin screamed in pain. He lay on the sawmill carriage. His mangled arm lay beside him, the fingers still twitching from the reaction of the severed nerves. His throat closed muffling his cries, then opened again as he screamed in pain.

"Oh, my God!" George shouted as he ran around the carriage to reach Alvin. A quick look at the arm told George that it was almost completely severed. Flesh on one side held it on.

"Somebody, get a blanket," George said as he pulled his shirt from his shoulders and wrapped the bleeding stump of the arm in the shirt.

Blood covered the shirt rapidly. Alvin was going into shock. His face was ashen. His breathing was too fast, and his blood pressure was dropping rapidly from loss of blood.

"Here! Here's the blanket, Uncle George," Henry said breathlessly. He had run all the way to the house and back in record time. He guessed his interest in physical activities at school had paid off. He was one of the fastest runners in the county.

"Spread the blanket out, son," George commanded as he lifted Alvin like a small child--although he was seventeen years old and weighed nearly two hundred pounds. George was careful to keep the mangled arm secure against Alvin's body.

George placed Alvin on the blanket and wrapped him carefully in it. "Go get the truck!" George commanded Henry.

Henry ran to the truck, grabbed the crank, inserted it in the slot, and pulled. The engine sprang to life. Henry looked around to see if there was anything else he needed to check.

"Pull the pin!" George shouted.

Henry jumped to the flatbed of the body, reached down, grabbed the ring on top of the bolster pin, and yanked with all his might. The pin was crooked. It wouldn't budge. Henry twisted it.

"Somebody hand me a crowbar or a cant hook!" He shouted.

A cant hook was in his hand momentarily. He inserted the hook through the ring and snapped the handle so that the pin flew out.

"Pull the truck out! Just let the trailer drop!" George shouted.

Henry did as he was told. The pole hit the ground as the truck leaped from under it. Henry brought the truck alongside as George picked Alvin up and mounted the truck from the right with a bound.

"Keep movin'. Don't stop for hell or high water!" George shouted as he hit the seat.

Henry drove as if the devil himself was after him. He splashed through the branch on his way to the main road to town. Sandy ruts made the narrow wheels of the Ford truck hard to hold. There was a lot of weave in Henry's driving, but George didn't say a word. Henry hit a long mud hole. Water sprayed all over the truck and its passengers.

They reached the graded road in two minutes or less. George

held Alvin close to himself. Under his breath, he was either praying or cussing--it would have been difficult to tell.

Henry swung onto the graded road. He had the throttle on the truck wide open. The Ford Model TT was designed as a work truck so its top speed wasn't that fast. Twenty-five miles per hour was about the best Henry could do. They met one or two cars and another truck on the five-mile run into town.

As they approached the edge of town, George spoke for the first time in a very long time. "Turn left at the next intersection. We'll take him to Dr. Comas."

Henry swung the wheel. The truck slid sideways as he made the turn. Another right turn brought them to the Doctor's home.

George was off the truck before it stopped. He ran as fast as he could go, with Alvin nestled in his arms. Mrs. Comas had spied them through the window. She had the door open as George bore his bloody burden into the front room of the house.

"Put him right over here," Mrs. Comas said pointing to the office door.

George laid Alvin on the table in the middle of the room. "Where's Doc?" He asked.

"He'll be back in just a minute. Went to check something in his drug inventory," Mrs. Comas answered.

* * *

Henry sat with his head in his hands. George sat on a chair across the room. His bloody clothes testified to the fact that he'd been involved in some brutal accident. His face was drawn. He had finally caught his breath. The shock had begun to catch up with him.

The door to the office was closed. There weren't any sounds coming from there right now. The last few hours had been harrowing as Alvin lay between life and death. Dr. Comas had administered morphine for pain. That had quieted the patient. Dr. Comas had then proceeded to amputate the arm at the shoulder.

He had cauterized the wound. That might have seemed extreme, but he knew the wound would heal better without the risk of infection.

There was just one problem. Alvin's vital signs weren't as good as they should have been. His blood pressure was too low. He'd lost a great deal of blood. Something had to be done.

The door opened, and the Doctor stepped out. George was on his feet immediately. "How is he, Doc?" George asked as calmly as he could.

"He's not doing well. He's lost a lot of blood. I hate to tell you this, but I'm afraid he'll die if we don't give him blood."

"How's that? What can I do?"

Dr. Comas frowned, "There's a procedure called transfusion . . . ."

"What do I have to do? I'll do anything. Just don't let him die." George interrupted.

"As I was saying, we can give him a blood transfusion, but we'll need the right donor."

"I'll give it. What do I have to do?"

"I must warn you," Dr. Comas paused, "it's risky."

"How risky?"

"Well, the donor has to have the same type blood as the receiver. What's your blood type?"

"Damned if I know. Why does that matter?"

"It might kill him if the blood types don't match."

George sobered, "What are we waiting for? Somebody in the family has to have the same kind of blood. I'll get the donor. You just tell me what you need."

"Why don't I type yours and Alvin's blood? I'll check it against Alvin's. That way I can be sure if they match."

"What if they don't match?"

"Then we'll have to find another donor."

"What about Henry's blood? Could you use it?"

Dr. Comas looked at the thin fourteen-year-old. "I could if

I had to, but maybe it won't be necessary. He's awfully thin to be giving blood."

"I'll do it, if it'll help," Henry volunteered.

"We'll cross that bridge when we get to it," Dr. Comas answered. He turned and walked back into his office. A small scalpel and a slide served his purpose.

"Come on in here," Dr. Comas said as he motioned to George.

George sat in the indicated chair. "Give me your finger," Dr. Comas said reaching for his hand.

George raised his hand for Dr. Comas. The Doctor pricked the finger and squeezed it enough to force a drop of blood onto the slide. George watched as he placed the open-faced slide on the platform of his microscope.

Turning to Alvin, the Doctor took a similar sample. Then he mixed the two drops of blood on a single slide. He peered through the microscope. His head shook a bit unsteadily as he concentrated on the view.

Finally, Dr. Comas lifted his head, sighed with satisfaction, and spoke. "It's a match. We can get started anytime you're ready."

The news delighted George, but he couldn't help being curious. How did Doc know they were a match? George said, "Pardon, Doc. But how do you know it matches?"

Dr. Comas smiled. He was accustomed to some people asking him questions, but the queries usually weren't technical. It was good to have somebody ask that type question. "The cells of the two blood types would have clumped together, if they had been unlike. They didn't clump. You want to see for yourself?"

"No. That's all right. I'll take your word for it. Let's get started. What do I do?"

"First," Doc said, "let's move this table over."

The two men placed the table next to the one Alvin lay on. Dr. Comas looked at the height of the table. It was too low. He pointed to the door that lead to the outdoors.

"There's some blocks out there. Would you mind bringing them in? We've got to raise this table at least six inches."

Henry, who had been standing at the inner office door, caught George's eye. He followed George outside. They found the wooden blocks near the door. The blocks were placed under the table legs. Doc checked the height. It was satisfactory.

"Climb up on this table. Be careful. It'll be a bit shaky, but that's the best I can do on short notice."

George mounted the table carefully.

"Lie down now. Put your head the same direction as his," Doc nodded toward Alvin.

Retrieving some tubing and other supplies, Doc returned to the table. He began to work, attaching one end of the tube to Alvin's arm. He talked as he worked.

"Let me explain what I'm doing . . ."

George nodded as if to say, "I'm listening."

". . . I'm doing what's known as a direct transfusion. Because the situation is so urgent, we'll save time, and we won't have to sterilize containers and such. Runs less risk of infection, too. I'll keep an eye on both of you. On Alvin, to be sure he's getting enough blood, and you so that I can be sure you're not losing too much."

The connection to Alvin's arm was complete. Doc turned to George and carried out a similar procedure.

"There, now. We can start," Doc said removing the clothes pin that had held the tubing closed.

Doc touched the tubing experimentally. The blood flow seemed to start all right. George's heart beat was far stronger than Alvin's. That, together with the gravity flow should deliver the blood to Alvin fast enough.

The vigil continued through breath-holding minutes. Slowly, Alvin's face began to show more color. Doc glanced at George. He seemed to be all right. A quick check of George's pulse told

Doc that his heart was still strong.

Henry stood by, shuffling on his feet. It was a helpless feeling. There was nothing he could do, but watch. What if Alvin died? Worse. What if Uncle George died, too? This transfusion thing was new to him. He'd heard about it before. Most of the old folks said it was a death warrant. The way they remembered it, everybody whom they'd known, who had it done, had died. The thought made chills run up and down Henry's spine.

Doc checked Alvin, then George. "That's enough," he concluded disconnecting the tube. Turning to George, he asked, "How you feeling?"

George opened his eyes. He had almost fallen asleep during the procedure. "I'm okay."

"I want you to sit up now. Easy."

George pushed himself erect on the table, swung his feet over the side, and sat there. The room slowly spun in front of his eyes.

"Dizzy?" Doc asked.

"Uh, huh."

"Take it slow. Don't move. You'll be all right. Just have to get your balance. It took a lot of blood to bring color to that young man's cheeks."

George moved slightly. He was still dizzy.

"Here, let us help you," Doc said motioning to Henry to catch George's other arm. Together they lowered him into a straight chair.

Doc checked his pulse, "How's that?"

"That's pretty good."

Doc glanced up to see his wife standing in the doorway, "Gladys, would you bring Mr. Reynolds a glass of milk and something sweet."

"That's not necessary," George managed to say, as Mrs. Comas disappeared.

"Nonsense, man. You've just done two, maybe three days work. You need some nourishment."

Mrs. Comas returned with the food and drink, momentarily. George accepted the offering.

Henry stood by watching. Mrs. Comas turned to him, "Would you like a bite, young man?"

"No, ma'am. I'll be fine."

"Are you sure?"

Henry glanced at Doc. Doc gave him a wink that meant, why not?

"I reckon just a bite," Henry said.

The lady left to get more food and drink.

* * *

Gussie was frantic with worry. George, Alvin, and Henry had been gone for hours. She sat and wrung her hands for a minute or two, then jumped up to do something she had suddenly thought of. This waiting was killing her. Her nerves couldn't take much more of this. Somehow she had to get some word about her oldest son.

She had considered sending Annie Lee to Pappy's. Pappy would let her have his horse and wagon, or he would take her to town himself. Pappy hadn't been feeling well lately--his arthritis had been giving him more than the usual hard time--but he wouldn't let that stand in his way.

She was thinking about this again, but she realized it was getting too late. It would be dark before they could get there. Besides, George might have had to take Alvin to Jesup or even Savannah. There was no hospital in Baxley. Each doctor had his own private room or rooms, but most patients who needed a hospital were sent out of town.

The sun was dropping below the tops of the tall Georgia pines when Gussie heard the rattle of the truck. Henry drove into the yard. Gussie bounded down the steps to meet him. She was standing by the truck before Henry could dismount.

Gussie's anguished face had anticipation written all over it. She was hoping for the best, but prepared for the worst. "Alvin?"

She asked.

"He's okay. Least ways, Doc Comas says so."

"Did he have to . . . ?" Gussie couldn't say "amputate."

"Yes'em. He took his arm off at the shoulder."

"Oh, my God!"

"It weren't no use, Aunt Gussie. The saw cut it in two. Bone and all."

Gussie's face went white. Henry thought she was going to faint, but she held up. Under her breath, she kept repeating, "Oh, my God. Oh, my God . . . ."

* * *

Alvin wasn't out of the woods yet. He spent several days at Dr. Comas' hospital room. When he finally gained enough strength, he was sent home. Needless-to-say, Alvin's life changed significantly. He had to learn to compensate for his missing limb. Simple tasks like tying a shoe or lighting a match now became major undertakings. Slowly, he mastered many tasks, including driving the truck.

George seemed to feel a great burden of guilt over Alvin's accident. So much so that he often favored Alvin above Henry and his other children--at least it seemed that way to Henry and his cousins. For example, Alvin now made trips with the truck that Henry would have made earlier. True, Alvin couldn't plow a mule like he once had--it took two strong hands to hold a cultivator straight in a row--but the favoritism seemed too strong to Henry. This attitude may have laid the ground work for future trouble.

* * *

The fall of that year brought more trouble in Henry's family. His mother and stepfather separated after Kenny, his mother's brother, and Mr. Liggit had a fight. Mr. Liggit's friends, members of the Ku Klux Klan, went to Henry's home looking for Kenny. Eva stood them off, showing a courage and determination Henry had never seen in her before.

Eva sent Henry to fetch George the next day. George promised to find out who was behind the attack and deal with them.

George found Kenny in town and urged him to go home with him, assuring Kenny he would be safe from the Klan. Kenny had accepted, giving George several days' work in the bargain.

The tire tracks of the Klan's car had been a dead give-a-way. All four was a different tread. George found out whose car it was. He was ready to confront him the next time they met.

The Model T Ford stopped on the street next to the Appling County courthouse. The driver got out of the seat with some trouble. George was standing on the courthouse square watching the man as he lumbered along the path to the courthouse.

"Mornin', Lem," George said, not unfriendly.

"Mornin'," Lem replied.

George fixed Lem with his gaze, "Understand you and some of your friends paid my sister-in-law a call the other night. That right?"

Lem swallowed hard, "Looka here, George. I ain't done nothin'. You can't go 'round accusin' folks o' things without proof."

"Proof? Hell, I've got all the proof I need. The tires on your car are just as plain as the egg on your face, you son-of-a-bitch!" George spat out the last words.

Lem's lower lip trembled. George knew it was him. It didn't matter a damn what he said. George was going to give him hell. Lem wasn't so brave without his hood, robe, and fellow Klansmen. Lem didn't say anything.

George continued, boring Lem's eyes with a stare. "I've got a flash for you and your buddies, Lem. That man you're looking for is at my house."

George paused for effect. "You boys are welcome to come and take him anytime you get ready."

Lem swallowed hard, twice.

George maintained his stance, "Just remember, y'all make damn good targets in them pretty white robes."

George walked off. Lem stared after George, his mouth hanging open.

The Klan decided the fight wasn't worth pursuing. George never heard another word, and the Klan never bothered Henry's family again.

* * *

The summer of 1929 came. Henry had more work than he could do. There were crops to plant at home and George had plenty of work for him, too. Farmers weren't making a lot on their crops, but times weren't as bad as they had been earlier in the decade.

One plus for some farmers was the growing of an old crop that had attracted new interest. In 1919 a farmer from Appling County had gone to North Carolina to study tobacco growing. The crop had become increasingly important. So much so, that new sales warehouses were built in Baxley about the middle of the decade.

Since George was involved in hauling farm products, the tobacco farming had provided him with additional work. He hauled for local farmers. Much of the product went to the new local warehouses, but some of it went out of town. Douglas, about forty-five miles southwest of Baxley, was a favorite market.

George picked up Henry one day, "I need him to help me with this load of tobacco," George explained to Eva.

Most of the day had been spent loading the trailer. George had rigged a body for his log trailer. It consisted of a board floor with sides attached. The body sat on the bolsters and could be removed for log hauling. It wasn't fancy, but it did the job.

The next day, George took Henry and Alvin with him to Douglas. The three farmers whose crop was on the load rode along, too. The tobacco was placed on the floor for the sale. It wouldn't sell until afternoon so the group hung around the warehouse waiting.

Finally, the sale was over. The farmers picked up their checks. They were well pleased. Their crop had brought almost a dollar a pound. Times were good. They could afford to splurge a little.

The thing that impressed Henry most was the new Model A's the farmers bought with their tobacco money. They rode home in style. Life sure was looking up for the folks in South Georgia.

* * *

October came. Henry and his family began to hear about the fall of something called "Wall Street." These unassuming folks knew little or nothing about finance, but they were to feel the pinch of this event for years to come. The nation's economy began a three-year collapse that would put millions out of work, and worse, in bread lines, as people began to feel the effect of what would become known as the Great Depression. This time would mold the life of all America, including Henry and his family.

The influence began to be felt almost immediately. Crop prices were among the first to fall. Goods sold for ten percent of their price just a year ago. Even farm jobs were not available. Farmers couldn't afford to pay anyone decent wages with the lower crop values.

Henry worked on the farm at home, of course, but there wasn't enough work to keep him occupied. George's business had fallen off so that he didn't need the workers he once had. When Henry could find work, the pay wasn't more than fifty cents a day--barely enough to buy grocery staples for his family.

That was one reason he took on the challenge when Weaver Long offered him ten dollars to break a wild horse he had bought. That ten dollars was like a month's pay on the farm or in the turpentine woods.

In addition to the money, Henry had become enthralled with

the movies. There was no sound yet and he didn't read very well, but he enjoyed watching the cowboy films. He usually found a nickel so he could go to the "show" on Saturdays. If Henry had been born in another time or another place, he would have been a cowboy--at least that's what he often told himself.

Mr. Long had given him a free hand with the horse. That is, he could come and go as he pleased.

"Just don't let 'im get out. Take yore own time and break him right. Start with the saddle if you like," Mr. Long had said.

Anytime he had an hour or so to spare, Henry went by to work with the horse. Henry made friends with the animal slowly. The horse was suspicious of any human. Henry worked over several weeks. Finally, Star--he had a beautiful white star between his eyes--would let Henry bridle him and lead him around the lot.

The saddle was another story. Henry tried several times, unsuccessfully, to get the saddle on the horse. After a number of failures, Henry decided to try just a blanket. Star turned around and pulled it off with his teeth repeatedly, but Henry kept putting it back on. Eventually, Star let it stay.

The day came when Henry tried the saddle. Star let him put it on this time. Henry hadn't fastened the cinch good before the horse was pitching wildly. Henry let him buck. Star finally decided he couldn't throw the saddle. He accepted it reluctantly.

Henry knew Star would have to become accustomed to more weight if Henry was ever going to ride him. A burlap bag partially filled with saw dust served the purpose. The weight was gradually increased until Henry thought the horse might be ready to ride.

The horse training had been in addition to other duties. It seemed Henry was always busy on the farm or working in the woods. Sometimes woods workers were given Saturday afternoons off, so they could buy their groceries. Henry usually took advantage of these times to go to town and see a movie or indulge in some other frivolous thing on the weekend. Today would be an exception. He needed that ten dollars. Mr. Long would only pay when the task was done.

Henry went to the Long home that afternoon. No one was home. They had probably gone to town to do their weekly shopping. Henry bridled and saddled Star. He walked him around the lot a couple of times.

The horse seemed to be content to let Henry lead him. Now's the time, Henry thought. If I'm ever going to ride him, it has to be now.

"Whoa, boy," Henry soothed the big animal with his voice. Henry pulled on the stirrup experimentally. Star didn't seem to notice. Henry placed his foot in the stirrup. When he pressed his weight on the stirrup, Star sidestepped slightly. Henry hopped on his right foot and swung into the saddle.

Star stood still for a brief moment. Henry held his breath. This was it. He'd committed himself. What was Star going to do?

Suddenly, Star put his head between his front feet and began bucking wildly. Henry stayed with him once around the lot, balancing himself with an outstretched hand like he'd seen the movie cowboys do it. On the second pass, Star stopped momentarily. Henry wasn't prepared for what followed. Star reared, plunged downward, and threw Henry toward the lot fence.

Henry's head hit a fence post. A knot on the post had punctured his skull. He lay still.

III
Duel with the Drug Demon

The Long family drove into the yard about five in the afternoon. They had been to Baxley for their weekly outing and shopping. Everybody piled out of the wagon as Weaver gave orders.

"You boys get that stuff in the house for your Ma. Pete, you put up the horse and wagon," he said as he handed the reins to his son.

The coker sack of groceries was lifted from the wagon bed. Herbert hefted it onto his shoulders as Pete led the horse toward the barn. The wagon was pulled under the shelter. The horse was unhitched and led to the main lot.

Pete was lifting the gate latch when he saw Henry lying still on the lot's floor. "Pa! Pa!" Pete called breathlessly, as he went bounding up the back steps into the house.

"What's wrong, son?" Weaver demanded!

Pete stopped to catch his breath. "It's Henry. He's lying in the lot. He ain't moving."

Weaver ran as fast as his legs could move. He approached the lot gate, threw it open, strode to Henry's side, and knelt beside him. A clot of blood had formed on the right front of Henry's skull. A trickle had run down his forehead and puddled beside his nose. His eyes were closed. Weaver was almost afraid to touch him. Weaver was sure that he must be dead.

Gingerly, Weaver touched Henry's wrist. He couldn't find

the pulse, but the body was still warm. If he was dead, he hadn't been that way for long. Weaver moved his finger slightly. There it was. He thought he could feel a faint pulse. Yes, there it was again. It was definitely a pulse.

"Pete!"

"Yes, sir!"

"Did you take the harness off the horse yet?"

"No, sir. Why?"

"Hitch the horse back up to the wagon."

"Yes, sir." Pete began to comply with his father's orders.

Weaver made his way into the house. "Dove, I'm gonna need a blanket and pillow."

His wife went to fetch the articles. Weaver shook his head and turned to Herbert. "Come help me get Henry in the wagon. We'll take him to his Ma's place."

* * *

Dr. Comas stood beside the bed examining Henry. The skull definitely had a fracture. The knot had broken the skull bone, pushing a fragment about the size of a half dollar into the skull. There were no other apparent injuries. All of his limbs seemed intact.

It was obvious to the doctor that an operation must be performed, but he was also aware that he didn't have the medical facilities or the expertise to do it. He was going to have to send Henry to a hospital somewhere. Even then, there wasn't much hope of recovery. His chances were somewhere between slim and none.

"What do you think, Doctor?" Eva asked, dreading the answer.

"Mrs. Liggit, I'll be honest with you. It don't look good."

"How bad is it?"

"He's got a hole in his skull. The brain has already started to swell. The pressure of the broken piece of skull on his brain may keep him in a coma for sometime."

"Can you remove it?"

"No, ma'am. That is, it can be removed, but I'd rather have a surgeon do it. I can do lots of things, but I'm not prepared for this kind of operation."

"Who can do it?"

Dr. Comas paused for a moment. It seemed like an eternity to Eva. "I'd like to send him to a surgeon in Savannah. He can do it. If he can't, he'll send him to somebody who can."

Eva looked worried. She could barely feed her family, let alone go to Savannah with Henry or pay for a major operation. How was she going to get Henry the help he needed? She thought.

"I don't know how I'll be able to do that," Eva said aloud.

Dr. Comas looked at Eva with compassion. "I understand," he sighed, "but he's going to die if he doesn't get proper treatment. I just can't do what needs to be done. I wish I could."

Eva looked thoughtful. "Maybe I could get my brother-in-law to help."

"Who's that?"

"George. George Reynolds. Henry works for George sometimes. I'm sure George would help us, if he knew."

"Would you like me to get in touch with him?"

"No, thank you. I'll send one of the young'uns for him."

"Don't take long. We don't have any time to spare."

Eva turned to leave the room, "Joe! Joe!" she called.

"C-comin', Ma," Joe answered.

* * *

The truck bounced over the rough road. Henry lay on a mattress with quilts and blanket covering him. He was still in a coma, so it would have been impossible to tell whether he felt any pain from the jolts. George was on his way to Savannah by way of Jesup, Doctortown, and Ludowici. He had just made the turn in Jesup.

George glanced back to check on his patient. He seemed to be resting peacefully. His eyes were closed. They remained that way most of the time. It was Sunday afternoon. A few stores were open in the small town, but most of them were dark and lifeless.

George looked down the road toward Doctortown. A cloud seemed to be building over the river. The new fill and bridge had been finished not too long ago. Up until just a few years ago he would have had to swing south to Doctortown to cross at the ferry. The new road was quite an improvement although it hadn't been paved.

The cloud continued to boil. The rain was going to catch them for sure, George thought. He needed to find a shelter before the rain came. It wouldn't do to let Henry get wet. There was enough trouble with him being injured, let alone getting sick from pneumonia.

A half mile or so down the road, George could see a building with a shelter on the front. As he drew nearer, it resolved itself into a small country store. The shelter provided just enough cover to get the truck under. George had barely stopped, when the rain came down in buckets. Good thing I stopped when I did, he thought.

The cloud rained itself out in a few minutes. George sat on the truck seat and waited patiently. There was nobody at the store, so he didn't have anybody to talk to. That was just as well. He needed to be on his way as soon as the rain slacked.

* * *

The hospital attendants lifted Henry from his bed on the truck. They took him to a small room, where they placed him on a stretcher. The doctor came, looked at him briefly, and turned to George. "You bring him in?"

"Yeah. Here, I've got some information for you from Dr.

Comas in Baxley."

The doctor grinned, "How is the old buzzard anyhow? I haven't seen him for sometime."

George reached into his coat pocket, "Doc? He's finer than frog hair. Just as mean and ornery as always."

"You sure we're talking about the same fellow?"

"I was just kiddin'. Yeah, Doc's fine."

George handed the handwritten notes to the Doctor. He looked them over before he said, "I see. How'd it happen?"

"Horse threw him as near as we can tell. Must have hit his head on a lot fence post?"

The Doctor examined Henry's skull. He pursed his lips and mumbled to himself.

"You think you can do the surgery?" George asked.

"Yeah, I can do it." Turning to the nurse, he said, "Let's get him upstairs. We'll need to operate as soon as possible."

* * *

George sat in the waiting room. It seemed like ages since he'd brought Henry in. He hadn't slept in several hours. The strain was beginning to show. He was nodding off in the chair when a nurse approached him.

"Would you like to lay down somewhere, Mr. Reynolds? I'll call you as soon as we know anything."

George considered the offer. It would be nice to put his head on a pillow, but a man of his height and size didn't just lay down anywhere. "That'd be real nice. You got someplace I could lay?"

"Yes, there's a couch in the solarium. It's right down the hall there," she said pointing to the room.

* * *

"Mr. Reynolds." George heard the voice as if in a dream. There it was again. "Mr. Reynolds, it's Dr. Swain. Can you hear me?"

George rolled over, sat up, and rubbed his eyes with the back of his hand. His eyes focused. There stood the doctor who had operated on Henry.

"How's Henry?" George managed to say.

"He's okay. He's still got a long way to go. But with proper care, he'll be all right. I've moved him to a room."

"Is he awake?"

"Yes. As soon as we were able to take the pressure off the brain, he woke up."

"That's good. Can I see him?"

"Yes. Now, remember, he's been through quite a lot. He may not recognize you at first. It takes a while for these things to clear up."

"I understand. Is there anything special I need to do?"

"No. Just humor him if he seems out of his head. He'll get over it soon enough."

"What about the pain? Is he in a lot of pain?"

"Yes, he's in quite a bit of pain. I've given him morphine for the pain. That's about the strongest thing I've got."

* * *

George eased into the room, his hat in his hand. The nurse stood by the bed tucking the covers in. She smiled at George as he stepped to the bedside. George looked at Henry. He lay on his back with a bandage wrapped around his head. His eyes were closed. George started to turn and leave, but he stopped in mid-step as the nurse spoke.

"He's not wide awake yet, but he can hear you, if you'd like to talk to him."

George smiled, "Thanks." He looked back at Henry, "Boy, how're you feeling?"

Henry didn't try to move, but he wet his lips before he responded, "Like I was kicked by a mule. Maybe run over by one of your trucks."

"You know who I am?"

Henry grinned weakly, "Yeah. I'd know your hide anywhere, Uncle George."

"That's good. Doc said you might be a little confused at first."

"Well, I ain't got it all figured yet. Where am I?"

"You're in Savannah in the hospital. Do you remember anything?"

"Nope."

"Did the horse throw you?"

"I reckon. I was sitting pretty for the first round or so."

The nurse looked at George, "You might want to take it easy now. Too much talk can wear him out."

George looked at Henry again. His eyes were closed. The drug was doing its thing. They could talk later. He moved away from the bed. The nurse turned to leave the room.

"Just have a seat. I'll be right back. The doctor wants me to keep an eye on him until he's wide awake."

George placed himself carefully on the chair. It didn't look as if it would hold his three hundred plus pounds.

* * *

Henry opened his eyes. They didn't focus well. He closed them again. When he reopened them, his vision was clearer. A vision of loveliness stood over him. He couldn't quite figure it out. She had on a nurse's uniform, but she was beautiful. Henry had always thought of nurses as old, ugly, and crabby. This one didn't fit any of those stereotypes.

She smiled at him, "How're you feeling?" She asked.

"Pretty good considerin' what I've been through, I reckon."

"I should think so. We weren't sure you were going to rejoin us for a while there."

Henry managed a weak grin, "Neither did I."

Henry grimaced. The nurse studied his face. "Are you

hurting?"

"Yeah, the pain's real bad. Could I have some medicine?"

"Let me check your chart. I'll be right back."

Henry raised his hands to his head. The bandage was still in place. He touched it gingerly. A sharp pain shot through his head. He was going to have to take it slow. The pain was still excruciating.

"Here," the nurse said as she placed the pill on Henry's lips, "take this." She turned and picked up the glass of water on the bedside stand.

Henry sipped from the glass taking just enough water to swallow the morphine tablet. "Thanks," he smiled. "That'll help."

The nurse looked at Henry. He looked back at her with probing eyes. She was young. Maybe just a little older than himself. Her dark hair was swept up in a knot at the back of her neck. The rest of her hair cascaded down her back. Her neck was thin. The muscles stood out when she turned her head. Henry thought she was very nice looking.

She smiled again. "I think you're doing much better."

"Yeah, I reckon you're right. When's the doctor comin'?"

"He'll be here later today. I'm leaving for now. I'll check back with you in a few minutes. Okay?"

Henry grinned at her, "Okay."

* * *

"Young man, how're you feeling?" Dr. Swain asked as he entered Henry's room.

"Not too bad. My head still hurts some, but I'm managing."

"That's good. How would you like to go home?"

"I'd love it. When can I go?"

"I think, most anytime."

"That's good, but I'm wondering about my pain."

Dr. Swain thought for a minute before he spoke. "The pain's likely to continue for sometime. You've had a serious injury.

Your brain had a piece of your skull pressed against it. To tell the truth, you're lucky to be alive."

"Just what did you do to me?"

"We removed the broken skull. Then we replaced the bone with a silver plate."

"How big?"

"Oh, about the size of a half dollar."

Henry thought about this revelation for a moment. "Then I'll have that plate the rest of my life?"

"That's right. Now, keep in mind, silver's not natural to the body, so it'll take time for you to get used to having it in your body."

"What am I going to do about the pain? Do I just suffer with it?"

"No. I'll give you a prescription for some morphine. You should be able to buy it at your local drug store."

Henry thought for a moment, "Thanks," he said.

* * *

Henry lay on his bed. He had been home for weeks now. It seemed more like a year. That's how time is when you don't have much to do. It seems a day, week, or month will never pass.

Henry couldn't read very well. His best efforts frustrated him. He would try to read a book or some pulp magazine, but it was always a lost cause. He had to spell each word before he could pronounce it. Silent reading was unthinkable.

On those occasions when he tried to stir from his bed, pain sent his head spinning. Sometimes a few steps made him so dizzy he had to stop and sit wherever he found himself. All the other family members were out in the field or gone to town or running whatever errands they needed to do. Not only did he feel the physical pain, he felt as if he wasn't making much contribution to his family. It seemed they didn't need him.

Things went all right until the morphine had started to run

out. Henry had searched every nook and cranny, all to no avail. He had taken all his medicine. There wasn't a single pill to be had. He finally decided to try other drugs he found. Aspirins were taken by the handful, all to no avail. Nothing relieved the pain.

At first, Henry was convinced that his pain was so great nothing would relieve it. It had not occurred to him that he might be addicted to the morphine. He seemed unaware that the problem was with the drug, rather than the pain.

Eva helped supply him with medicine. She wasn't familiar with drug addiction, so she tried to ease the pain the only way she knew. But she finally began to realize there was something wrong.

"Henry, we need to talk," she said one evening when she found herself alone with him.

"What about?"

"Your problem."

"My pain?"

"Yes."

"What about it?"

"I want you to see a doctor."

"I don't need to see a doctor. I just need my medicine."

"You've been taking your medicine for more than two months. The pain's still bothering you. Don't you think your head should be healing by now?"

"I don't know. Sometimes I think I'm better, then I start having pains again."

"That's what I mean. You should be healing. You're not."

"I still don't see why I need a doctor. All I need is my pain medicine."

Eva was silent for a long moment, "Henry, I know that you've been taking up all the aspirin in the house. I also know you've taken money from my purse. I assume it was to buy morphine. Is that right?"

Henry looked like a whipped puppy. His mother whipped him when he was a little boy. He couldn't remember how many times. But there were times when she said something that made those whippings feel like a pat on the back. He could deny her accusations, but he knew that she knew what was going on.

"Okay, Mama. I'll see the doctor."

* * *

Dr. Comas looked up from his desk. Henry sat across from him waiting to hear his verdict. The Doctor sighed before he spoke.

"Henry, I wish I could see inside your head. If I could, I'd be able to say for sure that you weren't healing. All the outward signs say you should be fine. I can understand an occasional swelling of the brain. We've known for sometime that the brain reacts to wet, humid weather. If that was the only time you had problems, it would make sense.

"I'm not sure why you are in pain. Maybe something's not working as it should. But, and I say this advisedly, you may have developed an addiction to the pain medicine. I would like for you to try and do without the morphine for a few days. That's the only way we're going to know whether it's the pain or the drug."

Henry looked at the Doctor. "I'm not sure I can, Doc. What if the pain gets too bad?"

"In that case, I'll see if I can give you a milder pain reliever."

Henry had gone for a day without the morphine. The withdrawal had put his entire body in agony. The next day he decided to try another doctor. His new doctor was not familiar with his entire case history. Henry told him just enough to make his case for the morphine. After several weeks, the second doctor began to suspect addiction. He refused additional medication.

Henry went from doctor to doctor in his continuing quest for the drug. Each doctor treated him for a while until it became clear Henry was an addict. Then the doctor refused to give him the medicine.

The local druggist had a good supply of morphine on hand. Henry knew it was possible to get the drug if the right person asked for it. He decided he would get the money from some source.

Henry went to work doing odd jobs. His strength was still not as good as it had been prior to his accident, but he managed to make a few dollars. To his credit, he had not yet resorted to stealing to support his habit, but every dime he could rake and scrape went for morphine.

He couldn't buy it himself, so he talked friends and acquaintances into getting it for him. Many of them were honest, returning any change he had coming, but others took advantage of his addiction to extort money from him. He didn't care as long as his habit was satisfied.

The addiction took its toll on Henry. His body had always been thin--probably because he had been so physically active. He was almost a skeleton now. His eyes had a hollow look, and he was so skinny, his bones showed in several places. His ribs were visible when he took off his shirt.

Food was of little or no interest to him. He ate as little as he could and still sustain life. Eva tried in vain to get food into him. He usually refused and went off to be by himself.

Not only did Henry avoid food, he separated himself from his friends. He had been a good mixer before his addiction. Most people seemed to like him. Now he became a recluse. Friends who had once sought him out for a good time, now distanced themselves from him. This act very likely made Henry feel less worthy, enhancing his withdrawal.

Even his friend, Bee, short for Benjamin Franklin Johnson, found it hard to relate to Henry. Bee was a likable young man, who lived across the woods from the Liggit place. He couldn't talk plain--he stuttered--but that didn't keep him from talking. You would have thought stuttering was a gift as far as Bee was concerned. He talked a blue streak, especially when he and Henry were alone.

"H-how ya f-feelin', Old Hoss?" Bee asked cheerfully.

It was a warm fall afternoon. Bee had wandered over the ridge through the woods to Henry's home. There was no hurry. The day was still young as far as Bee was concerned. He thought he'd visit Henry--you know, see how he was getting along. If he stayed long enough, Mrs. Liggit would ask him to stay for supper. There wasn't a better cook in the county than Henry's ma.

"Oh, pretty good, I reckon. How 'bout yourself?"

"C-can't complain, I r-reckon. Whatcha up to-to?"

"Nothing much. Just sittin' here soakin' up the fresh air."

Bee seated himself on the edge of the porch with his back against a post. "N-nice day, a-ain't it?"

Henry looked at Bee with a vacant stare. "I hadn't noticed, to tell you the truth."

Bee ran his hand through his sandy hair. This conversation was going nowhere fast. He'd have to do better than that if he was going to get anything out of Henry. "B-been g-galing lately?" Bee asked.

"Nope."

"I w-went over t' see that l-little trick l-lives down p-past the Veal place. Y-you know t-the one?"

Henry showed more interest. "I don't reckon I do. What's she look like?"

"Oh, she's g-got the pruttiest d-dark hair you m-most ever saw. And a f-figure, b-built like a b-brick outhouse. I t-tell you t-there ain't no f-finer tits on a cow t-than she's got."

Henry looked around. He was glad his Mama wasn't hearing this--at least he hoped she wasn't. He and his male friends talked about girls like that, but knew he'd catch it if Eva heard them.

"Keep it down, will you. If Mama hears that kind of talk, me and you'll both catch hell."

Bee grinned. He didn't mind too much. It would have been

worth it to get a rise out of Henry. That was the first time he'd shown any spunk since Bee had arrived.

Henry grinned, "Tell me more. What's her Pa like? He a hard case?"

* * *

A few days later, Henry went to town. He was sitting on the wagon seat waiting for his mother when he saw Bascomb Bayers come staggering out of the drug store. Bascomb was so drunk on paregoric that he couldn't walk straight. Henry watched him stumble off down the street.

Bascomb was a familiar sight on the streets of Baxley. He had once owned the local drug store. Then he had gotten hooked on narcotics. He had gone down hill from there. His drug addiction was now his main priority. He begged, borrowed, and stole to support his habit.

For some unknown reason a warning went off in Henry's mind. It seemed as if a voice spoke inside his head, "That's what you'll be like in a few years."

Henry pondered the thought for a few minutes before he said to himself, "No. I won't. I'm hooked, but I'm not going to stay that way."

IV
Lure of the Iron Road

The battle with morphine was far from over. Henry decided he needed to get back to work regularly, if he was to have any hope of winning his personal war with the drug. At first it seemed almost impossible to work. His strength had failed immensely since his accident and operation. He had to work for a few minutes, then pause to rest. It was hard, but Henry kept pushing himself. Each time he gained a little more strength.

The drug withdrawal was another story. He found himself craving the morphine constantly. Smoking had been a vice for Henry since he had turned nine years old. He had bought tobacco at that tender age by lying. He told people he was making the purchase for his father. He turned to the smoking habit as a substitute for his drug habit.

Even with the smoking, Henry craved the morphine. Day and night, he lived through hell, as he refused to satisfy his craving. Any substance was substituted for the drug. Rosin from tar faces in the turpentine woods, tree bark, and various and sundry leaves of plant were employed in an attempt to rid himself of the drug craving.

Slowly, but surely, Henry began to whip his craving. He still woke at night sweating from the withdrawal symptoms, but he didn't give in. Each time he thought he might succumb, he pictured Bascomb walking around in a drugged stupor. The vision always helped strengthen his resolve to kick his habit. After a matter of weeks, Henry was able to cease all of his substitutes except smoking. He hung to that one tenaciously. After all, smoking was socially acceptable. He could live with that.

During Henry's battle with drugs, he began to think about all the far away places he had never seen. The movies were enticing as they showed him pictures of places he thought he would never see. In addition, an occasional traveler would wander through Baxley telling of the exotic places he'd been.

Henry longed to travel--to see the world. He stood beside the railroad tracks in Baxley and tried to imagine what lay beyond the horizon. He had heard enough about the railroad to make it seem romantic. Swinging aboard one of those freights and riding west seemed the most wonderful thing he could imagine.

One Saturday afternoon, Henry and Bee came out of the movie house. The movie had been a western with lots of train action. They were still talking about it.

"Wouldn't it be great to ride one of them trains?" Henry asked.

"Y-yeah. A f-fellow could g-go all o-over the country o-on one of 'em," Bee answered.

They strolled around the corner of the building. A block away, the main line of the Southern Railroad ran east and west. The eastern end would take you to Surrency, Jesup, and finally to Brunswick. The western end was more fascinating. Hazlehurst, Lumber City, and Macon lay to the west. Henry's knowledge of geography was limited. He knew the plains of Texas lay in that direction, but he didn't know a lot about what lay in between. The more he thought about it, the more he knew he had to see for himself.

"Why don't we take a trip?" Henry asked Bee.

"Ya-ya mean now?"

"No, of course not. We'll have to make some plans. You know, get a little money and figure out what to take with us. Wouldn't it be a great adventure?"

Bee thought for a minute before he said, "I a-ain't too s-sure about t-that. W-what we g-gonna tell our f-folks?"

Henry grinned, "Tell 'em? Why, we won't tell 'em nothin' 'til we're back."

"I-I don't k-know. Are y-you sure a-about this?"

"Look here, Bee. Wouldn't you like to go off and see the country? Then, when we got back, we could tell tales about our travels. The trip would be interestin', but just think how you could perk up your stories. Why we'd be heroes if we did that."

"Yeah, may-maybe dead he-heroes."

Henry studied Bee's face for a moment, "Course, if you're afraid, I can get somebody else to do it."

That was a direct challenge to Bee's manhood. Henry knew he would have to put up or shut up. Bee screwed up his face before he answered, "I-I'll do 'er. D-damned if I'm go-gonna let you ca-call me a co-coward."

"We'll have to make our plans. First, let's decide when we're gonna leave. That'll give us something to work toward."

Bee nodded his head, "How-how 'bout a couple of we-weeks?"

"Yeah. Now we're gonna need some clothes. Just a changing mind you, but a changing at least."

* * *

The next two weeks seemed to drag. Henry found himself checking again and again to make sure he was ready. He wasn't an experienced traveler, but he had been away from home enough to know how to pack light. He had rigged himself a sort of knapsack using the sewing machine his mother had recently bought. The knapsack had a strap that allowed him to hang it over his shoulder. That would make it easier to hold on to his bag when boarding a freight.

His money supply wasn't much, but he felt sure that he and Bee could find work on the road. They'd be able to eat by working their way across country. The thing Henry hadn't figured on was how many other men and women were doing the same thing during these hard times.

Henry and Bee met the next Saturday to compare notes.

"You ready to go?" Henry asked.

"Aw-almost."

"How much money you gonna carry?"

"I-I ain't s-sure. I've g-got 'bout five d-dollars. I t-think maybe I'll h-have ten if I'm l-lucky."

"That'll be good. I had to rake and scrape, but I finally got seven together. We ought to be able to live like kings on the road. You got everything else ready?"

"Yeah, l-least ways I t-think so. You?"

"Uh, huh. By the way, don't forget to bring a jacket. It might get cold in the box cars."

"Okay. I h-hadn't thought about t-that."

"What time you gonna be ready next Saturday?"

"D-don't know. W-what 'bout you?"

"Why don't we meet at noon? I'll meet you down by the creek. We'll go to town and take in the show like we always do. Then about dark we'll slip down by the tracks and catch the train. How's that?"

"S-sounds okay to m-me."

* * *

Henry and Bee lay in the bushes along the westbound tracks of the Southern Railway. The freight was switching cars in the freight yard. The engineer gave three short blasts on his whistle to indicate he was backing up. Smoke poured from the stack as the engine pushed the cars back along the warehouse siding. The brakeman disconnected the last three cars after setting the brake on the first one.

The whistle blasted twice as the engineer eased the train forward. Restlessness settled over the two teenagers as they waited for the train to finish switching. It seemed to them the switch would never be done. However, the back and forth motion finally ceased. The section with the caboose was finally hitched. Two short blasts of the whistle, and the train began to accelerate.

The cab passed the boy's hiding place. Henry picked out a boxcar and pointed to it, "Let's see if we can get on that one."

The train picked up speed. It was running between five and ten miles per hour when Henry led the way. He ran to the front end of the car he'd selected. Grabbing the door handle as the car moved toward him, he swung himself into the open door.

Bee was right behind Henry. He grabbed for the door handle, missed his chance and was being left behind. Henry extended his hand. Bee ran alongside the car reaching for Henry's hand. Henry caught his extended hand and pulled Bee into the door. Bee's feet swung underneath the car. For an instant Henry thought he was going to lose his grip. He held on. If Bee were to fall, he'd wind up under the wheels of the speeding train.

Henry made one more supreme effort to pull his friend aboard. Bee's shins scraped as he was dragged into the open door. Both boys sat hassling for breath. They looked at each other.

Finally Bee spoke, "Thank y-you. I t-thought I was a g-goner."

Henry grinned, "You're welcome. I wasn't too sure myself. You all right?"

Bee ran his hands over his bruised shins, "Yeah. J-just skinned m-myself a little."

By now the train was nearing its full speed. The boys looked out the open box car door. Trees seemed to stream by in the late evening shadows. The wind whistled through the open boxcar door. Smoke from the engine and cinders from the track flew by and into their faces. This was going to take some getting used to.

The whistle sounded two long, one short, and another long. Henry looked ahead from the open door. There ahead lay a small town. The train sped through Graham without stopping.

Henry looked at Bee with a smile. "We're on our way," he shouted above the noise of the train whistle.

The train rumbled on through the night. There was a short pause in Hazlehurst, while a few cars were switched. Henry and Bee huddled out of sight in the front of their car. They were hoping the car they had chosen wasn't going to be sidetracked. That would present a problem. If that happened, they would have to find themselves a new car. They were in luck when the train pulled out again, they were moving right along.

Seven miles northwest of Hazlehurst, the engineer began to sound for the trestle over the Ocmulgee River. The boys looked out the boxcar door into the wide waters of the river. Lumber City lay on the other side of the river. The train hardly slowed down.

Towns like Helena and Cochran were short stops, then the freight headed for Macon. Henry knew there was a sizable railroad yard at Macon. Some of the hobos he had talked to had told him about a jungle, place where hobos gathered, there. His plan was to leave the train before they got to the yard, then try to find the jungle.

It was well after midnight when the train started to slow for the Macon yard. Henry shook Bee. Bee stirred, rubbed his eyes, and looked around.

"Where a-are we?"

"Just comin' into Macon. Quick! We've got to get off the train before we hit the yard."

Bee slung his pack on his back and followed Henry to the boxcar door. The train was still moving too fast to leave the car. Henry watched the telegraph poles slide by. Suddenly he realized they were passing the siding signal for the yard.

"We've got to jump. Remember now; we have to go with the motion of the train. Roll when you hit the ground."

Bee nodded in acknowledgment. He watched for Henry's

move.

As the train slowed, Henry looked for open track. You had to be sure you didn't jump off on a switch handle. That mistake could injure you fatally. He saw a good opening. He jumped. The forward motion of the train carried him several feet. He landed with a roll. When he had rolled half a dozen times, he came to rest and stood up. Bee had jumped right behind him and landed a few feet farther down the track.

Henry walked over to Bee, offered him his hand, and pulled him to his feet. "You all right?"

"Yeah." Bee shuffled a step or two. "I w-will be w-when I g-get my feet straight."

"Come on. We've got to get out of the yard before somebody spots us. We'll wind up talking to the cops if we don't."

The boys followed the track back to the yard gate. The cars of the train still flashed by. They were soon out the gate headed around the yard.

Henry wasn't quite sure where the jungle was. The best he could remember, an old hobo had told him it lay in the fork of the Atlanta and Columbus roads. That could be quite a walk. The boys made their way around the yard. They found the northwest track and walked along it toward what should have been Atlanta.

After while they saw a fork in the track. The other road crossed the one they were following at almost a right angle. The jungle should lie just to the west of the Atlanta track. They crossed the track, turned left, and worked their way between the tracks.

Sure enough, there ahead was a gravel path leading to some sort of camp. As the boys walked into the hobo jungle, they could see small fires burning. Several groups of hobos had built fires. They were either sitting and talking or sleeping. The hobo jungle was almost never without activity. There was always the anticipation that something might happen. A train might be leaving town. You had to be up and ready to catch it.

One fire seemed to have more hobos around it than the others. A set of forked sticks held a cross-stick. The cross-stick ran through the sides of a metal can, suspending the can over the fire. The smell of brewing coffee came from the can. The hobos were chatting until they noticed the newcomers.

Henry and Bee stood at a distance, not quite sure whether they should intrude or not.

"You fellers come on over," an older man said motioning to them. "Share our fire."

Henry and Bee moved closer to the fire. "You fellers care for a cup o' Java?" The old man asked.

"Don't mind if I do," Henry said. "That is, if it ain't too much trouble."

"No trouble atall." The old man reached for a bean can, wiped it with a rag, tilted the can on the cross-stick, and poured steaming coffee into the bean can. "Here ya are. How 'bout you, son?" He nodded at Bee.

"O-okay. Just a l-little, I r-reckon."

The old man repeated his procedure with a second can. He handed it to Bee.

"Where you boys from?"

Henry sipped the coffee. He wasn't quite sure how much he should tell the old man, but he seemed a friendly enough fellow. "Just down the road aways," he replied.

"Thought so. You boys look kinda green t' me."

There was silence as Henry and Bee sipped their coffee. The old man waited patiently for them to speak.

"We just left last night," Henry said.

"Yeah. New to the road then, huh?"

"Yeah."

"You boys let me give you some advice. There's lots t' learn on the road. The secret t' survivin' is knowin' what t' do and when t' do it."

Henry listened respectfully.

"First, don't give out your real name. Less you want to. Sometimes fellers that's leavin' somethin' behind just as soon you not know their name, an' they don't want t' know yours."

"You can call me, Slim," Henry said.

"That's good," the old man smiled. "You've got the picture."

Henry pointed to Bee. "This is my friend Bee."

The old man smiled again. "My name's, Smokestack. Most folks just call me Stack."

"Glad to meet you, Stack," Henry offered, extending his hand. Bee nodded in agreement.

The old man swept his hand over the crowd, "Meet the crowd. Fellers, this is Slim and Bee, like in yore bonnet, I reckon."

The group acknowledged Henry's and Bee's introduction with a nod of their heads.

"Which away you fellers heading?" The old man asked.

"We thought we'd try west. Understand there's lots of wide, open spaces out there," Henry offered.

"That's for sure. Which route was you figurin' on takin'?" Smokestack asked.

"Don't rightly know. What's the best way?"

"Depends."

"Depends on what?"

"Whether or not you want t' ride the high iron."

"What's the high iron?"

"Boy, you're greener 'n a gourd. High iron means the main lines. The rails are a bit higher on them routes than they are on spurs and such."

"I see. Which would you recommend?"

"Well, if I wanted t' go somewhere's in a hurry, I'd take the high iron. If I wanted t' loaf along I'd take any road that struck my fancy."

"We'd like to get to Texas. What's the best route?"

Smokestack grinned, "The high iron's best followed by goin'

t' Atlanta. Catch the westbound for Birmingham, then you can head by way of New Orleans. Just kinda follow your nose after that. That'll get you to the plains o' Texas."

* * *

Dawn broke. Henry and Bee had passed the night in the hobo jungle. They were awakened by the activity around them. Many of the hobos were preparing to leave. Some strolled down the Columbus track hoping to catch a westbound. Others went east toward Brunswick. Still, others strolled toward Atlanta. Many stood around drinking coffee from bean cans or tin cups. You were considered well off if you owned a tin cup.

Smokestack was stirring the fire. He added another piece or two of wood before he noticed Henry and Bee rubbing the sleep from their eyes. "Mornin', boys. Sleep good?"

Henry stretched himself before he answered, "Yeah, pretty good. And you?"

"Oh, 'bout as well as an old man could expect. Come on over and have a cup."

Henry sat by the fire as Smokestack poured a can of coffee. Bee followed suit.

"What you boys got on your minds?" Smokestack asked.

Henry took a sip of his coffee before he answered, "Thought we'd try for the Atlanta train. You wouldn't happen to know when it leaves, would you?"

"Yeah, there's one leavin' in about an hour."

"Thanks. We'll try to be on it."

Smokestack studied Henry's face for a moment. He could see himself in this young lad. There was the yearning for adventure in his eyes. He seemed open to possibilities. It would be a pity for him to lose his life on the tracks. Maybe the youngster would let him teach him a few tricks of the trade.

"Tell you what," Smokestack said. "Why don't I tag along with you boys? I was thinking of headin' for Birmingham anyhow. Mind if I throw in with you boys?"

Henry thought about his proposal. It would be nice to have an old hand around, at least until they learned the ropes. "I don't see why not. Might be nice to have company."

"It's settled then. Finish your coffee. I know a good spot to catch that north bound freight."

* * *

The train eased out of the freight yard headed for Atlanta. The three men hunkered down behind the bushes just off the tracks. When half a dozen cars had passed, Smokestack urged Bee, then Henry to board the train. He ran along behind until they were safely aboard, then he mounted the moving car.

When they were settled, Smokestack looked at his pupils. This was as good a time as any to give them a lesson. He spoke.

"You fellers done pretty good, but you need to pay more attention to your boarding technique. Slim, you almost broke an arm back there. You got to catch that hand rail so's the motion o' the train don't slam you against the car. Always go with the motion o' the train. That-a-way you can pull yourself up without being slammed against the car."

Henry felt his arm. It was hurting from the force it had taken. Maybe Smokestack was right. He'd listen to this veteran of the iron road. Maybe he could learn something from him. "Thanks. I appreciate your help. I'll remember that."

"Just tryin' t' be helpful. There'll be other things, but we'll talk about 'em when the time comes."

When the train began to slow for the Atlanta freight yards, Smokestack picked up his bindle, hobo's pack, and turned to Bee and Henry. "Time to get off. You don't want t' ride into the yards if you can help it. There's lots o' Bulls in them yards."

Henry looked at Smokestack. He wasn't familiar with this talk. There was lots to learn on this new adventure, Henry decided.

"What's a Bull?"

"Oh, I forgot. You're new. It's a railroad policeman. You don't wanta tangle with 'em. Most of 'em are twenty-four carat bastards. They've been known t' kill hobos just for the hell of it."

* * *

The westbound train rumbled out of Atlanta. Henry, Bee, and Smokestack were resting comfortably in the front of a boxcar whose last load had evidently been brick. The straw still smelled of the red clay.

"Boys, this's travelin' in style," Smokestack said as he nestled down in the straw. "We'll have a smooth ride all the way t' Birmingham."

Henry lay back and enjoyed stretching out on the straw pile. Bee didn't quite have the spirit of the trip yet, but he was beginning to act more like himself with each new turn. Henry wasn't worried. He knew he would be able to count on Bee when the chips were down.

Smokestack reached in his pocket, extracted a stub of a cigar he'd been saving, and lit up with the aid of a match scratched on the boxcar wall. The end of the stogie glowed as he puffed away. Soon he was blowing smoke rings.

Henry watched as Smokestack puffed on the stub. He wondered what kind of flavor the smoke had. Cigarettes were his smoking staple. He'd been around cigar smokers, but he couldn't remember ever taking a puff.

Smokestack looked at Henry. He could almost read Henry's mind. "Care for a puff?"

"Don't mind if I do."

Smokestack handed Henry the weed. Henry took a drag on the cigar. He inhaled, unaware that cigars were never intended for inhaling. The smoke burned his throat and then his lungs. Choking on the smoke, Henry's face turned green. He struggled to exhale the strong smoke. He gasped, spat, and expelled the smoke.

Smokestack slapped Henry on the back as he coughed on the smoke. "You ain't supposed t' inhale. You just take the smoke in your mouth and kinda roll it around."

Henry coughed again. The smoke still burned his insides. He finally managed to speak, "Thanks for tellin' me. I didn't know that."

"You're welcome, Slim. Wanta try again?"

Henry shook his head, "No. Not right now. Maybe later."

Smokestack took the cigar, looked at it as if he was considering what to do next, and snuffed it out. "Think I'll save some for later."

Henry didn't say anything. Bee, who had been quiet all this time looked at Henry, "D-damn if you a-ain't green a-around the g-gills."

"Yeah, reckon I am. I'll get the hang of it though."

* * *

The train rolled into Birmingham. Late afternoon shadows told the travelers they didn't have much daylight left. Smokestack prepared to leave the train. He watched for a hill. There should be one coming up soon. There it was ahead. He led the way as the trio left the comforts of their boxcar.

"You boys'll want t' catch the next train headin' west, I reckon. Remember what I've told you 'bout catchin' them cars. Y'all be careful now. I'll be seein' you around."

Henry and Bee watched as Smokestack headed north into the city. They turned to skirt the freight yard and made their way to the west side of Birmingham.

When the westbound left Birmingham, Henry and Bee were on it. The train rumbled and rocked along as the drive wheels grabbed each rail like some giant climbing a ladder. The smoke from the stack swept over them leaving the scent of coal in their already soiled clothing.

Henry thought they weren't doing too bad. They had learned

a lot in the last couple of days. Too bad Smokestack hadn't decided to go with them. It would have been nice to have an experienced traveler, but that didn't concern Henry too much. He could take care of himself.

The train made a stop in Tuscaloosa, then another near Akron, Alabama. Henry and Bee had been lucky. The car they were riding hadn't been sidetracked. Henry was usually vigilant when they came to towns with open freight yards, but he and Bee were getting tired. They had been on the road for sometime without much rest. The adrenalin had been flowing in their excitement. They were nearing exhaustion.

The train pulled into Meridian, Mississippi while they were sleeping. Unknown to them, the boxcar they inhabited was sidetracked near a warehouse. The shippers would load it for shipment in a week or so. Meanwhile, it would sit unnoticed.

The train had been gone only a short time when a warehouse-man decided he ought to check the cars. He didn't want the local kids playing in them, so he walked along the track closing each car as he went.

When the warehouseman closed the last car in the line, Henry woke up. He stood up and moved cautiously to the door. He could hear the man walking away from the car. Henry tried the door. He couldn't budge it.

"Bee," Henry called in a soft voice.

"Yeah, whatcha w-want?"

"Help me open this door."

Bee was on his feet immediately. They both strained at the door. It didn't move. Bee looked at Henry, his eyes big as saucers. He voiced their worst nightmare, "H-henry, we're t-trapped."

V

Trapped in a Railroad Car

Bee's words slowly sank in. Henry looked at the door. There was no inside handle. The boxcar locked from the outside. A small opening between the wall of the car and the door let in a sliver of light. If they could find some kind of lever, they might be able to open the door.

Henry began to feel his way along the wall of the car. The light was so dim; he couldn't see very far ahead. Perhaps half way around the car, Henry found what he was looking for. Somebody had left a piece of two-by-four in one corner of the car.

A few steps brought him to the door. He attempted to insert the lever into the small slot. It was too large. Henry pulled it back. "Let's try the other door," he suggested.

The second door was even tighter than the first. Henry's lever wouldn't work there either. What to do? They might be able to trim the lever down so that it would fit the slot. That was it. He would trim it down.

Henry reached in his right front pocket. His hand closed on his pocket knife. He pulled it from his pocket, opened it, and began to whittle away at the wood. It was slow going. For one thing, he could barely see in the dim light. In addition, the wood was hard. Henry wasn't sure; it might have been oak.

Bee stood by waiting. He had felt panic when he first realized they were trapped in the car, but he was settling down. He decided to see if he could help. "W-wonder if t-this car's got s-skylights?" He asked out loud.

Henry paused his whittling for a moment. "That's a good question. If one of us could get through, he could climb down and open the door from the outside."

"I'll t-take a l-look," Bee offered.

A quick search revealed no skylights. Some boxcars had them for ventilation or sometimes top loading. This boxcar didn't.

"Well, it was a good idea," Henry said.

"Yeah, too b-bad it d-didn't work," Bee moaned.

Henry attacked his piece of two-by-four again. Slowly he began to take the edge off. The wedge shape began to emerge as Henry whittled. After what seemed like hours, Henry inserted the lever in the slot. He had plenty of lever, but it soon became clear he wasn't going to move the door.

"Damn thing's locked from the outside, looks like. Why the hell weren't I paying attention when we pulled into this siding?"

"It a-ain't your f-fault," Bee stammered. "I-I coulda b-been watchin'."

"That's water under the bridge, as they say. What the hell are we gonna do, Bee?"

"D-don't know. Maybe w-we could yell or s-something."

Henry filled his lungs with air. "Heyyyyy! Anybody out there? Can you hear me?"

Both boys listened. There was no reply. The interior of the car was as quiet as the inside of a tomb. Henry waited a few minutes before he tried again.

There was no response.

Bee tried, but he met with the same result.

"We'll have to try different times of the day. Somebody has got to hear us," Henry decided.

"Yeah," Bee agreed.

The day dragged on. Henry began to feel thirsty. They didn't have a drop of anything to drink. Why didn't I think to bring something to drink, Henry thought? He would have given all the money he had in his pockets for a canteen of fresh water--hell, he would have given it for stale water.

The sun set. Night enfolded the boxcar. The interior slowly cooled. Henry and Bee sat in the dark wishing for a light. There was none to be had. Henry had some matches in his pocket, but he didn't have anything to burn. Even if he had, it would foul the air they had to breathe. It was best not to strike a match. They both would have given a dollar for a candle.

Finally, both boys fell asleep from exhaustion. They slept fitfully. Ever so often, Bee would talk in his sleep. He was apparently dreaming some terrible nightmare. The noise woke Henry a time or two. He listened until he was sure Bee was the source of the noise.

Once during the night, Henry thought he heard a rustling noise outside the car. He strained to be sure. There it was again. There was definitely a noise. He shook Bee until he woke.

"Bee, there's somebody out there. Maybe we could get their attention," Henry said quietly.

Both boys yelled at the top of their lungs, "Heyyyy, get us out of here!"

There was no response. They both listened quietly. The rustling noise came again. They shouted again. Silence reigned again.

"Must have been some kind of animal," Henry volunteered.

"Yeah, r-reckon so," Bee replied.

Dawn came. The sun gave the boys some small relief from the darkness, but their troubles were just beginning. Hunger pains came. Their stomachs rebelled, demanding food. There was none to be had. Henry hadn't planned on carrying food. They would either buy their food or work for their meals. This wasn't going according to plan.

The hunger pains passed, but thirst was another matter. For a while they were able to summon saliva from their glands, but as time wore on, their bodies began to dehydrate. Their mouths became dry, and their lips began to swell.

Another night passed increasing their torture. Dawn only served to enhance their agony. The light revealed how far they were from freedom physically, yet not how far away they were in fact. Their shelter had inadvertently become their prison.

As time wore on, the boys tried to summon someone to help. Their cries went unanswered. The exertion only made them weaker. They were slowly dying. Their bodies began to feel the long-term effects of deprivation.

During the third night of their captivity, the lightning began to flash. Powerful rolls of thunder followed sounding as if some giant were rolling barrels around in an attic. The boys lay listlessly listening to the cacophony of sounds. They had almost given up hope.

A bolt of lightning hit somewhere near the boxcar. The thunder was so close it shook the car. Both boys were shaken. They looked at each other as if they were surprised that they were still breathing. The smell of burning wood came to them. The lightening had started a fire nearby, but it was impossible to tell where. The acrid smell grew stronger.

When it seemed the smoke would seep into the car asphyxiating them, the bottom fell out. Rain poured from the sky in torrents, just in time to douse the fire before it spread any farther. The water washed over the top of the car and swept through the small crack between the closed door and the roof. Henry saw what was happening. His mind was sluggish from thirst and hunger, but he realized they had been given a reprieve. If they only had some way to catch the water.

His hat. Where was his hat? He thought. Feeling around, he found it. Pressing it against the door, he was able to catch part of the drip that came through the crack. When he thought he had enough to drink, he pulled it back and drank from the hat. The water was refreshing to his thirsty, swollen lips. He pressed his hat against the door again.

Bee was hardly conscious of what was happening, it seemed.

"Bee, get over here. We've got to catch all this water we can."

Bee roused. He found his hat and held it under a second drip. The rain continued to fall. The boys were able to drink their fill from the drips. They were even able to retain some water in their hats, but a felt hat doesn't hold water very well, so they couldn't keep it for long.

The drink of water had refreshed them. They both felt better. Maybe they were going to survive this ordeal after all.

The rain passed, then returned for several hours. Musty smells came from the boxcar. The rain had washed the outside air giving it a clean, clear smell. The contrast served to remind the boys that they were confined to the limited space of the boxcar.

The sun rose. The dim light of the car was little comfort, but Henry was cheered by his drink of water. Maybe he could do something about their situation, he thought. He decided to try the lever again. Pushing it as far as possible, he strained to force the door open. If I could pop the lock loose, I might just be able to move the door. Alas, the lock was not responding to his work.

Bee looked on while Henry tried the door for the umpteenth time. "Ain't n-no use, I r-reckon."

Henry cursed under his breath. "I guess not. You'd think somebody would come along, wouldn't you?"

Bee shook his head, "Don't l-look like n-nobody's gonna."

"Well, if it rains, we can get water, at least."

"Yeah."

* * *

One day faded into the next. Each effort to open the car door met with the same result. The boys were now so weak from hunger and thirst that they no longer moved unless they were trying to find a more comfortable position.

Hunger passes after the third day of a fast. The body becomes accustomed to the lack of food. Then the mechanisms of nature take over; the body begins to deplete its own fat and muscle. This leads to a weakening of the muscles. Contrary to popular belief, one loses muscle as much as they do fat under fasting conditions.

Henry nor Bee had that much excess weight. Both boys had a high metabolism, which left them thin. Therefore, their bodies depleted their fat and muscle more rapidly than they could really afford. Historically, men have been known to survive for more than a month without food. Low activity helped, but both boys were rapidly approaching starvation.

Such deprivation sometimes plays tricks on the mind. Bee had been having nightmares almost from the beginning. Now Henry began to experience some of the same things. His mind played tricks on him. He often thought he was back home or even a small child again. He dreamed or hallucinated frequently as his body suffered the early stages of starvation.

* * *

Henry stood at the window, in his dream. He could see the small, furry animals playing in the light from the kitchen lamp. The rabbits, at least that's what he thought they were, frolicked, chasing one another around the yard. One would flash through the light occasionally. Henry, a boy of five, could see them plainly.

"Pa, see the rabbits," Henry said to his father.

Gus stood up and went to his son's side. "Where, John?"

"Out there! See! One just ran through the light. Did you see him?"

"No, son, I didn't. Where is he now?"

"He went behind the well curb. See! There's another."

Eva, Henry's mother, turned from the stove where she was cleaning a pot in preparation for supper. "John, are you playing that game again?" She asked.

"What game?" Gus asked.

"He's been seeing rabbits for sometime out there. He mentioned it the other night when you were gone."

Gus looked again, "Son, I don't see anything. Are you sure you see rabbits?"

"Yes, sir. Just as plain as day."

Gus picked Henry up and sat him on his shoulder. "Let's go see."

The man and boy went into the night. Gus stood there waiting. "Do you see them now?"

Henry seemed perplexed, "No, sir. I can only see them from the window."

Gus scanned the yard for any sign of life. He walked around the well. There was nothing there. He put Henry on the porch. "Son, I want you to stop this."

"But, Pa. I seen 'em," Henry protested.

"Maybe you did, maybe you didn't. But you're worrying your Mama. Now promise me you won't talk about this anymore."

Henry put his head down, "But, Pa."

Gus's voice grew more stern, "Listen, John, if you don't stop this, I'm gonna have to spank you, you hear?"

"Yes, sir."

But the rabbits had not stopped coming--that is, until Gus died. Henry could hear the sounds of grief and mourning in the house. His father lay a corpse, having died of pneumonia. A few days later the family had attended the funeral at his Grandpa Hester's place. Henry had always associated the vision of the rabbits with his father's death.

* * *

Henry woke with an uneasy feeling. The dream was so vivid. It was as if he'd been living that part of his life over. What did the dream mean? He had been told all his life that dreams were significant--hadn't Joseph had them in the Bible? Could this dream mean he was about to die? There was no way to know. It was best, if he put it out of his mind. But that wasn't easy. You don't throw off a life time of teaching so effortlessly.

The sun rose high in the sky. Its penetrating rays warmed the outer skin of the boxcar. As the outside warmed, the interior of the car seemed to heat rapidly. Actually, the heat was no worse than the boys had experienced previously. Their weakened condition probably just made it seem that way.

Henry, who lay flat of his back gazing upward to the small crack above the door, suddenly felt as if he couldn't breathe. He sat up, attempted to catch his breath, and gasped for air.

Bee raised himself on one elbow and looked at Henry. "You o-okay?"

"Can't breathe," Henry gasped.

Bee moved cautiously to Henry's side. He wasn't quite sure what to do. Suddenly, he summoned all the strength he had and slapped Henry on the back.

"W-why'd you do that?" Henry said with some anger in his voice.

"I-I ain't s-sure. T-thought it might h-help you b-breathe."

Henry caught himself on the chest. He coughed once before he spat up white phlegm. His breath came easier.

"Thanks, that seems to have done the trick."

"Y-you're welcome."

"I wonder what brought that on?"

"Don't k-know."

"We ain't been moving around much. Do you reckon I'm taking pneumonia?"

Bee shook his head in bewilderment, "Damned if I-I k-know."

The heat continued to build. Both of the boys broke out in sweat. They were so dehydrated that there wasn't much, but they were definitely sweating. The temperature in the boxcar was stifling. It seemed the heat of the day would never pass, but it finally did. The falling shadows were a welcome reprieve from the overpowering heat.

Night came again. Henry and Bee could hear the trains as they came and went. Both of them could imagine the car they were in being opened by a railroad brakeman or even a Bull. At this point, they would have welcomed the devil himself, if he had opened the door. But no one came.

* * *

The drunk came wandering through the freight yard. He had just finished a bottle of cheap whiskey and was looking for a place to sleep it off. Several boxcars beckoned as he strolled along the track. Occasionally, he stumbled up to one, checked out the door, and went on to the next.

Near the end of the line, three boxcars stood still fastened together. There ought to be at least one of them open. He swung on the handle of the car. The door wouldn't budge. Oh, well, that was okay. There were plenty more. The second car was the same as the first.

The third car's door had something stuck in it. What the hell was that anyhow. Looked like a piece of wood, he thought.

"Now, who in the hell'd stick a piece of wood in a boxcar like that?" He asked himself with a thick tongue.

He listened. There wasn't a sound. He slapped his hand on the car door. The sound startled Henry.

"Who's there?" Henry asked with surprise.

"Hey, anybody in there?" The drunk demanded.

"Yes. Can you open the door?"

The drunk staggered against the door again. "What thu hell you all doing in there?"

"We're trapped in here. Can you open the door?"

It was impossible to tell whether or not the drunk understood him. He paused while the man muttered to himself. "Can you open the door?"

"What you want the door open fer?"

"So we can get out. We're trapped in here, dammit."

The drunk coughed a time or two. He reached for the door handle, grasped it in his drunken, clumsy hands, and fell to the ground. After a few minutes, the drunk rose shakily to his feet.

Henry had been listening intently. "Can you open the door?" He repeated.

The drunk wove on his feet, "Damn thing's stuck. Can't move it. Why the hell'd you lock it so tight?"

Henry's frustration level was growing by the minute. Wouldn't you know it? They had waited an eternity for some one to rescue them; now they had a drunk half out of his mind with pop-skull whiskey. Henry decided to try another tack.

"Look, can you go get some help? Do you hear me?"

Henry paused. The drunk didn't respond. Henry repeated himself. "Go get some help. Get us out of here, please."

The drunk spun around as if he were on a Ferris wheel. "Yeah, I'll get somebody."

Henry could hear his footfalls as he stumbled away from the car. Time passed slowly, but the drunk never returned.

* * *

The dream was so real it seemed as if Henry could hear the sounds of the playing children. Where was he? He seemed to be in the school yard. Turning, he could see the door of the school house. Sure enough, it was Hamilton School. The boys were playing a game of stick ball, the closest thing to baseball they knew. The teacher stepped to the open door and rang the hand bell. School-time again.

Henry sat at his desk. The lessons were boring. Spring beckoned out the window. He gazed at the bright green colors at the edge of the woods. They were so beautiful it seemed a pity to be stuck in a school room. Then the lessons were over. He and his friends were on their way home.

Henry could hear Jimmy Lee singing in his high-pitched little boy's voice:

"Glory, Glory, Hallelujah. Glory, Glory, Hallelujah."

It was Jimmy Lee's favorite song. They always sang it in school.

Henry smiled as he dreamed. He loved music. Some of his most beloved memories were of music. His Grandpa Hester played the banjo. His memory took him back to times when they had sat for hours listening as Grandpa played one tune after another. Sadly, Henry wondered if he would ever hear music again.

Suddenly, a big boy came running up to Henry. He slapped him behind the head and ran away taunting Henry as he ran. Henry gave chase. The syrup bucket in his hand became a weapon. When he was in striking distance, Henry let go with the bucket. A gash appeared on the side of the boy's head. Blood flowed. Henry backed off and watched as his enemy clasped his head in anguish. Henry had won his fight.

The dream faded into another scene. Henry could see the face of his former school teacher. Bob Wolf seemed to taunt him from a distance. He held a rod in his hand, swinging it against his leg as he challenged Henry.

"Young man, get yourself up here," the voice seemed to say.

Henry shrank back at first, then he went forward to challenge his tormentor. The teacher put a whipping on the pupil, but Henry walked away with victory in his heart. Power flowed through him, giving him renewed strength.

Again the dream changed. Old man Liggit, as Henry usually thought of him, was in the dream, but Henry wasn't sure why. Maybe it was because he had often thought of the man as stealing his mother's affection.

One after another, Henry's enemies--at least those he perceived as enemies--seemed to parade through his dreams. There seemed to be no rhyme or reason to the dream. If there was one unifying theme, it would have been Henry's ability to triumph in the face of adversity.

* * *

Henry tossed in his sleep. Suddenly, he woke. What was happening? Where was he? The dream had seemed so real. He looked around. A thread of light came through the boxcar door's crack. Henry looked at Bee. His friend seemed to be resting. His breaths came in regular rhythm.

Henry came back to the present. He was locked in a boxcar without hope of escape. Rescue, maybe? Escape, never. But the dream must mean something. Why would he dream such things if they were meaningless? Instantly, it came to him. Maybe the dream was a message from some unseen power. Henry was no expert on theology, but he'd been told all his life that God did things mysteriously. Perhaps God was trying to tell him something. Maybe the dreams meant he was going to live in spite of his peril.

* * *

On the sixth night, the rains came again. Surely, this was a message from Heaven. Why else would they be given water if they were meant to die? The waters helped revive their spirits as well as their bodies, but their troubles were far from over. They had grown so weak that they were now unable to try opening the door. Both boys grew weaker by the hour. Henry thought somebody had better find them if they were going to live.

The next day the sun rose high in the sky bringing the heat to torture the suffering boys. They lay still now; their bodies so weak they could hardly move. As far as they knew, this could be their last day on earth.

* * *

The shipping clerk looked at his records. They had to get that shipment of grain out today or tomorrow. Orders were so far behind that they wouldn't catch up this week. This was costing the company money. Those railroad cars sitting on the track had to be paid for. The railroad charged rent for them whether they were rolling or sitting on the siding.

The foreman came into the office, retrieved a cup from the shelf at the water jug, and drew himself a cup of water from the tap.

"Looka here, Don. I want you to get them cars on the end of the siding loaded today. We've got to get our orders filled. If we don't, we're gonna be outa business. We can't afford that in these times," the clerk said.

The foreman tossed his cup of water down, "Yeah, I'll see to it right away. Me and the boys been busy gettin' that new bin fixed, but we oughta be able to load 'em today."

The foreman strolled out of the office heading for the loading dock. He spotted two men sitting on a stack of grain sacks. "You boys come with me. We got orders to load them cars down on the end of the track."

The two men stood, stretched themselves, and followed their foreman down the steps to the railroad siding. They came to the first car. Both men stood waiting for specific orders.

The foreman looked at first one and then another of the cars. "I reckon we better open 'em all. They'll need to dry some from the rain we've had lately. I don't reckon it'll hurt to let 'em air some either. Go ahead and open this un'."

The two men unlocked the latch and strained to push the door open. Stale, musty air met their nostrils as the door slid reluctantly back.

"What the hell's the big hurry, you reckon?" One of them asked.

"Don't know. These cars ain't been here more 'n a week," his companion answered.

The next car was opened in a similar fashion, but the third car was another matter. There was a piece of wood jammed in the door. The lock wouldn't spring loose.

"Who the hell left that wedge in that door?" The foreman demanded. "It'll take an axe to drive it out."

One of the men went for an axe. He returned shortly and drove the wedge back into the car. This time the lock wasn't so tight, but it was still hard to open. A lick with the axe popped it loose. The men swung their weight on the door handle bringing the door open two or three feet.

"Push it all the way. We'll need to get the truck backed up so's we can load it easier," the foreman directed.

One man jumped into the opening. Heaving his weight against the door he pushed it wide open. He was about to jump down when he turned. There lay two teenage boys.

"Hey!" the worker shouted. "They's two bodies in this car."

"What?" The foreman asked.

"I said 'there's two bodies in this car.'"

"What do you mean, bodies?"

"Two boys. Looks to me like they're dead."

VI
A Girl Called Avis

Henry opened his eyes. Where was he? It was hard to remember. The last thing he recalled was going to sleep in the boxcar. The room he lay in wasn't familiar; it smelled like medicine. Where was Bee? They had been together in the car. Was Bee dead?

Henry mustered enough strength to raise his head and look around. There were two or three more beds in the room where he lay. Somebody lay on the bed next to him. He wasn't sure if it was Bee or somebody else.

"Bee, is that you?" Henry asked weakly.

There was no answer from the other bed. Henry tried to speak louder, but he couldn't raise his voice above a whisper. As he tried to speak again, a man dressed in a white coat entered the room.

"Well, young man, how're you feeling today?" The newcomer inquired jovially.

"Not too hot," Henry replied. "Where am I? Where's Bee?"

"Take it easy, young feller. One thing at the time, you and your friend had a close call."

Henry stared at the man, "Is he. . . . Is Bee all right?"

"Well, he's not going to be running any foot races for a while, but I'd say he'll probably recover just fine. That's him in the next bed. He's sleeping like a baby."

Henry looked across to the next bed. The sleeping form

didn't move, but you could see a slight movement of the chest if you looked close enough. "How'd we get here?" Henry asked.

"Hands down on the track found you two in a boxcar. You were both near starved to death. Any idea how long you'd been there?"

Henry frowned. He tried to think. "Must have been a week or more."

"I thought so. Now you rest. You're going to be fine, but you need rest. Could you eat something? I'll order you some soup if you want it."

Henry had been so long without food that he wasn't sure whether he was hungry or not, but he was weak. He had to gain his strength back. "Yeah," he answered. "That'd be fine."

* * *

The doctor examined Henry, poking and probing here and there. Henry wished he'd get it over with. He was feeling much stronger and was ready to get out of there. The doctor stepped back before he spoke.

"Young man, you've made quite a remarkable recovery. Are you ready to go home?"

"You bet. When can I go?"

"Right now, if you like."

"What about Bee?"

"Sure, he can go, too. I can't tell you what to do, but I suggest you get a ticket to ride the next time you decide to take the train. At least stay out of locked boxcars."

"You don't have to worry about that. The boxcars, I mean."

"That's good." The doctor turned to go.

"Wait a minute, Doc. What do I owe you?"

"Nothing."

"Huh?"

"That's right. The grain company paid me. The foreman said somebody at the company locked you in. They figured they'd better pay, or you might come back looking for blood."

Henry grinned, "I might have at that."

"You take care of yourself and your friend. You hear?"

"I will," Henry answered as he swung out of bed. "Bee, you ready to go?"

"Yeah. I c-can't wait t' g-get home."

* * *

Bee and Henry came back home as heroes, at least in their minds. Each of them had a ton of fun telling their tale. Of course, they told it with lots of embellishment. They were always in control, even when they told about being trapped in the boxcar. They made life on the hobo circuit seem glamorous.

The boys' trip might have been high adventure to them, but Eva, Henry's mother, didn't see it that way. Henry would recall, years later, that Miss Eva had given him hell for taking off like that. It had been irresponsible of him according to her. Not only was he endangering his life and that of Bee, but he had left them to carry his work load.

Henry let the lecture go in one ear and out the other. He laughed and called Eva an old hen that was trying to keep him in the nest. After all, Henry was seventeen; seventeen-year-olds know all the answers, even though they might not have heard all the questions.

Henry would never have admitted it to anybody, but he was happy to be back home. His narrow escape from death had been close enough to make him appreciate his home and family. It was even good to be back in the old neighborhood.

There was one new reason he was glad to be home. She had just moved in down the road. Her family had come from Nichols, Georgia. They had moved into the Dunn house across the field where her father was going to share crop for Mr. Dunn.

Henry spotted her one Saturday evening on his way to town. There were at least half a dozen ways to town. He had taken this one out of curiosity. The new neighbors had been there for a while, and he hadn't had a chance to meet them.

She sat on the front porch of the frame house. The porch ran the entire length of the house with a swing suspended on the north end. The dark haired, brown eyed girl of perhaps sixteen sat in the swing. She had a dress draped across her lap. The hem had come loose, and she was taking careful stitches as she tacked it back in place.

She hadn't noticed Henry, who was approaching from behind her. Suddenly he was standing in the yard. She glanced at him. Her first impulse was to go into the house leaving him standing in the yard, but on second thought, she decided to see what he wanted. She met his gaze boldly.

"Hello," she said. "What can I do for you?"

"Hello," Henry answered looking deep into her brown eyes. "I'm your neighbor from down the road."

She looked a bit confused, "Which way?"

"Back up toward the pecan grove. Our house sits in the corner of the grove."

"Oh, yeah. I seen it the other day when we come by there. It's got that strange looking roof. Looks like it's wearing a hat, don't it?"

Henry laughed, "Yeah, I reckon it does. You're new around, ain't you?"

"Yeah, we just moved in."

"My name's Henry. Henry Reynolds. What's yours?"

She blushed slightly, "I'm Avis. Avis Jackson."

Henry gave her his most charming smile, "Glad to meet you, Miss Jackson." He had always found it better to be a little formal at first. You could get familiar later.

"Oh, you can call me, Avis."

"Thanks, you can call me, Henry."

The conversation took on an awkward pause. Neither of the young people seemed to know what to say. Finally Henry broke the silence.

"What you sewing?"

"Oh, this? It's just an old dress. The hem come loose. I was trying to fix it."

Henry had found something to talk about. "I've been learning to fix clothes, too."

Avis couldn't believe her ears. It was unusual for a boy to sew, but it was more unusual for him to admit it. "That's nice. What do you sew?"

"Oh, one thing and another. Mostly I fix up my clothes. You know they don't always fit like I like 'em, so I patch 'em up to suit myself."

"I know what you mean. I don't recollect the last time I had a new dress. Most of 'em are hand-me-downs. 'Specially my everyday things."

"Tell me about it. It seems like all I've ever had was hand-me-downs. Mama used to try and make me wear my sister's old shoes."

Avis grinned, then laughed out loud. Henry thought the sound of her laugh was musical. This was a charming young woman. He'd like to get to know her better.

"I bet that was a sight," Avis said merrily.

"I wouldn't know. I only wore 'em 'til I was outa Mama's sight."

Avis smiled again showing a mouthful of white even teeth. "What did your Ma say about that?"

Henry smiled back at her, "She didn't say nothin'. Just tanned my hide for doing it."

"And you kept right on doing it, I bet."

"Yeah. Why not?"

They both laughed heartily. Henry wanted to find out more about her. He'd heard neighbors talking, but he wanted to hear it from the horse's mouth.

"Where'd y'all move from?" He asked.

Avis paused as if she wasn't sure whether she should tell him or not, but she finally decided it wouldn't hurt. "We're from Nichols."

"Your Pa gonna farm for the Dunns?"

"Uh, huh."

"I reckon we'll be neighbors for a while then."

"I reckon."

Henry wanted to ask her for a date, but he wasn't quite sure how to do it. "You ever get to town?"

"Once in awhile."

"You like the picture show?"

Avis paused again. She seemed at odds with herself. Should she let this strange boy know how sheltered her life was? Again, she decided to open up her life. "I ain't never seen a picture show."

"Is that right? Well it's a lot of fun. 'Specially since they added sound to 'em. They've got this vita-phone sound they call it. It's just like you was settin' there listening to the people talk. Some folks call 'em 'talkies'."

"It sounds like it would be lots of fun."

"Oh, it is. Would you like to go sometimes?"

"I don't know. I...."

"I'd be glad to come by and pick you up. Mama might let us use the wagon to go to town."

Avis seemed confused again, "I . . . I can't."

"How come?"

"Well Pa . . . He won't let me go to the picture show."

Henry was stumped for a moment, but he recovered quickly. "How 'bout dancing? There's a frolic most every week around some place. Will your Pa let you go dancing?"

Avis wanted to say yes so badly she could taste it, but she was afraid of her father. He was strict on her. Things had been bad enough before they had moved to Appling County, now he had really tightened the reins. "I... I don't know. I'll have to ask him."

Henry thought for a minute. He wasn't going to let this dark haired girl get away that easy. He could tell there was something wrong between Avis and her father. The way she weighed each question before she answered was enough to tell him she wanted to say 'yes,' but was afraid to.

"Could I come calling sometime?"

"I'll have to ask my Pa."

"Okay. Why don't I check with you in a day or two?"

"That'd be fine."

"Bye, then. I'll see you later."

Avis watched as Henry walked off toward the branch. He seemed like a nice enough young man. Perhaps she could persuade her father to let him court her. After all, she was sixteen. Lots of girls were married at sixteen.

Henry made his way across the branch, stepping carefully to keep from wetting his shoes. His mind was on Avis. He was going to find a way to see her. It didn't matter what her Pa was like.

* * *

The year went by slowly. Henry had recovered from his ordeal on the railroad. He was working on the farm again and in the woods. It felt like old times, he thought. The young tend to heal fast. Their aches and pains are soon forgotten in the rush of new experiences. Optimism springs eternal in the bosom of youth.

Avis's father, Clint, had denied her the privilege of seeing Henry. But any parent who is alive soon realizes that it's impossible to prevent such things. Avis was always finding excuses to go to the Liggit house across the field. The Reynolds girls, Lorene and Alice, were sometimes used as a reason for the visits. The old man probably knew in his heart that he wasn't going to keep a rein on Avis forever, but he was too stubborn to admit it.

Avis and Henry also developed a system that enabled them to meet in secret. Telephones were unknown in the common household of that day, so neighbors communicated by calling to each other with a special 'holler'. These signals could be heard for miles. In those days there wasn't that much noise to interfere with the sounds.

Avis might be hanging clothes on the clothesline. Henry would step out his back door and give a holler. She could hear his voice a half mile away. She usually responded with a prearranged signal that meant she could or could not meet him. If the signal was positive, Henry would stroll through the pecan orchard. Once through the field, he crossed to the three-path road that led to the Daniels' farm. They had a prearranged meeting place. Henry usually sat there and waited for her.

By and by, Avis would come striding along the road as if she had urgent business down there somewhere. Henry often hid himself and came up behind her, grabbing her around the waist. She would pretend she was frightened, and they would wrestle, rolling in the pine needles and wire grass. This tussle usually ended in a smooching session.

Finally, Avis would push him away with some reluctance. "Is that all you ever want to do?" She asked with a sparkle in her eye.

Henry grinned, "No. Sometimes I want to just sit and look at you, but not often."

"Henry, you're awful."

"Am I?"

"Yes."

"All the time?"

Avis laughed with a teenage giggle, "Most of the time."

"But you like me that way, don't you?"

Avis frowned playfully, "God help me. I reckon I do. I'd probably run the other way if I had any sense."

Henry reached for her again, "I think you're as crazy about me as I am about you."

"You're probably right."

The evening would pass while they strolled the woods. If the moon was full, they stayed late into the night. Avis found herself wanting to stay with Henry. It would be nice not to have to go back to her father. She loved him, but he seemed to have little appreciation or sentiment for her feelings. His main concerns in life seemed to be those things that satisfied him.

Finally, one day Avis decided to bare her feelings to Henry. At first, she found it hard to talk about her troubles, but the talking helped her live with them.

"I'm worried," Avis said one quiet evening while she and Henry were walking.

"What about?" Henry inquired with genuine concern.

"It's Pa."

"Is he sick?"

"No. At least, I don't think so."

"What's wrong?"

Avis thought for a minute before she said, "I ain't sure. You know he don't want us to see one another."

Henry didn't say anything. Avis continued, "Well, it seems like he's got worse lately. Every time I tell him I was with your sisters, it's like he's seein' right through my story. I'm afraid he's gonna catch me. If he does, he's gonna beat me. I just know it."

Henry put his arm around her in an effort to comfort her. "Why don't I just have a talk with him? Maybe we could come to some kind of understandin'."

Avis frowned, "I don't think so. His mind's made up."

"Maybe I could make him listen to reason."

"You don't know Pa. He ain't one to listen to reason. That's why we had to move to this town. He got in trouble with the law back home. The sheriff give him the chance to move out of the county and not come back or go to jail."

"What happened?"

"Pa and this other man got into a row."

"What about?"

"Pa said he owed him some money for a horse."

"Did he?"

"I don't rightly know."

"Did they have a fight?"

"Yeah. It was awful. They say Pa nearly killed the other man."

Henry paused. He didn't know what to say. Finally he said, "Your Pa must have been pretty mad."

"He was. Fact is, he's still mad. That's what worries me. I'm afraid he's gonna do something like that again. I'd just die if he was to hurt you, Henry."

I might, too, Henry thought.

* * *

Even though Avis and Henry had to slip around to see each other, they sometimes had an opportunity to be together at Henry's home. One Sunday afternoon the family was sitting around. Avis had come over on the pretense of seeing Lorene. It was a lazy afternoon. The warm sun almost put the group to sleep.

A horse and rider came up the road from the west. Henry heard the sound of hoof beats and stood to go to the fence. It was one of the Crosby boys on his new horse. The Crosbys lived down the road about a half-mile to the west.

"Evenin', folks," Ben Crosby said as he reigned his horse to stop at the gate.

"Evenin', yourself, Ben. How are ya?"

"Can't complain."

Henry looked at Ben's mount, "Fine piece of horse flesh you got there, Ben. Mind if I take a closer look?"

Ben slid from the saddle, "Help yourself."

Henry walked around the horse admiring his muscled body. "How fast can he run, Ben?"

"Pretty fast. He's a race horse. At least he was born of racing parents."

"Is that a fact? Did you ever time him?"

"Nope. T' tell the truth, I ain't had him too long."

"Mind if I ride him a piece?"

Ben passed the reins to Henry, "Help yourself."

Henry stepped into the saddle and urged the horse forward with a stroke of his heels. The horse broke into a run. Henry sat in the saddle and the animal moved smoothly over the sandy, wash-boarded road. After a sprint of perhaps a quarter of a mile, Henry turned the beast around and rode him back to the front gate.

Henry dismounted, "Bet I could out run him in a hundred yards."

Ben shook his head in disbelief, "You can't neither."

Henry paused thoughtfully, "I got a dollar says I can."

"I don't want t' take your money."

"You won't be taking it. If he outruns me, I'll give it to you."

Ben scratched his head, "On second thought, maybe I ought to take your money just t' teach you a lesson."

"It's okay by me. Tell you what. Let me mark off a hundred yards, then we'll give it a try."

Ben nodded in agreement as Henry paced off one hundred steps down the road. As he came back, Henry stretched himself and prepared to run. He was in good shape again. His accident with the horse and his ordeal on the railroad were behind him. He felt confident he could win the race.

"Ready," Henry asked.

"I was born ready," Ben bragged.

"Okay, on three. One, two, three."

Henry was in motion instantaneously. His quick start was the advantage. He put all his energy into the sprint. It seemed he might lose his wager at first, but he was able to maintain enough lead to finish first.

Ben reined his mount to a stop, "I'll be damned. If somebody had told me this, I wouldn't have believed them."

Henry stood there blowing from his exertion. He finally caught his breath. "I wasn't too sure myself for a minute. He's fast, really fast. You oughta enter him in some of the local county fairs."

Ben grinned, "Not after the word gets around you out run him."

"Sure, that'll make folks think he's a sure thing not to win."

"Might work at that," Ben laughed. He handed Henry his winnings.

Henry strutted back to the front porch. He knew Avis had seen the race. She smiled at him, letting him know she approved of his demonstration. He grinned back at her. Young love was in bloom. The sun might set, but they had each other to give off light.

* * *

Henry and Avis continued to see each other into the spring of the next year. Avis continued to worry about her relationship with her father. She talked to Henry about it frequently. Henry decided he would see what he could do about the dilemma. They were walking together when Henry dropped his bombshell, although it wasn't entirely unexpected.

"Avis, I need to ask you a question."

"What's that?"

"Let's stop for a minute."

The couple stopped and sat on a dirt bank where the water had washed out the road. When they were seated comfortably, Henry continued, "I want you to marry me."

"What?"

"I want you to be my wife."

"That's sweet of you, Henry, but Pa's not gonna let me marry you."

"He won't have a choice if we don't ask him."

"What do you mean?"

"I mean, let's run away and get married."

"Are you serious?"

"Just as serious as I can be. Cross my heart and hope to die."

"Don't say that," Avis said with confusion written on her face. "How would we live?"

"I've been thinking about this for sometime. I've saved some money for us to start. We could stay with Mama for a while before we found us a place of our own. What do you say?"

Avis didn't answer right away. She was confused. Her life left much to be desired, but she wasn't sure she wanted to break with the family she knew to start a new one. "I'll have to let you know."

A few days later the plans were made. Henry and Avis planned to elope in two weeks. She would pack a few things and meet him just as they had met so many times on the road to the Daniels' farm.

* * *

Clint Jackson wasn't oblivious to what was happening between his daughter and that neighbor boy. He knew they were meeting somewhere. She made too many trips to the Liggitt farm to suit him, but he hadn't been able to catch them together. He became suspicious when Avis came home one day. She went to her clothes closet and pulled out a couple of dresses. She washed them, but she didn't hang them back up. It wasn't clear what was happening. He decided it was time to confront her.

"Avis, come here," Clint demanded.

"What is it, Pa?"

"I want to know what's goin' on with you and that Reynolds boy."

Avis was taken aback, but she tried not to show it. "There ain't nothin' goin' on Pa."

"Don't lie to me, girl. You've been seein' that boy on the sly, ain't you?"

"No, Pa."

"I know better. You're not to leave this house, you understand."

"But, Pa. Why can't I?"

"'Cause I said so. I'm gonna put a stop to this foolishness right now."

Clint strode through the house to the back bedroom. There against the wall stood a double-barreled shotgun. He picked it up, opened the breech, and pushed two shells into the barrels. Placing the gun over his shoulder, he picked up his battered felt hat, slammed it on his head, and walked out the back door.

Avis watched helplessly as her father made his way across the field toward the woods. Avis knew that her father knew Henry was working in the woods behind their field. Her heart sank as she realized her worst fears. How could she stop her father from killing Henry--at least beating him up? There seemed to be nothing she could do, but she decided to follow him. She might be able to warn Henry.

Henry was working turpentine for the Dunns. The high faces on the trees required the use of a tool called a 'puller'. A puller was set in a six- to eight-foot handle which could be used as a weapon if necessary. Henry heard the squeak of the wire fence as Clint stepped over it into the woods. Henry continued to work, moving from one tree to the next. As far as he could tell, Clint wasn't aware Henry was watching him.

Avis stood at the fence watching her father stalk Henry. Henry stepped behind a palmetto patch and watched as Clint eased through the gallberry bushes. Henry could see Clint clearly. Easing around the palmetto patch, Henry came up on Clint from the rear.

"You lookin' for me?" Henry asked evenly.

Clint turned to face Henry, cocking one of the hammers of the shotgun. As Clint lifted the weapon, Avis yelled, "No! Pa!"

VII
Riding the High Iron

Clint had the shotgun halfway up when Henry reacted. The puller handle came down across Clint's hands knocking the shotgun from his grasp. A look of surprise came over Clint's face as he realized he no longer had the upper hand. Clint cursed as he dropped the shotgun.

"I'm gonna kill you for that, you son-of-a-bitch."

Henry didn't say anything. He watched Clint to see what his next move might be. Clint rushed Henry, but Henry sidestepped and pushed the puller handle in front of the charging man. Clint fell like a ton of bricks, cursing as he hit the ground.

Henry retreated, waiting for Clint to make his next move. Clint rushed him again, but Henry's evasive maneuver didn't work this time. Clint managed to knock the puller handle from Henry's grip.

Henry was bowled over into a gallberry patch. The rough bark and limbs of the gallberry bushes scratched him as he fell, but he rolled over in spite of the pain. Clint tried to kick Henry. Henry was able to evade the blow by rolling over once again. He came to his feet prepared for the next rush.

Clint was the larger man, but he was handicapped by his weight. Henry was more agile. His reach was better, too. He could move quickly enough to avoid Clint's attempts to bear hug him. Clint would come at Henry with both fists flailing. Henry would punch him in the stomach eliciting a grunt from the larger man.

Over and over, Henry pounded Clint's abdomen. Clint was never able to quite get a grasp on Henry. The fight continued. Both men were tiring, but they both persisted. The wire grass and pine straw looked like it had been trampled by two ferocious animals.

Finally, Clint began to tire noticeably. Henry was able to sidestep his rushes more easily each time. Clint rushed Henry again. Henry sidestepped the rush and brought both hands down on the back of Clint's neck. Clint stumbled into the fence. He turned to try and stand up, when Henry hit him under the chin with both hands. Clint fell backwards over the fence and lay on the ground. He didn't move.

Henry stood by breathing hard. Avis ran to her father, picked his head up, cradled it in her lap, and spoke to her father, "Pa! Pa! You okay?"

Clint didn't respond.

Avis glared at Henry, "You've killed him," was all she said.

* * *

Two short blasts of the whistle told Henry the train was about to leave the freight yard. He crouched in the bushes by the track and waited. The engine passed him puffing steam like some kind of primeval dragon. He swung on board the first empty boxcar, pulled his pack from his back, and threw it on the floor of the car near the front. Henry turned and lay down, using his pack for a pillow.

He was alone this time. He could have asked Bee to come with him, but he really didn't want company. Life had been a living hell for him since he had fought Clint Jackson. Avis had flatly refused to see him. He had tried a number of times, without success, to get her to talk to him.

It was frustrating. Henry didn't understand how somebody could take abuse from another person, and, at the same time, refuse to leave him. In his naivety, he didn't realize that many people abide in an abusive relationship because they're afraid to change it. In the words of one sage, "They prefer the devil they know to the devil they don't know."

Anyhow, Avis had dumped him. This was his chance to get away. He still wanted to see the Western United States for himself. His trip with Bee had fallen far short of his expectations. They hadn't seen the plains of Texas or gotten anywhere near them. It was about time he saw some of the world for himself. To hell with Avis anyhow. What hurt most was the fact that Henry loved her. She was really his first love. He didn't know it, but hoboing around the country wasn't really going to remove her from his mind.

The train blew for the crossing. Graham, Hazlehurst, Lumber City, and McRae all slipped by. The freight was headed for Atlanta. Henry decided he would ride her straight through.

Henry considered his situation. He was better equipped for this trip than he'd been with Bee. He had all the money in his pocket he'd saved for his and Avis' wedding. It might as well be put to good use. He sure as hell wasn't going to spend it on a wedding.

The train paused in Macon to switch cars. Henry dropped off the car before the train hit the yard. There was no need to take unnecessary chances with the railroad Bulls in the yard. There would be plenty of time to get a bite to eat, too.

Henry found a greasy spoon café that hadn't closed. From the looks of it, it was never closed. He sat at the counter and ordered a hamburger and cup of coffee. The sound of the trains coming and going in the freight yard could be heard distinctly. Henry knew he'd have to hurry to make the next freight going north. He finished his sandwich, tossed down his coffee, and headed for the north side of Macon. The train left with Henry riding a boxcar.

Henry decided to take the familiar route out of Atlanta. He

boarded the Southern Freight for Birmingham. A few hours later he was headed southwest toward New Orleans. The train rolled on through the night, then the next day.

Henry was developing a rhythm that allowed him to sleep and wake refreshed. He soon found he could awaken when the train made a change in speeds, especially braking. Actually, it was rather simple. The cars sort of bumped each other as the engineer applied the brakes. The motion was the clue. This new alertness helped Henry feel less anxious about falling into the locked boxcar trap. He'd had more than enough of that scene. He didn't care to repeat it.

It was broad daylight when the freight rolled across the wide Mississippi. Henry gazed on the broad river with awe. He'd seen pictures, but this was a totally new experience. Henry dropped off the train before it reached the freight yard. He walked through unfamiliar streets with unfamiliar sights, sounds, and smells.

New Orleans was the biggest city Henry had ever seen. It was quite an experience for a country boy from the backwoods of Appling County, Georgia. Henry spent hours just taking in the sights. He found himself in the French Quarter briefly, but he didn't linger. This was all very interesting, but he wanted to go west. He'd better find somewhere he could get information.

Henry knew he had reached the end of the line for the Southern Railroad. What he had to find, was what line to follow to reach Texas. There was no better place to learn this than in a hobo jungle. He made his way back to the tracks. Strolling along westbound tracks, he had to find a jungle sooner or later.

The day was well spent when Henry saw the smoke of a fire. Sure enough, there just to the right of the westbound tracks lay a hobo jungle.

Henry made his way to one of the fires. A nondescript group of men sat around the blaze laughing and talking. Henry's presence was acknowledged. A hobo, who seemed to be serving as temporary cook, offered him a tin cup with coffee. Henry took the cup, sipped the hot steaming liquid, and listened as his companions bantered each other.

When Henry finished his coffee, he pulled a pack of Prince Albert from his pack, rolled a cigarette, lit it, and offered the pack to another man. The hobo took the pack, then passed it on to the next man. The pack made the rounds until each man had a smoke. These men were following the law of the hobo jungle. If one man had something, they all had it until it was exhausted. It was given freely and received likewise.

Henry took a puff before he asked his leading question. "Any of you gents know which road I'll need to take to get to Texas?"

One grizzled man with a stubby beard grinned, "Texas is a mighty big place, young feller. Reckon it depends on what part o' Texas you want t' git to."

Henry grinned back at the man, "It don't matter much. I've got a hankering to see San Antone, though."

"Why didn't ya say so?"

"Well, I'm kinda new to this part of the country."

The hobo spat in the fire before he replied, "Yeah, I reckon ya are. Don't hurt t' ask questions though. Hell, if'n a feller didn't ask questions, he wouldn't learn nothin'."

Henry nodded his head in agreement, "So what's the best road to San Antone?"

"Just catch anything that's got Southern Pacific painted on it. That'll take you to Houston and right on to San Antone."

"Thanks."

"Don't mention it."

* * *

Houston was a Texas oil town. The depression had put a damper on the industry, but the automobile was here to stay, and the locals were making the best of it. The city was fast becoming a seaport for oil exports although it lay fifty miles from the Gulf of Mexico. Inland waterways made it possible for ships to harbor there where they were loaded with oil and other local products.

Houston was also an important railhead. The same products that were shipped on the seas found their way onto rail cars of one kind or the other. Henry rode into this town along with a number of other hoboes and bums. The depression had bred a wandering population that never seemed to cease moving. Men, who were rather stable just a few years before, were now roaming the country hoping to find that place where they could earn a living. Many of them were family men who hoped to better themselves, then send for their families. The hopes and dreams had remained elusive until many of them had given up their goals. They had simply become wanderers.

Henry found Houston fascinating, but it was still a big city. He longed to see the West that had been glorified in Hollywood. With this objective, he continued westward toward San Antonio. The rails of the Southern Pacific made it possible for him to gaze on the plains of Texas from the door of a boxcar. What surprised Henry most were the trees of Southern Texas. Mesquite grew as far as the eye could see. None of the trees were over twenty feet tall, and Henry couldn't conceive of any possible use for them-- except, maybe firewood, even that didn't seem to be very good, on second thought.

Henry stood in the boxcar door watching the mesquite trees pass before him as the train rolled into San Antonio. When the train had slowed sufficiently, he jumped from the car and made his way along the tracks to a road intersection. He stood beside the road while a Model-A Ford and a couple of trucks lumbered by, their wheels kicking up little puffs of dust. Turning, he followed the road toward the main part of town.

San Antonio was a modern nineteen-thirties city--hardly what Henry was expecting. As he gazed on its buildings, he wondered where the wild west he'd seen in the movies was. Henry was unaware that Hollywood movies were made in Southern California for the most part. He was learning fast that movie sets and the real world bore little resemblance to each other. Well, I might as well have a look, he thought to himself.

The San Antonio River wound through the center of the town. Its pleasant waters were cool, and the willows that stood on its banks cast an inviting shade for a weary traveler. Henry seated himself on a willow root, removed his boots, and soaked his feet in the cool flowing stream.

As he sat there letting the weariness soak out of his body, a teenage Mexican girl came down to the water's edge across the river with a bucket in her hand. She stooped to lower the bucket into the sparkling water of the river. Henry's form caught her eye as she gazed across the river. The waters were narrow at this point--less than thirty feet. She smiled at the gangly lad with his feet draped over the riverbank.

Henry slowly became aware that someone was watching him. He raised his head and searched for the observer. There she was, almost straight across the river.

"Hello!" Henry called.

The girl kept her gaze fixed on the young man. "Buenos Dais," she replied.

Henry wasn't sure he understood her. He had heard the words in the movies before, but he wasn't sure what they meant. "Do you speak English?" Henry asked.

The young lady looked at him a bit perplexed, shook her head, retrieved her bucket of water, and went on her way.

"Hey, wait," Henry called after her.

She continued to hurry until she was out of sight.

Henry thought on this chance meeting. It would have been nice to talk to her--get to know something about her--but that was out of the question now. Oh, well, he couldn't speak her lingo anyway, he thought. It was just as well.

The young woman aroused thoughts of Avis in Henry. He had tried to put her out of his mind since he'd left home. Sometimes it worked; other times she returned to haunt him. Time to move on, Henry thought to himself. That'll get her off my mind.

As Henry strolled through the streets of San Antonio, he chanced on a row of stores across the street from an old Spanish church. There in the window hung a suit of clothes. The pants and jacket appeared to be made of leather. Henry had most of the money he'd saved for the wedding in his pocket. He decided to see how much the shop keeper wanted for the clothing.

"Can I help you, young man?" The proprietor asked as Henry walked into the store.

"Yes, I wondered how much you wanted for the leather suit in the window?"

The shopkeeper looked at the young hobo. He didn't know for sure, but he'd have bet a plugged nickel this young man didn't have more than a dollar on him. Oh, well. Might as well find out if he was serious. You couldn't afford to pass up a sale with things like they were. The suit had been in the store window for months now. The shopkeeper was beginning to wonder if it was ever going to sell. This young man could be his chance to get rid of what had become something of a burden.

"How much you willin' to pay?"

Henry hesitated. Anybody who answered a question with a question came under suspicion immediately with him.

"Not one cent more'n you're askin'," Henry replied.

The shopkeeper smiled, "That's a good answer, young feller. Tell you what. You try it on. If it fits, I'll let you have it for five dollars. How's that?"

"Sounds okay to me. Where can I try it on?"

"Just happen to have a room in the back. You can see if it fits back there."

The shopkeeper took the suit from the rack, led the way to a back room, handed the suit to Henry, and said, "Right in here."

"Thanks."

Henry closed the door of the small room. A dim light overhead cast shadows around the room as he stripped down to his underwear. He picked up the suit and started to slip the pants on when he made a discovery that delighted him. The suit was reversible. One side was a black leather; the other was a tan colored cloth. This would be like owning two suits of clothes. He could mix and match the pants and jacket any way he wanted.

The trousers fit him well enough. Given a sewing machine and time he could tailor them to suit his taste. The short jacket met the top of the pants forming a neat fit. Henry liked the results immediately.

"You've got a deal," Henry told the shopkeeper as he emerged wearing the suit with the leather side exposed.

"Looks like a right good fit at that," the shopkeeper responded.

Henry handed over the five dollars. The shopkeeper accepted the money, turned, and put it in his cash drawer.

"Will there be anything else?"

"I don't think so."

"Come back and see me."

"Thanks, I will."

Henry started for the door of the shop. He paused just inside and looked at the building across the street. He thought it looked familiar, but he couldn't be sure. Turning to the shopkeeper, he asked, "What's that place across the street?"

The shopkeeper stood to his full height raising his shoulders to emphasize his pride, "That, young man, is the Alamo."

"The Alamo. I've heard of it. Even seen pictures, but I never expected to actually see it."

"I'd be surprised if you hadn't heard of it. The Alamo's the most famous place in Texas."

"Didn't Davy Crockett die there?"

"Yep. Him and about one hundred eighty other fellows. In March of 1837, him and Colonel Travis led the defenders against thousands of Mexicans under the command of General Santa Anna."

Henry thought for a moment, "Bowie? Wasn't there a fellow

named Bowie there, too?"

"Sure, Jim Bowie. He's the one had the famous knife, you know."

"Yeah, I heard about the knife."

The shopkeeper stood gazing reverently toward the old Spanish church, "Legend has it, that knife was made from metal taken out of a meteorite."

"What's a meteorite?"

"It's a piece of rock from space."

"You mean it just fell out of the sky?"

"That's right. At least, that's what they say."

Henry mused for a minute, "Ain't that something?"

"It sure is, but the courage of them fellows at the Alamo has been an inspiration to Texans for nearly a hundred years. I reckon that's almost as amazing."

Henry respected that. It seemed to him he was standing near sacred ground. If you thought about it, you could almost feel the presence of those men who had defended the Alamo. With a little imagination you could hear the sounds of gunfire as the Mexican army rushed the wall of the ancient structure over the very ground that he stood on. The feeling was uncanny.

"Thanks for telling me about that, mister," Henry said almost reverently.

"You're welcome, young man. It's an important lesson, I think."

Henry took another look at the ancient building, "Be seein' you," he said as he walked out the shop door.

"So long, young man," the shopkeeper said with a note of sadness in his voice.

* * *

Henry's encounter with the Alamo gave him a new insight into history. He began to develop a new sense of the events that had happened around him in the past. With this appreciation, he spent more time exploring his surroundings each place he went.

Wherever he went, he talked to people. Some were aware of their surroundings and how history unfolded there. Others were oblivious to their environment. They couldn't have cared less about history. Their minds were filled with more immediate concerns--making a living, for instance.

Hobo jungles provided a place to sleep, and often Henry found useful information to guide him on his travels. His money began to run low, so he tried to find work from time to time. Often a farmer or rancher would hire him for a day's work in the fields. Sometime a merchant would give him a day's work unloading a freight car or some other form of manual labor.

Henry learned how to read hobo signs--these were frequently left to inform fellow travelers about local conditions. He found out how to offer his services for a meal. He adhered to the hobo code. A hobo never panhandled. He was often given a meal or other accommodations when he asked, but he always offered to work for the things he needed.

San Antonio whetted Henry's appetite for more of the West. He began to appreciate the vastness of this area of the country. When he caught a train, it took hours to make the journey to the next town. Many places consisted of a water tank with coal bins for refueling. There might be a lone house or house/general store combination nearby. Sometimes there were grain elevators where rail cars were filled with local farm products for shipment to larger cities and towns.

Henry caught a westbound out of San Antonio. He had learned that Del Rio lay to the west near the Mexican border. He was curious about Mexico; maybe he could take a short trip over the border. The idea was intriguing.

The train pulled into Del Rio. Henry dropped off well before the engineer stopped in the freight yard. The landscape had begun to change here. There were still plenty of mesquite trees, but there were more rolling hills. The hills gave way to the flat of the Rio Grande south of the town. Henry stood and gazed at the shallow river. It wasn't at all like he had it pictured in his mind's eye.

Hollywood had led him to believe the Rio Grande was some kind of big river. It looks more like Ten-Mile Creek back home, Henry thought. It was the dry season, and the waters resembled a muddy ditch more than a river. Another illusion gone bust. This wasn't as surprising as it would have been a short time ago. Henry was beginning to learn that much of what he saw in the movies was an illusion.

Henry found his way back toward the town. He was able to buy a meal by cleaning out a few stalls in a farmer's barn. The man offered to let Henry sleep there in addition to the meal. The next day, the family offered him breakfast before he went on his way.

* * *

The train chugged up one hill and flew down the next in the West Texas hill country. The rolling hills were barren here except for the grass that covered them like a huge blanket. More than one person who knew the region had said, "God put West Texas there to hold the rest of the world together." There were seldom any buildings in sight. Once in awhile, a lonely farm or ranch house could be seen as the train struggled to climb the next grade.

At night the stars shown in a wide expanse of sky that could be seen from horizon to horizon. The moon appeared several times as large as it had at home--leastwise, Henry thought so. If you listened closely, you could hear the howl of a coyote. When Henry first heard it, he thought it was one of the most mournful sounds he had ever heard. The sound seemed to linger in the air as if it were suspended in time, haunting the listener.

It seemed it might take forever to reach the next outpost of civilization. Most stops were made for coal and water, then the train moved slowly over the tortuous terrain. Day and night came and went as the train wound its way toward El Paso. Nine hundred miles separate the borders at Orange Texas and El Paso.

Henry was not more than half way.

So far, so good. Henry had been able to avoid a run in with the railroad police. These men, known as 'Bulls', were hired by the railroad to prevent hobos from riding their trains. Most of them had reputations for being tough, a status they deserved for the most part. Hobos jungles were filled with men who told tales of murder by the Bulls. Men, who had been beaten to death, had been left along tracks where they were thrown from the train.

The Bull was making his way along the top of the boxcars. He kept a sharp eye out for unwelcome riders. He hadn't seen anybody get on at the last stop, but he was double checking just in case. He came to a boxcar, knelt to look in the car door, and surveyed the scene. Nobody there.

The next car he checked was empty, too. But he found what he was looking for in the next car. There lay a young hobo asleep with his head on a bundle. The hobo hadn't heard him, evidently. The Bull swung down through the car door, landing on his feet. He pulled his billy club from its holster.

"Okay, Weary Willie, get on your feet," the Bull said with contempt in his voice.

Henry had awakened at the sound of the Bull's feet, but he lay still. He stirred now, rolled over, and got to his feet. The Bull stood with his club ready to swing. Henry eyed the Bull warily as he picked up his pack.

"What thu hell you think you're doing, Weary Willie?" The Bull demanded.

"Just hitchin' a ride," Henry replied.

"Well, thu free ride's over. When we get to the next hill, out you go."

"How far is it to the next town?"

"Don't know. What's more, I don't give a damn."

"You can't leave me out here in the middle of nowhere."

"Thu hell, I can't. I can do as I damn well please."

"You can't leave me to die."

"You oughta thought o' that afore you hopped this here freight, Willie."

"Just let me ride to the next stop. Then I'll get off."

"Like hell you will. You're goin' over the side right now."

The Bull swung his club at Henry's head. Henry ducked, but the Bull kicked him in the stomach with a follow-up blow. Henry doubled over landing on the boxcar floor. The Bull picked him up by his jacket collar and shoved him through the open door. Henry fell from the train.

VIII
Rambling with Hobos and Outlaws

Henry rolled end over end as he hit the ground. His momentum took him away from the train which continued to rumble westward along the track. Finally, he came to rest among the cinder blackened brush along the track.

The Bull looked back at his handy work, grinned and said to himself, "That'll teach you to listen to your betters, dammit."

Henry lay still until the caboose of the train passed. When he was sure he was alone, he stirred. The fall from the train had scuffed his clothes, but he was all right otherwise. He got to his feet experimentally. There didn't seem to be anything broken. At least I'm alive, he thought. That was more than many men could have said after such an encounter.

Henry dusted himself off before he began to walk westward along the tracks. He could hear the sound of the locomotive whistle in the distance. It sounded two long, one short, and another long. That meant there was a grade crossing not too far ahead. Maybe there was some kind of town there.

As Henry ambled along the tracks, his mind wandered back to his Uncle George's home. He could almost hear the sound of Annie Lee's Gramophone as Jimmie Rodgers, the singing brakeman, plaintively sang "All Around the Water Tank." The words ran through his head:

All around the water tank, just waitin' for a train.

I'm a thousand miles away from home, sleepin' in the rain.

Nobody seems to want me, or to lend me a helpin' hand.

I'm on my way from 'Frisco; I'm goin' back to Dixieland.

Henry smiled grimly. Those words seemed to fit him well. At least the part about being a thousand miles from home. He really didn't know how far he was from home, but it had to be at least a thousand miles.

How did the rest of that song go? He thought to himself. Now he remembered. He began to sing to himself:

"Walked up to a brakeman to give him a line of talk.

He said 'If you've got money, I'll see that you don't walk.'

Well, I haven't got a nickel, not a penny can I show.

'Get off, get off, you railroad bum.' He slammed the boxcar door.

"He put me off in Texas, a state I dearly love.

The wide-open spaces all around me, the moon and stars up above.

Nobody seems to want me, or to lend me a helpin' hand.

I'm on my way from 'Frisco; I'm goin' back to Dixieland."

As Henry sang to himself, he topped a hill. There before him lay a small town. The grain elevator stood out against the cloudless sky. Not more than two or three miles, Henry thought, as he resolutely began to walk toward the town.

Henry had been walking for an hour or more when he topped another hill. The town seemed as far away as when he had first noticed it. Unaware that one can see long distances across the plains, Henry had mistaken the distance. He would soon learn that one's eyes can deceive them in such terrain, especially if they're unfamiliar with it.

Another two hours of walking finally brought him to the small town. A sign near the edge of town informed him he was entering Hog Town, Texas, population twenty-five.

Henry couldn't have been more delighted if he'd walked through a time warp. The small town resembled a Hollywood movie set. The dirt street was lined with false-fronted buildings.

A grocery store, a saloon, and various other buildings bordered the only street. Board walks with weathered timbers fronted the buildings, joining them with steps.

The few men who were about wore what Henry identified as western wear. Their hats, jeans, and boots marked them as cowboys. The saloon door stood open, inviting everybody to drop in, including the flies.

Henry stopped in front of the saloon. He looked around before he made up his mind to enter. A sign on the bar proclaimed that one could buy a meal in the establishment. Henry didn't read well, but he could make out enough to tell what the sign said.

A bartender stood at the end of the bar polishing a glass. He looked up as Henry walked through the batwing doors.

"Howdy, mister. What'll it be?" The bartender asked civilly enough.

"What you got to eat?" Henry asked.

"Got some stew and cornbread."

"Sounds good. Bring me a plate."

The bartender disappeared through a back door. Henry looked around at the interior of the saloon. He half-expected Tom Mix or Hoot Gibson to walk through the door any time. The bar ran along the back of the room. A mirror, flanked by bottles of whiskey lined on shelves, hung behind the bar. It was quite an elaborate place for a small backwater town in West Texas.

Henry would learn that the saloon was a staple of western towns. Even prohibition had failed to rid many towns of their watering holes. The people of the area often ignored the law, and the law enforcers were reluctant to try and enforce it in small towns. They had neither the time nor the people to do so.

The bartender returned with a steaming plate of stew topped with a generous slice of cornpone. He sat the plate before Henry, "That'll be two bits."

Henry fished in his pocket for a coin, found a quarter, and

handed it to the man. The bartender checked the coin to be sure it was U. S. He sometimes had men try to pass Mexican coins, which were worth considerably less, as U. S. mint. Satisfied that the coin was negotiable, the bartender returned to his station behind the bar.

Henry ate his meal in silence. The quiet of the shadowy saloon seemed to lull him after his long hot walk in the blazing sun. It was good to find shelter from the elements.

Men came and went quietly for the most part. There was an exception, however. A disheveled man with a scraggly beard slammed the batwings back as he burst into the room.

"Howdy, ever'body," he yelled at the top of his voice.

The bartender looked at the man. The newcomer was obviously drunk, although it was only the middle of the afternoon.

"Say, Samson, how 'bout holding it down?" The bartender said quietly.

"How come?" Samson asked with a thick tongue.

"'Cause I got customers."

"Hell, they too good to drink with me?"

"I don't reckon, but most of 'em want it quiet and peaceful. So how about keeping it down?"

"Keep it down, hell. I can whip any man in this room," the drunk staggered in his tracks.

Henry listened as the drunk argued with the bartender. Nobody moved. The drunk wasn't satisfied. He felt his challenge should be answered. What the hell did these people mean anyhow, ignoring him?

"Hell, I can whip any man in this county," Samson raised the ante.

Still, no one answered his challenge.

"Didn't you jackasses hear me?" Samson continued. "I can whip any man in this state. Ain't nobody got the guts to say otherwise?"

The bartender looked at the table where a long, lanky cowboy sat smoking a homemade cigarette. A drag on the cigarette made it glow in the twilight of the room. The bartender nodded his head in response to the cowboy's questioning glance.

With one swift motion, the cowboy was on his feet striding toward the noisy Samson. The tall man grabbed the drunk by the shoulder, spun him around, planted a boot on Samson's butt, and sent him sailing through the batwings into the dusty street.

Beneath the batwings, Henry could see the man lying in the street. Samson slowly got to his feet, brushed himself off, and staggered down the street. As he reeled off, he said, "Huh, I took in too much territory."

* * *

The train slowed for the turn. A hill ahead made the winding serpent of cars slow to a walking pace. Henry swung aboard a boxcar with ease, made his way to the front, and lay down using his pack for a pillow.

The engine huffed and puffed as the engineer opened the throttle. The fireman glanced at the glass that told him how high the water was in the boiler. He pulled the cord attached to the handle that would allow fresh water to enter the tank. When the tank was sufficiently filled, the fireman loaded his shovel with coal, stepped on the treadle, and tossed the shovelful of blackened carbon into the yawning mouth of the roaring dragon. He repeated the operation until the blue flames licked at the boiler with the fury of a miniature hell. The train's speed increased slightly. It topped the rise and plunged down the opposite side.

El Paso lay ahead. Barring some kind of trouble, Henry thought, he should be there in another day or less. He'd learned his lesson. The Bulls were going to find it harder to toss him from a freight the next time.

* * *

Henry found El Paso interesting, but he was more fascinated by his short trip across the border to Juarez, Mexico. There he found a world unlike anything he'd experienced. Poverty was very familiar to Henry, having been raised in the woods of South Georgia, but he was unprepared for the squalor he found in the streets of Juarez.

Men lay in the streets smelling of cheap wine. Harlots plied their trade in the open on the streets, ragged children begged for money and any morsel of food they could spy. Raw sewage ran in the street, rendering the smell intolerable to anyone unaccustomed to the scent. Henry didn't dare eat or drink anything in the city for fear he might come down with some dreaded illness. It didn't take long for him to get enough of this skid row city.

Back in El Paso, Henry found the hobo jungle. It seemed like a haven of cleanliness compared to what he'd witnessed south of the border. He fell into companionship with the other hobos easily. The chatter always turned to where they had been and what they had seen. Henry sat for hours and listened as one after another seasoned traveler told of his exploits. That fed Henry's appetite for more travel and adventure.

The next day another hobo, known as Sidetrack, persuaded Henry to accompany him north along the Golden State Route. Henry liked traveling alone, but he welcomed the chance to share his experiences with another person. The two caught a northbound train for Alamogordo.

North of Alamogordo, the desert gave way to the Capitan Mountains. Past the mountain range, the land flattened again as they crossed Lincoln County, the site of the famous Lincoln County War and home of Billy the Kid. A long hot, boring ride took them through a whistle stop known as Tucumcari.

They were soon back in Texas crossing the panhandle. A short while later, they crossed the Oklahoma panhandle into Kansas. The duo decided to leave the train for a while at Liberal. A few hours of work brought them the reward of a hot meal and a dollar in their pocket. To a hobo, that was high living.

The next train through Liberal wasn't due until late at night.

Sidetrack and Henry sat by the tracks and waited patiently for their ride. There was a full moon, and you could see forever across the prairie. A column of smoke rose from the approaching train, revealing its presence before the sound reached them.

The train paused briefly at the Liberal station. As it moved out, Henry and Sidetrack boarded a boxcar, climbing the ladder near the end. As they made their way along the top, they discovered the car had a skylight. One by one they slid through the opening. As soon as both were inside the dark car, a light appeared at one end of the car. The glow revealed a group of twenty to thirty men.

Sidetrack hesitated briefly, "Is this car full?" He asked.

This was a standard greeting among hobos. They never intruded on each other's solitude. Even when there was one man in the car, he could have it all to himself by answering, "This car's full." A reply of "no" was an invitation to join the rider.

A tall muscular fellow sitting near the front of the car eyed the two men in the flickering light of the torch that had been lit. "No, this car ain't full," he answered.

Sidetrack looked at the speaker, "Thanks."

Suddenly a look of recognition crossed Sidetrack's face. "Is that Jeff Davis?"

The muscular man looked at Sidetrack for a moment before he spoke, "Who wants t' know?"

"I go by the handle, Sidetrack."

"Yeah, Sidetrack. I'm Jeff Davis. Have we met?"

"Uh, huh. One time down near New Orleans. It were in a jungle. You had a pretty little gal a travelin' with you."

Jeff Davis thought for a minute. Finally he said, "I can't rightly remember, but, hell, I've met so many folks it's hard t' keep 'em all straight. Say, who's your pal, Sidetrack?"

Sidetrack turned to Henry, "Goes by the name o' Slim. Georgia Slim, I reckon. He's outa Georgia."

Jeff Davis nodded at Henry, "Glad t' have you on board,

Slim. Glad t' make your acquaintance. Won't you boys join us?"

Henry and Sidetrack found a seat in the circle. Jeff Davis began introducing the men around--rather he called on each one to introduce himself. A list of pseudonyms as long as Henry's arm was given. A hobo hardly ever used his real name.

When the introductions were complete, Jeff Davis addressed himself to Henry, "Say you're from Georgia?"

"Yeah."

"What part?"

"South part."

"I've been in Georgia a couple o' times."

The crowd chuckled. One of them said what they were all thinking, "Hell, Jeff, you been ever'where a couple o' times."

His companions laughed again.

"Yeah, that's how come they call 'im King of thu Hobos," somebody else chimed in.

Jeff Davis grinned. He liked the title. It wasn't official, of course, but it was good to have the recognition and admiration of your friends and companions.

"You boys been on the road long," he asked good naturedly.

Sidetrack took a drag on his newly lit cigarette, blew a smoke ring, and said, "Hell, I was born on the road. Seems like it anyway. I don't know 'bout Slim. We met down near El Paso. Thought we'd see something 'sides desert and tumbleweeds."

"I've been riding the high iron for some weeks now," Henry volunteered.

"Say," Sidetrack asked, "how's the Bulls on this road? Anybody seen any on this train?"

Jeff Davis grinned, "A Bull'd be crazy t' mess with this many 'bos, wouldn't he, boys?"

Cheers of "Hear! Hear!" went around the group.

"Tell us 'bout the Bulls you've run into, Jeff," one of the hobos prodded.

Jeff Davis had the gift of gab. That was one of the reason

men liked him. Everywhere he went, he spun tales of adventure that made his listeners sit up and take notice. Davis warmed to his topic.

"This road ain't bad. Oh, there's a few s.o.b.s just like anywheres else, but they ain't that bad."

"What's the worst one you ever seen, Jeff?"

"Well, there's this stretch up in Idaho that's so bad they call it 'Dead man's mile.' Seems like there was this one fellow, name of Sam Hill. All the 'bos said he was the worst of the lot. They say he killed a hundred 'bos and dumped 'em on that mountain road."

"You don't mean it! A hundred, you say?"

"It was probably just talk. You know how stories like that gits told 'til they're bigger'n life."

"What happened, Jeff?"

"The way I hear it, a car full o' 'bos got together and punched his ticket. Sent him off on the westbound."

The statement meant he was dead. To say someone had gone on the westbound was to announce his demise.

An old, bearded hobo broke the train of thought with a question, "Say, Jeff, you ever been to Canady?"

"As a matter of fact, I have. Would you like t' hear about it?"

"Yeah, I would."

Jeff Davis continued to entertain his audience as the train rolled through the night.

* * *

Henry had thoroughly enjoyed meeting Jeff Davis. He told himself it was a once in a life time chance to meet a real folk hero. It would also make a great story to tell when he got home again. Actually, Henry had begun to think of home more and more lately. So, when he reached Topeka, he determined to head south again. His ultimate goal was to return to Georgia.

"Sorry t' see you go," Sidetrack said as they said their goodbyes.

"I'm kind of sorry about it, too. But I been thinking I ought to get home and check on my Mama."

"I understand. Well, it was great t' meet you. Maybe we'll cross trails again sometime."

"I wouldn't be surprised."

Henry shook Sidetrack's hand and answered the call of a south bound out of the Topeka freight yards. The train took him into Oklahoma. Near Muskogee, he decided to leave the train for a while. Family tradition said he was descended from the Cherokee Indians. He wanted to visit the Indian Nations briefly while he was in the area.

It didn't take long to convince him that he wouldn't want to live among the Indians. The poverty of the tribes was one thing, but their customs were totally strange to him.

The most impressive thing he saw was the Indian method of cooking fish. The fish was wrapped in wet leaves, then covered with mud. The mud-covered fish was then placed on a bed of hot coals. The heat baked the fish rather nicely. Henry thought the meat tasted delicious, but he couldn't quite forget how the food had been prepared.

After a brief trek among the Indians, Henry again made his way south. He had been advised that he could make connections at Fort Smith, Arkansas to head east.

With this in mind, he was walking along a dusty Oklahoma road about mid morning when a black Ford Roadster overtook him. The car flew by leaving him in a cloud of dust. Suddenly the driver applied the brakes, bringing the sleek car to an abrupt stop. The transmission ground as the car was backed toward Henry. He stepped to the side of the road in time to avoid being hit by the car.

As the dust settled, Henry could see a man and woman in the car. The man was driving. The woman sat beside him on the seat grinning at Henry. The man was a skinny, somewhat pimpled young fellow. Henry thought he looked as if he could use some sunlight. His face looked pale.

The woman was a slight built blonde. Her face was almost the color of her hair. She don't eat too good, Henry thought.

"Hey, buddy, how 'bout a ride?" The pimpled young man said with a grin. "You look kinda hot 'n tired."

Henry studied his face for a moment before he answered. It wasn't a good idea to accept a ride with some folks. He'd heard of people who'd gotten themselves robbed and killed when they rode with strangers. What the heck, he was hot and tired. This once wouldn't hurt.

"Don't mind if I do," Henry replied reaching for the door handle.

The blonde slid over next to the driver. Henry seated himself, placed his pack on the floor between his feet, and closed the door. The driver engaged the clutch, and the car sped away with a shower of dust and gravel.

The blonde grinned at Henry. He thought he caught a look of disapproval from Pimples. Blondie ignored him.

"So, where you headed?" Pimples inquired.

"Fort Smith."

"Well, I'll be damned. Ain't that a coincidence, Sue?"

The blonde looked at him, but she just grinned.

"We was just talkin' 'bout goin' that way ourselves. By the way, my name's, Sam. This is my sister, Sue. What's your name?"

"You can call me, Slim."

Pimples grinned at Henry. "Name sure fits you. You're a long, tall one if I ever saw one."

The trio rode on in silence for a while. Pimples drove as if he had to be somewhere yesterday. Henry kept an eye on the speedometer. It seemed to him the needle might twist off at anytime. Henry began to wonder if accepting this ride had been such a good idea after all.

Pimples sped through a little one street town. As they

whizzed by, a black car with a red light on its roof pulled out behind them. The sound of a siren pierced their ears as the cop pursued them down the dusty road. Henry glanced at Pimples. He showed no sign of slowing down. A glance back at the police car told Henry that they were out distancing the cop easily.

"What kind of engine you got in this buggy, anyhow?" Henry asked.

Pimples grinned as he concentrated on his driving, "V-8," he responded.

The car bucked as it crossed a small rise in the road. Henry looked for the police car again. It was nowhere in sight. Pimples glanced back over his shoulder, "Looks like we lost 'im."

"Yeah," Henry answered, making a note to get out of the car as soon as the opportunity presented itself.

Half an hour later they rolled into a somewhat larger town. Pimples slowed down here, driving as if he were on a Sunday afternoon excursion. The change was almost schizophrenic. Pimples pulled the car into a service station, stopped before the gas pumps, and killed the engine.

"Me and sis got some business to attend to, Slim. But if you'll meet us on the other side of town. You're welcome to ride on to Fort Smith."

"Thanks," Henry responded. "I think I'll go to that café and get a bite to eat."

Henry picked up his pack and strolled off down the street. He had no intention of riding anywhere else with Pimples and his sister, if she really was his sister. Henry had become suspicious of their relation by the looks they had exchanged.

Henry seated himself by the window of the café. Across the street, Henry could see the service station attendant as he filled the fuel tank of Pimples' Ford. Pimples had gotten out of the car and was strolling around. Henry noticed Pimples had a slight limp. Pimples paid the service man, then he and the blonde got back in the car. The Ford disappeared around the corner of a brick building.

Henry ordered a hamburger and a cup of coffee. The waitress brought his food. She was about to turn around when she looked out the window. A thin, bald man was running toward the café. He burst through the door out of breath.

"W-where's the chief?" The newcomer gasped.

The waitress looked him square in the face, "Don't know. I ain't seen 'im since early this mornin'. He come in about seven. Had some coffee and pie. Then he left. What you want 'im fer?"

The man gasped for breath again, "I think somebody's robbin' thu bank."

"No!"

"Yeah. I just seen a man and a woman go in there."

"What's so strange about that?"

"They was carryin' guns."

The waitress's face changed colors. She didn't quite know how to respond. Finally she found her voice, "Try the drug store. The chief stops in there for a soda sometime."

"Thanks," the man said as he dashed out the screen door.

Henry looked out the window. There wasn't much going on in this sleepy little town, but a hush seemed to have settled over it even more. A few people moved about the streets on their business, oblivious to what might be happening around them.

Two pistol shots sounded. They echoed off the walls of the buildings resonating across the small town. Henry saw the Ford Roadster with Pimples at the wheel. It came from behind the corner building at breakneck speed. The tires were laying rubber as the car careened down the street.

Somewhere in the distance, Henry heard the boom, boom of a shotgun as both barrels were discharged. The Ford was out of sight momentarily.

Nobody in the café moved. They all sat as if they were models for some still photo or painting. Suddenly, a man burst through the door.

"The bank's been robbed!" He announced with emphasis.

"Who done it?" Somebody in the crowd demanded.

The man looked at the inquirer, "We're all lucky t' be alive."

"Who was it robbed the bank, dammit?"

"Bonnie and Clyde!" he announced firmly.

IX
Effie and the Airplane

Henry was hiking through South Carolina. He had worked his way across Arkansas, Tennessee, North Carolina, and into South Carolina without incident. Each time he thought about the incident in Oklahoma, he shuddered to think how close he had come to getting caught up in that bank robbery. That was something you saw in the movies or read about in the papers. Things like that didn't happen to ordinary people. He considered himself ordinary. It would be all right with him if it never came that close again.

There was no way to know whether the culprits had been Bonnie and Clyde. The locals in Oklahoma had thought that's who the couple was. They could have been anybody as far as Henry knew. It didn't matter. He was just as glad to be clear of them.

While Henry thought on these things, he heard a scream. It sounded like a woman. Yes, it was. He couldn't quite make out what she was saying. Stopping for a moment, he listened. The cry was more distinct now.

"Help me! Somebody help me! He's killing me!"

The sound came from somewhere off to the right of the road ahead. Henry hitched his pack up tighter and broke into a trot. The call grew louder as he ran. He could hear sobs of crying in between the words.

Perhaps a hundred yards ahead, he saw a man and woman

struggling with each other. They were in front of a weather-beaten house situated in an oak thicket. The man appeared to be beating the woman. Henry saw the man raise his hand and strike the woman a blow on the face. She fell beneath the impact, rolling in the sandy yard. The man reached for her again as Henry approached.

"Hey, what's going on here?" Henry demanded.

The man turned his fury on Henry, "Stay the hell out of this. It ain't none of yore business."

"We'll see about that."

The man swung at Henry, but he missed. Henry sidestepped the swing easily. The man recovered and rushed Henry again. They both went sprawling into the sandy soil.

Meanwhile, the woman lay sobbing in the sand where she had fallen. She seemed to realize that she was no longer under attack. Looking carefully under her arm, she saw the man locked in combat with a stranger. She pushed herself to a sitting position, scrambled to her feet, and ran into the house.

Henry rolled his opponent over and slugged him with his right fist. The man was dazed enough for Henry to stand. Henry pulled him to his feet. The man started to swing again. Henry evaded the swing and caught him from behind. Momentarily, Henry had his adversary in a full-nelson. The man struggled, but to no avail.

"Now what's this all about?" Henry asked again through a gasp of breath.

The man spat before he answered, "Mister, just who the hell do you think you are, interfering in a family fight."

"Family, did you say?"

"Yeah. Family. This is between me and my wife."

"Well, maybe somebody oughta teach you not to beat up on women."

"Who's gonna do it? What goes on between a man and his wife ain't nobody's damn business."

Henry had his back to the door of the house. He didn't see

the woman. She came through the front door carrying a two-pronged meat fork she had retrieved from the kitchen. Without warning, she approached Henry and plunged the fork into his back just above the shoulder blade.

Henry lost his hold on the husband as she pulled the fork from his flesh and started to plunge it in again. The pain was excruciating. Henry tried to reach his back, but the wound was out of reach. He stumbled a step or two. The husband grabbed his wife's hand as she tried to stab Henry again.

"No! Don't! You've done him enough damage," the husband shouted.

The woman stood with the fork poised, ready to strike again. Henry took another step or two, gathered his pack in his hand, and walked slowly off down the road. The man and his wife stood with their arms around each other's shoulders watching him go.

* * *

Henry lay by the roadside. The pain in his shoulder felt as if it would never go away. He had felt plenty of pain in his life, but he'd never quite felt pain like this. He was sure he was going to die.

The pain made it impossible to think clearly. The one thought that kept running through his mind was, why? Why the sam hell had she stuck him like a pig? It was her husband who was beating hell out of her. It just didn't make sense.

Henry decided he wasn't going to die after all. He got to his feet and began to walk along the road. By shifting his pack to one side, he could bear the pain. He gritted his teeth in determination.

After Henry had walked for a half hour or so, he came to a small creek. He laid his pack on the grassy bank, removed his shirt and pants, and eased his aching body into the stream. The water was cool to the wound. It helped tremendously. He lay there letting the soreness seep out. After an hour or so, he came out of the water, searched his pack for clean underwear, changed, and hung his wet clothing out to dry.

* * *

The red rooster hopped up on the fence. He sat there for a moment as if he was trying to remember what he was supposed to do. The rising sun cast its rays over the horizon. The rooster spread his wings and let out a long, powerful crow. Not satisfied with the first rendition, he emphasized his point with a second, then a third.

Henry rolled over in bed. He sat up on the side of the bed before rising to go to the window. He could see the rooster sitting on the fence post, flapping his wings and making enough noise to wake the dead.

Henry was still sore from his encounter with the man in South Carolina. His back hurt, and he was still tired from his trip. The last thing he needed was that noisy chicken.

"Shut your damn mouth," Henry yelled, "or I'll put you in the supper pot."

The rooster cocked his head to one side as if to say, what did you say? He crowed one more time just to make his point, then hopped off the fence.

Henry returned to the bed, sat down, and reached for his can of tobacco. He proceeded to roll himself a cigarette. It was good to be home, even if that stupid rooster had awakened him from a perfectly good sleep. He finished rolling the cigarette, reached for a match, struck it on the box, and lit his smoke.

Henry sat there in his underwear smoking and thinking about his adventures. The trip had been exciting, but a fellow could stand just so much excitement. After awhile, it became like a drug. You built up a tolerance for it. It took more and more of it to satisfy you. Well, he'd had enough for the time being. Life had to go on. Right now Henry felt as if there wasn't any thing he couldn't do.

The sounds of Eva making breakfast could be heard in the kitchen. Henry decided to join her. He pulled on his pants and shirt. A few steps took him to the warm kitchen where the smell of baking bread filled the air.

"Morning, Mama," Henry said, seating himself at the dining table.

"Good morning. How are you feeling today?" Eva replied.

"All right. What do you need me to do today?"

"The two acres needs plowing. The grass is 'most as high as the corn."

"Okay, I'll do it. Anything else?"

"I'll let you know. Let's take one thing at a time."

"Okay. Say, do you have some coffee made?"

Eva handed him a cup, then filled it with steaming hot coffee.

"Thanks."

* * *

Life fell back into its usual humdrum routine. Henry really didn't mind. It was good to get back to old familiar habits. He plowed the fields along with his brother Joe. He even enjoyed talking with his sisters. Marie was growing into quite a cute young girl, and she thought there wasn't another person in the world like Henry. He was thirteen years her senior, so she almost thought of him as a father.

Henry went back to work in the turpentine woods. He worked for the Dunns now and then, but it was too painful to work the area where he and Clint Jackson had fought. He really wasn't over Avis. It didn't matter that she and her family had moved--somewhere across town he'd heard. Each time he thought of her, he felt the pain return.

Not long after Henry came home, he learned that his fight with Clint had brought him a certain notoriety. One man in particular would cross the street when he saw Henry coming. Henry learned the reason for this strange behavior from his friend, Bee.

The way Bee told it, Aaron McMillan had known Clint before he came to Appling County. Clint's reputation as a fighter made him a feared man in Coffee County. Aaron was among those who went out of his way to avoid trouble with Clint. Bee told Henry, with laughter in his eyes, that Aaron had supposedly said, "I don't want to walk on the same side of the street with the man that can whip Clint Jackson."

Henry took some comfort in those words, but they did little to help alleviate the pain of losing his first love.

Time, however, does have a way of healing old wounds. Henry began to take an interest in girls again. He was determined he wasn't going to get serious about anybody, but that didn't mean he had to miss all the fun. He would just play the field--play mostly.

The Oxenwine family had lived down the road from Henry's home place for as long as he could remember. Nole, the man of the family, farmed and did other odd jobs around the community. He had a reputation as a fairly good carpenter.

There were two children in the family. The oldest was a boy named Jay. Henry always thought of Jay as peculiar. Jay led a sheltered life due to his mother. Mattie was very protective of her boy. As a result, Jay was teased by nearly every one of his age group. In addition to his mother's over protectiveness, Jay suffered from a tendency to be clumsy. Henry often observed that Jay couldn't walk and chew at the same time.

One night Henry and Bee had been at a party. Jay was there carrying on in his usual bumbling way. The evening had gone pretty well, but Jay had been particularly annoying to Henry. Finally, Bee and Henry left the party while Jay hung around trying to court the host's daughter.

Henry and Bee weren't too far down the road when Bee made a suggestion, "Why d-don't we f-fix ole Jay?"

"How do you mean?"

"Well, y-you know he's a s-scared of his own s-shader."

Henry eyes gleamed, "Yeah, you're right. What'd you have in mind?"

"C-come on, I'll s-show you."

Bee led Henry to a neighbor's house. There on the porch they found a sheet or two of an old newspaper. A roll of twine lay on the wash shelf nearby. Bee appropriated that as well. They headed for the path they knew Jay would take to his house.

About two hundred yards from Jay's house, a small creek ran through thick, bushy woods. The narrow path made a perfect place for Henry and Bee's trick. They set up their trap. The sheet of newspaper was attached to the twine, then the twine was wrapped around pine trees on opposite sides of the path. A complete loop in the twine made it possible to slide the newspaper across the trail. As the twine slid over the bark of the pines, it gave off a scraping, whining sound.

The boys tried their "ghost" a time or two to be sure it worked, then they settled down to wait for Jay. They weren't disappointed. Jay came sauntering along the trail whistling. Apparently he had had quite an enjoyable evening.

Henry stood in the bushes on one side of the trail, while Bee took a similar position on the other side. When Jay was about twenty feet from the twine, Henry pulled the "ghost" across the trail. The twine sang as the paper danced up and down. Jay stopped in his tracks. His overactive imagination was trying to get a fix on the spook.

While Jay stood in a state of confusion, Bee pulled the "ghost" back to his side. Jay began to moan as if he were in pain, "Lordee! Lordee! Lordee!"

Jay's heart leaped to his throat, skipped a beat or two, then hammered until he could feel the blood pounding in his ears. How was he going to get by that thing? The bushes were too thick to go around. He would have to run right by it. That prospect didn't appeal to him, but he didn't exactly have a choice. He'd wait until the ghost was on one side, then he'd make a mad dash for home.

The best he could remember, the foot log was on the right side of the path. If he waited for the ghost to move to the left, he might be able to make it. He watched while the ghost made another pass across the path. As soon as it reached the other side, Jay let out a scream and ran within two feet of Henry. Jay hit the string, breaking it. The broken string caught around Jay's neck. His eyes bulged with terror. He was sure he'd been attacked by the ghost.

Jay's flailing hands broke the string and the ghost ceased to follow him, but when he reached the foot log, he lost his balance and plunged into the shallow creek. He picked himself up and splashed on through the water to the other bank. As soon as he was on dry ground, he began to run with renewed vigor, screaming as he ran.

Henry and Bee watched with great amusement as their victim fulfilled their wildest hope. The darkness hid their mule-eating-briers grins. As one person, they broke into a run, pursuing Jay as he ran at top speed toward his house. They negotiated the foot log successfully and followed Jay home.

Jay's breath was coming in great gasps as he neared his house. The yard had a wire fence about three feet high designed to keep cows and hogs out of the yard. Jay jumped the fence like an Olympic athlete, clearing it easily. He made a bee line for the back porch of the house. However, the pitcher pump sat in the yard just off the porch. Jay's trajectory took him into the pump. He howled with pain as he ran into the pump, but his momentum was scarcely slowed.

The back door of the house presented a momentary obstacle. Jay twisted the door handle. It seemed to be stuck. After what seemed an eternity, he pushed the door open and fell over a chair that had been left near the door.

Henry and Bee stood near the fence listening to the commotion. A light came on inside the house. Mattie's voice could be heard as she called to Jay.

"Jay, son, is that you?"

"Yeah, it's me, Ma."

"What in the world's the matter?"

"Nothing, Ma, just comin' home."

Henry and Bee looked at each other and doubled over with laughter.

The tale was too good not to tell. It wasn't long before the whole community knew about Jay being chased by the "ghost." Finally, Henry and Bee owned up to being the culprits that created the "ghost." Needless to say, Jay wasn't amused, but a lot of other folks thought the incident rather funny.

Jay had a younger sister named Effie. Henry had been around her all his life, it seemed. She had always been a gangly, long-legged slip of a girl. Henry had often thought her legs would have been better placed on a bird. He had never given her a second look, except to tease her about her legs or some other timely thing.

When Effie reached puberty, the ugly duckling became a swan. Her body began to take on a rounded pleasing shape. Her legs became well shaped and muscular. Her black hair shown, while her blue eyes were beautiful enough to drown a young man. At sixteen, she was a knock out.

This metamorphosis took place gradually, of course. So gradually, that Henry had scarcely noticed it. Suddenly, it seemed, he found her attractive. The attraction was mutual, so they began to see each other as something other than childhood acquaintances. Effie, of course, had quite a bit of growing up to do. Henry didn't stop to consider that. He took one look at the package and decided he liked what he saw.

They went to parties together. This was accepted because Mattie considered her daughter properly chaperoned in such situations. Henry didn't mind at first, but he soon became annoyed by the constant attention they had when they were together. This lead to furtive meetings and an occasional breaking of the rules so that they could be together. Henry finally succeeded in getting Effie to go to the movies with him. It was a big step.

Henry had forgotten his promise to himself not to fall for another girl. He was headed for a new heart break, but he was totally oblivious to the fact. The old adage says: "Love is blind," but others know it's also insane.

* * *

The barnstormers came to town. These intrepid men of the air had been making irregular visits for years now--ever since Lucky Lindy had flown from New York to Paris. The typical scene went something like this:

A lone pilot would fly into the area, land his biplane in a farmer's pasture, and request the owner's permission to set up rides for the locals. It was unusual for any farmer to refuse since he usually got some monetary compensation as well as a ride in the airplane--assuming he wasn't scared to death to take it.

Several people had been heard to say, "I don't want t' git no higher than pullin' fodder, or no lower than diggin' taters." But that didn't keep the more adventuress from flocking to the fields. Many of them just came to watch. They didn't have the money to pay for a ride, but it didn't cost anything to watch. Entertainment wasn't easy to come by, so these people took it where they found it--especially when it was free.

Henry had never ridden in an airplane himself. He'd been to plenty of barnstormings, but he had been one of those who watched, mainly because he could ill afford to spend the dollar or two the pilot charged for the ride. Old man Liggitt's boy had been killed in an airplane crash a few years before, and that hadn't helped any either.

One fine Saturday afternoon, a fellow who called himself "Buzz" Branigan landed his sputtering biplane in Clint Crosby's pasture less than a mile from Henry's home. Mr. Crosby went out to see if he could be of any assistance. Buzz informed him that he would like to use his pasture as a landing strip to give folks a ride. They made a bargain and the word went out that there would be airplane rides on the following afternoon.

Buzz knew he was in the Bible Belt, but he figured he could draw a fair crowd after everybody had gotten their weekly dose of preaching. He'd run into some people who considered his services a possible spiritual experience. Like the old black woman who had approached him once with the question, "Mistuh Branigan, how much would you charge t' take me up t' heaven and leaves me dere?" Buzz had tried not to laugh as he explained that his plane couldn't go that high. The old lady had walked away, disappointment clouding her brow.

Sunday came. Henry had gone to Effie's home before noon. They had managed to get away alone. Effie was having a fit to go to the barnstorming.

"Let's hurry," she urged, "we'll be late."

"What's the all fired hurry?" Henry demanded. "It'll be there when we get there."

"But I don't wanta miss anything. Something might happen before we get there."

"Like what?"

"How should I know? Let's go," Effie grabbed Henry by the hand, almost dragging him down the sandy road toward the pasture.

As they approached the intersection of two rutted roads near the Crosby place, several other people met them. Every youngster from miles around had come to see the airplane. They were not more than a hundred yards from the pasture when the plane took off. Buzz flew low over their heads. The wind from the propeller fanned their hair as he soared by.

Effie turned her head and watched as the plane passed them. Her face told Henry she was thrilled to be this close to a real airplane.

"Did you ever see one before?" Henry asked.

"Not this close up. Goodness, it's big."

"Yeah, it's pretty big."

"You know what I want?" Effie said grinning from ear to ear.

Henry was almost afraid to ask, but he managed, "What's that?"

"I want to ride."

"What?"

"I want to ride in the airplane."

Henry thought about it for a minute. He wasn't too sure about this thing. For one thing, he didn't have much money in his pocket. The pilot usually wanted two to three dollars for a ride. He had five dollars, but he'd been saving it for weeks now. There were other things he would have rather spent it on. Secondly, what if something happened. Thoughts of Wright Liggitt's death still flashed before his eyes. Effie's mother would never forgive him if anything happened to her daughter.

"Are you sure? Those things are dangerous."

Effie wiggled her hips and radiated the warmest smile she'd ever given Henry, "Of course, I'm sure. What's the matter? You afraid?"

Henry's manhood had been challenged. That was the one thing you didn't do--no matter who you were--man or woman--especially a woman.

"No. I'm not afraid for myself, but what if something happened to you?"

"Don't be silly. What could happen?"

Henry could think of several things, but he declined to elaborate. He didn't see how he was going to get out of this one. "Why don't we just watch for awhile?"

"Okay, but I wanta ride later."

Henry and Effie mixed with the crowd. Buzz took the plane up several times. A number of people had come with the express purpose of riding the airplane. It didn't matter that it was going to cost them as much as a week's wages.

Buzz taxied to his loading place. He stepped down, grabbed his gas can, and poured five gallons in the fuel tank. "Who's next, folks?" He asked as he turned to the crowd.

Henry looked around. There wasn't anybody else rushing up to ride. "I reckon that'd be us," Henry said handing Buzz a five-dollar bill. "How 'bout givin' us the special," he winked.

Buzz returned the wink, "Sure thing."

Buzz stood back while Henry and Effie seated themselves in the front seat. When they were belted in, Buzz climbed in, taxied off from the crowd, accelerated, and the biplane lifted off.

Effie was grinning from ear to ear as the plane rose above the trees. "Oh, look," she exclaimed.

Corn and cotton fields looked like plaid pieces of cloth beneath them. The wind whipped their hair, and the sensation of flight made them feel light as a feather. In fact they both had the feeling that their stomachs had moved up to their throats.

Buzz gunned the engine. The plane climbed another two or three hundred feet. When it reached this point, Buzz took it into a loop. Effie screamed to the top of her voice as they hung suspended upside down. The sound pierced Henry's ears. Buzz came out of the loop for an instant. The plane leveled off, rushing straight forward.

Suddenly, Buzz dropped the plane into a sideways dive. The wings on the plane quivered under the stress. Henry thought they looked just like a bird flapping his wings. Trees came into view as the plane swept low over the pasture. Henry stole a look at Effie. She was holding her breath. Her face was almost purple.

Buzz climbed once more and did a second loop. As they went into the loop, Effie caught her breath long enough to scream, "Nooooo!"

The crowd on the ground was enjoying the show immensely. They stood transfixed as Buzz put his plane through its paces. To the crowd, the show seemed to last only a few seconds, but Effie could have sworn it was an hour.

When the plane taxied to a stop, her face was flushed with either fear or anger. It was impossible to tell which. Buzz jumped to the ground. He gave Henry a hand as he dismounted from the wing. Henry turned to help Effie down. She glared at him. If looks could have killed, he would have been a dead man. She ignored his extended hand.

"You . . ." she said, her thoughts going to that place where all thoughts go when we are unable to express ourselves.

Buzz grinned, "Hope you folks enjoyed your ride."

Henry laughed, "We sure did."

Effie shot Henry another dagger with her eyes, "Speak for yourself you. . . ." Again her thoughts were inexpressible.

Effie stepped onto the wing, slid to the ground, and turned to face Henry. She straightened her skirt. Looking hard into Henry's eyes, she said emphatically, "You dog!"

Effie turned to walk away. As she paced off in anger, a wet circle was visible on the back of her skirt.

X

Logging the Alapaha River Swamp

Henry raised the tongue of the timber cart high enough to lay the "dogs" on top of the log. He waded through the bushes and hooked the dogs to the piece of timber. A crack of the bullwhip and a shout of, "Hup," told the ox team to pull the cart down. As the cart tongue came down under the force of the four-cow team, the butt of the log lifted slightly off the ground. The oxen's muscles bulged as they strained to move the timber.

Henry cracked his whip again as he called "Baaack." The team took a step or two backward allowing the timber cart tongue to rise. Henry had placed a small limb under the log to keep it from settling back to the wet soggy soil of the swamp floor. He took another hitch with the dogs before he cracked the whip.

The straining team pulled the cart. The log moved a little farther under the tremendous force of the team. The secret to moving the log from its mossy bed was to keep the team in motion. Henry followed in the path of the log as the team made their way to the hill. They were soon on a beaten path. The log cart, along with its burden moved slowly, but surely, up the path to the logging brow.

Henry called a loud, "Gee!"

The oxen swung right, depositing the log neatly alongside several others that lay waiting to be loaded on the truck.

"Baaack," Henry commanded.

The team gave enough slack to disengage the dogs of the

cart. Henry kicked the dogs loose with one blow of his foot, cracked his whip again, and commanded the oxen to move forward. "Hup."

The team stood patiently waiting for their next command. This team was well trained. They would wait until they were out of harness before they did anything other than by command.

Henry made his way to the water barrel. He picked up the dipper from the rack, filled it with water from the tap, and drank his fill. The water refreshed him. Better get a move on, Henry thought. Old man Fletcher wanted to load another truck before sundown. The old man considered it a waste of time and energy if his log truck wasn't loaded when it left the woods for the night. Henry uncoiled the bullwhip, cracked it, and commanded the oxen to move.

He'd been driving the team for a few weeks now. Jim Fletcher had let it be known that he was looking for a cart man. Henry had jumped at the chance to do this new kind of work. He'd done some work with oxen before, but he'd never handled a timber cart. This was a new challenge--one he had looked forward to.

It was good to get away from home. Effie had given him the cold shoulder after the airplane ride. She hadn't spoken to him for weeks. When she finally did, it was to tell him that she didn't want to see him anymore. On top of that, Nole, her father, had made it clear that he didn't appreciate Henry putting his daughter's life in danger. Henry pointed out that he was in just as much danger, but Nole hadn't considered that a valid excuse for what Henry had done.

Henry didn't worry about it too much. After all, she had gotten what she wanted as far as he was concerned. She had challenged him with that remark about being scared to ride in the plane. He had shown her who was scared. Now there, let her get huffy. He couldn't have cared less.

* * *

The logging crew worked from Monday morning to Saturday noon. Men who lived close enough to the camp usually went home leaving the camp deserted for the weekend. The arrangement went well except for the stock. Somebody had to tend the stock on the weekend. Henry had gone home every couple of weeks in the beginning, but he lived too far away to make a regular trip. It was just too expensive. When Mr. Fletcher offered him extra money to stay and feed the stock on weekends, Henry accepted.

His new responsibility gave him more money to send home. Eva had agreed for Henry to go to the logging camp with the understanding that he would send money home to help her pay the mortgage and other bills. He had done his best to fulfill the bargain.

Needless to say, the weekends could get boring, but Henry soon found ways to entertain himself. The small town of Ocilla, Georgia lay not too far from the logging camp. It had a movie house and two or three joints where a man could get a drink and meet a woman.

But there were other mundane chores that had to be done, too. One Saturday afternoon, the crew had left for home. Henry fed the stock and prepared to do his laundry. A creek ran into the river not too far from the camp. He decided to take his clothes down there for a wash.

Arriving at the creek bank, Henry stripped off his clothes, all except his undershorts. He then proceeded to sit in the small stream as he laundered his clothes. His mind was totally on the task at hand when he heard a horse snort. There, not fifty feet away, sat a woman on a horse. There was no where to hide. Henry continued to wash his clothes.

The rider spotted Henry sitting in the stream. She smiled to herself as she called, "Howdy."

"Howdy do, ma'am," Henry responded.

The young woman looked him over carefully. His muscular

body was attractive to her. She knew he must be one of the loggers working the swamp, but she really had no idea who he was.

"My name's Jane Fletcher. Who might you be?" She asked with a smile.

"Henry, Henry Reynolds," Henry answered.

"Looks like you're catching up on your wash."

"Uh, huh. I didn't have a clean stitch to my name. Decided t' get some cleanin' done while I weren't nursin' cows."

"Oh, so you must be working for my Pa."

"If your Pa's Jim Fletcher, I am."

"That's him, all right. How long you been working with Pa?"

"About a month. I stayed on to see about the cows this weekend."

"I see. What do you do for fun around here?"

Henry squeezed out a shirt, threw it over a limb, and reached for a pair of pants. "Don't have a lot of time for fun. Too busy workin' most of the time. What do you do for fun?"

Jane dismounted from the saddle, "Oh, I go riding in the woods a lot. It's a great place to get away and think about things."

"Yeah, I know what you mean. There's lots of quiet, and you have lots of time to think. That's one reason I like to stay on weekends."

"Do you ever get to town?"

"Sometimes. I've been to a movie once or twice. Do you ever go to the movies?"

"Sure do. I like all kinds of movies. What kind do you like?"

Henry wrung out another piece of clothing, "I guess you might say westerns are my favorite. But I like jungle stories, too. Tarzan's my favorite in the jungle stories."

"I like Tarzan, too. He's so handsome and muscular."

Henry didn't answer that one. He concentrated on his laundry. Best not to let her know how flustered he felt. She had him at a disadvantage.

Jane grinned at Henry again, "Well, I reckon I'd better go and let you finish what you started. I'll see you around sometime."

Henry was in an awkward position, but he seldom let that keep him from making a point with a good-looking woman, "Say, would you like to go to a movie sometime?"

Jane looked thoughtful for a moment, "Yeah, I'd love to. When did you have in mind?"

"What's playing tonight?"

"Ken Maynard, I think."

"Good, he's one of my favorites."

"Mine, too."

"There's just one problem. I don't have a car."

Jane grinned, "Oh, heck, that's no problem. Why don't I pick you up about sundown?"

"Okay. See you then."

* * *

The date had turned out to be lots of fun. Ken Maynard had rounded up the bad guys within the hour. The second feature hadn't been quite as interesting, but Jane and Henry sat through it anyhow. Afterward, they found time to go to a local eatery. The food was too greasy, but they both enjoyed the drinks.

Henry drove Jane's car back to the camp. They sat and chatted for a while. The stars overhead seemed extra clear–a night made for courting. Jane began to drop hints that she had to go. Henry was reluctant to let the evening end. He decided that he had to know how her lips tasted before she got away.

"How about next Saturday?" Henry asked.

"I'll let you know."

"Good. I'll look forward to hearin' from you."

Henry reached for her. Jane didn't move toward him, but she didn't pull away either. That's a promising sign, Henry thought. Henry kissed her cheek experimentally. She didn't try to pull away. He moved to her mouth. She offered him her lips as his arms tightened around her. The kiss was not long, but Henry felt he'd found out what he wanted to know.

"Good night," Henry said as he slid out of the car.

"Good night," she answered. She drove away into the night.

The taste of her mouth lingered on Henry's lips.

* * *

The logging continued. Fletcher hired more men as the work progressed. Soon the logging camp had a score of men working on a somewhat regular basis. The larger crew led to a problem. Fletcher had hired a cook, but the men had found so much fault with his culinary skills that he had left the camp. The men decided they would each cook their own food. This led to a logistical problem. How could twenty men use the cooking facilities that were available? It soon became clear that this was not working.

"What we gonna do about this situation?" Fletcher asked during a crew meeting one evening.

"Looks t' me like we gonna have t' hire another cook," one of the crew volunteered.

"Where's he gonna come from? You boys has got a reputation for runnin' off cooks. I can't hire nobody from town. They won't take the job."

The crew sat silently for a moment. Henry spoke, "I'll cook if the pay's decent."

Fletcher turned to Henry, "What do you consider decent?"

"A dime a day per man."

"A dime!" Delton Hardwick said.

"Yeah, a dime a day!" Henry emphasized.

Delton counted on his fingers, "That two dollars a day for cooking. That's more than I make pulling a crosscut saw."

"That's my offer. Take it or leave it."

Fletcher surveyed his crew, "How 'bout it men? You willing t' pay Henry a dime a day t' cook?"

Everybody nodded their agreement except Delton. "Damned if I'll pay. I'll cook for myself."

So Henry became crew-cook. He still drove the team, but Fletcher allowed him to take off long enough to prepare a meal before the men came back to camp. Henry's pay was the highest in the camp, and Delton continued to resent it.

One evening the crew came in. Delton had gone off to the sleeping shed saying he was too tired to eat, but later he came plundering around to see if there was any left over food. Henry caught him in the act of taking a piece of bread and some meat.

"Thought you were too tired t' eat," Henry said accusingly.

"I was. I'm feelin' better now."

"How 'bout doing your own cookin' then?"

"Aw hell, can't a man have a bite of leftovers?"

"Not if he's not payin' for the cookin'."

Delton was hungry. He'd put in a long day pulling a crosscut saw, and he wanted to eat badly enough to fight for it. He considered doing just that, but decided against it. Henry's reputation as a fighter gave him second thoughts. He fumbled in his pants pocket, pulled out a coin, handed it to Henry, and said, "Here. Here's a damn dime."

Henry took the coin, feeling he had made his point. From then on, Delton paid his dime a day. He may have continued to resent it, but he was smart enough not to let Henry know.

* * *

Henry's experience as camp cook led him to experiment with other things. During the week he prepared such culinary delights as bacon and beans, but the weekends gave him an opportunity to try his hand with more exotic foods. One day he decided to try baking a cake. The problem was, he didn't have an oven. Henry decided to try and make one.

There were some pieces of galvanized tin in the camp, probably left over from some other project. Henry cut four posts, cut the tin to size, and constructed a makeshift oven. A piece of tin served as the top while a second piece sat on braces six inches or so below the top. The griddle would be placed between the sheets of tin.

Henry mixed his cake with flour from the barrel where he usually made hoecake. He added eggs and a bit of flavoring he had brought to camp for occasional use. He tasted the batter. All in all, it didn't taste too bad.

A griddle full of batter went on the bottom layer of tin in his homemade oven. A shovelful of coals from the oak wood fire was piled underneath, and another on the top sheet of tin completed the process. Actually, it worked quite well. You had to keep a close eye on the procedure, but the bread baked all the way through in a matter of minutes.

Each layer was carefully baked in the oven. A frosting made from egg whites gave the finished product an appetizing appearance. Henry sat his cake in a well-covered place to cool.

On Sunday afternoon, Fletcher and his daughter came to the camp with a load of hay for the oxen. Henry helped them unload the hay, then invited them to have a cup of coffee with him. Jane sat and chatted with Henry. Fletcher was off wandering around the camp, checking on things in general.

Meanwhile, Henry brought out his cake, cut a slice for Jane, and poured her a cup of coffee. Jane tasted the cake experimentally. She licked her lip to remove a piece of frosting.

"Hmm, that's good," she commented.

"Thank you. I baked it myself."

"You did? How in the world? I didn't know you had an oven out here."

"I don't. I made one."

"That's interesting. How did you manage that?"

Henry explained his method to her. She was amazed at the ingenuity Henry had employed. It was as fascinating to her as the taste of the cake.

When Fletcher returned, she couldn't wait to share the story. "Here taste this cake, Dad," Jane said, offering him a small bite of the piece she was eating.

Fletcher tasted the morsel, licked his lips, and said, "Think I'll have a piece, if you don't mind."

"Help yourself," Henry urged.

Fletcher cut a piece of the cake and savored it along with a cup of coffee. When he had finished, he wiped his mouth.

"Say, you mind if I have another?"

"Go right ahead."

The trio sat there while Fletcher consumed most of the cake. Henry decided he'd have to bake another if he wanted much cake, but the old man's relish told him his experiment had been a success.

* * *

The storm clouds had been gathering for more than an hour. Black clouds boiled over the river. Lightning flashed and thunder rolled. The oxen were penned in a wooden corral down the hill from the camp. They stirred restlessly as the storm grew more intense.

A flash of lightning hit a nearby oak sending splinters flying. A limb fell across the corral fence. The restless cows turned their backs to the wind and crowded together against the opposite fence. Another bolt of lightning rent the sky striking a few feet from the corral. Suddenly the oxen pushed at the corral fence. Ordinarily the fence would have held, but the combined weight of the cows forced it to collapse. The oxen trampled the fence rail as they ran from the corral in panic.

Henry heard the commotion. He realized there was something wrong, but he wasn't inclined to get out in the flashing lightning to investigate. He hovered under the palmetto lean-to while the rain began to pour from the inky sky. It came down in sheets. The wind came up, rushing through the trees, sending limbs flying through the air. The cows would have to wait.

After an hour or so, the storm blew itself out. The sweeping clouds moved to the east; the sun returned low in the Western sky.

Henry went to inspect the broken fence. He would have to

repair it before he brought the oxen back. Otherwise, they would just wander off again. He found a hammer, some nails, and a few replacement boards. The sun was low on the horizon when Henry finally had the corral repaired enough to hold the cows.

"Just as well go hunt'em," Henry said to himself.

He trudged off toward the stand of trees near the river. It was unlikely that the animals would cross the river. Sure enough, their tracks were there, but the cows were no where in sight. Henry began to track the oxen in the fading light. After a half hour or so, he decided that it was useless to try any longer. He would return to the camp.

The night was dark. The moon wouldn't rise for another three or four hours. Ordinarily, Henry had an excellent sense of direction. He could find his way through some of the worst circumstances, but he soon found himself at a loss to make his way back to the camp. The trees had been cut in this part of the woods; everything looked the same.

He had been walking for an hour or more. The day had already been a long one. He was tired from repairing the fence, and it seemed he couldn't take another step. Finally, he decided to rest for a while.

Black clouds continued to obscure the sky. There wasn't a star in sight. Henry knew how to follow the North Star. He could find his way on a clear night, but this night was anything but clear, leading him to the conclusion that he was totally lost.

As Henry sat thinking about his predicament, the clouds cleared momentarily, but not enough for him to find the Little Dipper. He knew the star at the end of the handle would point him north, but he had to find the constellation first--no such luck.

Henry decided to try once more. The visible stars made it possible for him to travel in a straight line, but they were soon hidden by the boiling clouds. Henry walked on in hopes he might be able to stumble on his camp by chance. When another hour or more had elapsed, Henry thought he saw a familiar tree stump.

Yes, it looked very familiar, as well it might. He had passed it not more than fifteen minutes ago. There was no doubt about it; he was going in circles; he was hopelessly lost.

Henry had been told any number of times that the best way to handle this type of situation was to simply stay in one place until daylight. That, he decided, was about the only thing he could do. He sat down by the stump, closed his eyes, and tried to sleep.

He awoke with a start. The morning had dawned. Birds sang across the river swamp in a symphony of beautiful music. Henry stirred. When he stood up, he looked around to orient himself. There, not more than a hundred yards away, lay the camp. A short walk took him there.

Henry decided he needed to get his breakfast. Then the cows would have to be rounded up. Old man Fletcher would have a fit if he came back tomorrow and the oxen were not in the pen.

Henry prepared his food over the fire. As he sat eating his meal, he heard the lowing of a cow. Looking toward the south, he saw the oxen slowly trudging along the three-path road toward the camp. They made a bee line for the corral and started to munch the hay in the feed rack.

Henry looked on in amazement as the cows filed into the corral. "I be damned," he said to himself. "They knew where to find their grub better than I did."

* * *

Jane picked Henry up early one Saturday afternoon. They were planning to spend the day in Ocilla and maybe even ride over to Fitzgerald. During the afternoon, they stopped at a hardware store. Henry wanted to see what they had in the way of a gun. He'd been planning to buy one for sometime, but his funds hadn't been adequate before. Now that he was making some extra money, he felt he could afford one.

The selection wasn't too big, but Henry finally settled on a 32-caliber Smith and Wesson. It had a six-inch barrel and felt right in his hand. He bought it and a holster along with a couple of boxes of cartridges. That would be enough to begin. He wanted to practice his shooting.

Henry and Jane spent the rest of the day just driving around on the sandy South Georgia roads. It was good to get away from the camp for a while. Henry hadn't been home for sometime--to tell the truth, he was getting bored with cows for company.

Once they stopped on the side of the road. Henry wanted to try out his new weapon. An old tin-can furnished a usable target. Henry set the can on a stump, backed off ten steps, pulled the pistol from the holster, and fired. The bullet kicked dirt just short of the target.

Henry stepped forward slightly and tried again. His shot went over the target. I'll have to try something different, Henry thought. He held the pistol in both hands and squeezed the trigger. The bullet tore a hole through the can. Settle down now; Henry told himself. He tried one hand again. The bullet ripped into the rusty can. That's more like it, Henry thought.

When Henry returned to camp, he stored the pistol in his bedroll. That would keep it handy for future use. He had no idea how soon he would have need of the weapon.

* * *

There were a variety of wild animals in the swamps of South Georgia during the nineteen thirties in spite of the expansion of towns and farms. The black bear could be seen rambling among the trees. Alligators were common in the rivers and their surrounding swamps. Beaver dammed creeks and built their nest in the midst of the resulting lakes. Each of these creatures roamed at will and was left pretty much to themselves. An occasional sighting was all that let people know they were anywhere near.

The black panther was also present. This big cat was more elusive. The most common evidence that one was present was the trail the feline left when it slaughtered stock. Farmers often hunted them, but they continued to harass the country side pretty much as they pleased.

Henry knew there was something disturbing the cows. On weekends especially, when he was the only person in the camp, the cows were often upset by the presence of some wild animal.

Once, Henry had seen a small bear running from the vicinity of the corral. He had fired a shot to scare the animal away. The small pistol wouldn't have been powerful enough to kill the bear, even if Henry had wanted to kill it--which he didn't.

Henry began to suspect that he was getting visits from another creature soon thereafter. He found large paw prints not too far from the corral on more than one occasion. He wasn't sure if they were panther tracks, but he wasn't taking any chances. He told old man Fletcher what he suspected, but the old man just laughed it off. He told Henry he was seeing things. Henry hadn't said another word about it.

One Sunday morning, a brilliant dawn came. Henry knew it was daylight by the sound of the birds, but he lay still with his eyes closed. He wanted this tranquillity to last as long as possible.

A bird flew near to the tree Henry was sleeping under. The bird gave a squawk and flew away. Suddenly the forest grew strangely quiet. Henry sensed something was wrong. He opened his eyes slightly. The cows were stirring restlessly down in the corral. As his eyes became accustomed to the light, he saw a dark form directly over head in the branches of the tree.

The black cat's eyes shown, even in the bright morning light. Red looking eyes watched Henry as if he were a mouse. The cat's tail twitched as if he were angry. The big feline sat like a knot on the limbs he occupied.

Henry watched the animal. Its eyes were fixed on what it obviously considered its prey. Henry had a problem with being breakfast for the huge cat. He considered what to do. He had laid his gun under his pillow. If he could reach it in time, he might be able to shoot the big cat. There was just one problem. He had to be a dead shot; otherwise, he could still be mauled by the huge cat. That prospect wasn't pleasant.

Henry moved a hand experimentally. The cat's eyes followed his movement. Henry decided that whatever he did it was going to have to be quick. Well, he wasn't going to lie here and play cat and mouse all day. He was going to get this over, one way or another.

Henry turned to retrieve his weapon. As he moved, the panther sprang from the tree directly toward him.

XI
The Ghost in the Haunted House

Henry rolled over reaching for his pistol at the same time. He pulled it from under his pillow and cocked the hammer as he brought it up. When he was on his back, he found himself looking at the breast of the panther. Lifting the pistol, he squeezed the trigger.

The bullet hit the huge cat in the left breast, plunged through his heart, and lodged in the beast's shoulder. When the panther hit the ground, blood splattered everywhere. Henry rolled over one more turn before gaining his feet. He stood there looking at the big cat, astonishment written all over his face. His body trembled from the rush of adrenalin. That had been a lucky shot. There was no way he could have aimed and hit the animal, especially with him in motion. Henry decided he'd settle for a lucky shot.

The big cat trembled as his life's blood flowed from his body. He gave a final sigh as he died. The blood continued to flow freely.

Henry considered what to do next. He had to get the cat off his bedroll. It would have to be washed. What was he going to do with a full-grown panther? He thought he might bury it, but he was going to wait until old man Fletcher had seen it. He would laugh out of the other side of his face now.

Henry dragged the carcass down near the corral. The cows lowed nervously when they caught the scent of the cat, but they calmed after a bit. Henry threw a tarp over the carcass, laid a few pieces of wood around the edges to hold the tarp in place, and went back to the task of cleaning his bedroll.

That afternoon, Fletcher and Jane came bringing the usual load of hay for the cows. Henry helped them unload before he mentioned his adventure. When they had finished, he broached the subject.

"Mr. Fletcher, I've got something to show you."

"What's that, son?"

"Remember, you said there weren't any big cats in this swamp."

"Uh, huh. I recall."

"Well, I shot one this mornin'."

"What?"

"That's right."

"What'd you do with 'im?"

"He's right over here under a piece of canvas."

The two men walked over to the canvas-covered carcass. Henry kicked a couple of pieces of wood off the edge and lifted the tarp. Fletcher's eyes bugged out.

"Whew! I'll be damned if that ain't a big 'un. Where'd you shoot 'im?"

"He was sitting in the limbs of that oak over there," Henry pointed to the tree. "He looked to me like he was plannin' to have me for breakfast."

"I'll be damned."

"Yeah, I damned near got eat. If it hadn't been for a lucky shot, I'd probably be dead right now."

The crew heard the story when they arrived for work the next day. The most common comment Henry heard was, "I'm glad it was you instead of me."

* * *

Henry's experience with the panther made him more cautious. His pistol was his constant companion in the woods. He wore it everywhere except to town. It took a while to get used to it, but he soon became accustomed to having it strapped to his hip. Some of the men started to make fun of him for carrying it, but he gave them a look that suggested they had best keep their mouths shut.

Not only did he carry the pistol, he became an expert at handling it. Several boxes of cartridges were expended practicing. In the beginning, Henry used still targets, like a can. Later he graduated to moving targets. Soon he was shooting pine cones in the air. He threw the cone with his right hand, drew the pistol from his hip with the same hand, and fired two or more rounds into the flying target before it hit the ground.

Many Saturday and Sunday afternoons were devoted to target practice. Jane would sit and watch while Henry demonstrated his skill with the weapon. She was impressed enough to ask him to teach her to shoot.

Henry started her lessons using both hands with a still target. She mastered the double-hand technique shortly, but her skill with one hand remained somewhat poor. They were practicing one Saturday afternoon. Henry was holding her arm, trying to help her get the hang of using one hand. She pulled the trigger, the gun spat fire, and the bullet plowed into the stump that held her target.

"I'm not doing so well, am I?" Jane sighed, laying the pistol aside.

Henry grinned at her, "Oh, I don't know. If I was a stump and you had both hands on the pistol, I'd be scared to death."

She kicked him in the shin playfully, sticking her tongue out at the same time. Henry reached for her, and she took off running. He caught her and wrestled her to the ground. They rolled in the wire grass until they were both exhausted. She finally gave in. Henry held her hands down on the ground as he sat over her gazing at her face. A ghost of a smile crept over the corners of her mouth. As Henry leaned over to kiss her, she broke into a laugh, but the laugh gave way to a pucker as Henry's lips touched hers. They lay in each other's embrace.

Finally, Jane said between kisses, "If I don't practice I'm never gonna learn to shoot."

"I'll do the shooting for both of us," Henry said as he kissed her again.

*   *   *

The work of removing timber from the Alapaha River swamp continued. Days were filled with hard, backbreaking work, and nights were used to rest as only a laboring man could. The task of sawing the trees with a crosscut saw was rather boring, but it paid the rent and made it possible for a man to enjoy himself on the weekend.

Most of the hands lived from one payroll to the next. They were paid Saturday at noon. By Sunday night they were broke again. Many asked their employer for an advance on their coming wages so they could buy smoking tobacco or some such item until their next payday. The cycle never ended.

Henry was doing quite well. He seldom spent any money, except for taking Jane somewhere on the weekends. Most of Henry's pay was sent home to his mother. She had expenses that she found almost impossible to meet without Henry's help. Farming wasn't a money business. You could grow your own food and fiber. You could get by, but paying a mortgage was another matter. The depressed state of the nation's economy didn't help any either.

Henry took a weekend off once in awhile, but he continued to stay in camp for the most part. Staying there cost less, and he wasn't weary from the trip home after the weekend.

One Saturday Fletcher came to the woods for the usual morning's work. He had a dog with him. The animal was chained to the back of Fletcher's hay truck. Henry was curious about the dog, but he didn't get a chance to ask about him until the payroll had been distributed. Everybody had boarded the log truck for the trip to Ocilla except Henry. He was staying in camp for the time being.

Fletcher made a note in his accounts book, blew on the ink to assist in drying it, and closed the book.

"Well, that's another week's work brought to a close," he said to no one in particular.

"Mr. Fletcher," Henry said tentatively, "I noticed the dog you brought. Is he yours?"

Fletcher got to his feet before he answered, "Yeah, he's mine."

"What kind is he?"

"Oh, I suppose you'd call him a German Shepherd. Why do you ask?"

"Just curious. He's about the most beautiful animal I've ever seen. What's his name?"

The old man looked a little uncomfortable, "Satan."

"Satan? How come you named him Satan?"

"'Cause he's got a mean streak a mile wide."

Henry grinned. He liked the sound of the name. "How come he's so mean?"

"Wolf."

"Huh?"

"He's got wolf in 'im, boy."

Henry had heard of wolf dogs before, but he'd never actually seen one. He was unaware that so-called experts claimed a dog and a wolf had never mated. It didn't matter. Henry wouldn't have been impressed by expert opinion.

"Is that so?"

"Yeah, it's so. Fact is, he's got so much wolf in him, I'm gonna have t' do away with 'im."

"You mean kill him?"

"Uh, huh. I brought him out here t' do just that."

Henry looked at the magnificent animal again. He was strong and muscular with a fine shaped head. His eyes were penetrating and intense. The dog was not unfriendly. Henry approached him with extended hand. The dog sniffed the back of the offered hand, wagged his tail, and allowed Henry to touch him.

"He seems okay to me," Henry said.

"Yeah, I know what you mean. He seemed okay t' me up until the other day. Then he damned near took my hand off when I went t' feed 'im."

Henry looked at the animal again. He couldn't picture this beautiful dog attacking anyone unless provoked.

"Can I have him?"

Fletcher stood there looking thoughtful for a moment. "I don't know. Like I said, 'He's got too much wolf in 'im.' He's liable to turn on you when you least expect it. If he does, he could kill you, boy. You sure you want 'im?"

Henry looked at the dog again. The tail wagged almost unnoticed, but Henry thought he saw a flicker of warmth in the animal's eyes. "Yeah, I want him."

"Okay, he's yours, but don't say I didn't warn you."

"He'll be just fine. I'll train him. You'll see."

"Okay. You can keep the chain, too. Just be sure he's chained up when I come around."

"I will. He'll be handy to have around the cows, too."

Fletcher didn't say anything to that. He wasn't so sure about the statement. Henry was a trifle too trusting of the animal to suit Fletcher. He wasn't sure he was doing the right thing. Henry will have to butt with his own head, Fletcher thought. Maybe it would work out.

* * *

Henry began training Satan immediately. The dog responded to his new master favorably. Henry's touch was gentle. He didn't want to antagonize the animal so he took the training sessions slowly.

Henry learned a good deal about dogs while training this one. For example, always using the animal's name made a command more specific. When he gave a command like sit, it was given in the context: "Sit, Satan." or "Satan, sit."

Henry discovered something else quite by accident. Dogs respond to imagery. That is, if you picture in your mind what you want the animal to do, he is more likely to carry out the act. As time went on, this imagery became more and more important.

A game of fetch was among the first lessons Henry taught Satan. They were soon enjoying this game on a regular basis. Other little things like shaking hands followed.

One of Henry's favorites was the counting trick. He held a morsel of food in his hand with a number of fingers extended. Satan would sit there with his tongue hanging from the side of his mouth--saliva dripping from the tip. Satan would eye the scrap of food with hungry eyes. Henry gave the command, "Count, Satan." Satan soon learned to bark for the bite of food.

It was confusing at first, but Satan soon learned that three extended fingers meant three barks were necessary to get his reward. Soon, Henry had taught Satan to count up to five.

Other lessons followed. Henry spent several weekends teaching Satan to do tricks. After work during the week, Henry tried to spend some time with the dog so that the lessons were re-enforced regularly.

Most of Henry's coworkers steered clear of the animal. Satan was a one man dog. He took orders from Henry alone. Others, who tried to command him, found themselves either ignored or looking at a mouthful of teeth. Satan wasn't necessarily antago-nistic; he just didn't take orders from anybody but his master.

Fletcher watched from afar as Henry trained the dog. He was impressed with the change in the dog's attitude, but he was far from convinced that the animal's base nature had really changed. As far as Fletcher was concerned, the canine was a bomb waiting to explode. Just wait, he thought to himself, that dog's gonna be trouble yet.

Jane saw more change than anybody except Henry. She sat and watched as Henry put Satan through his paces on weekends.

"Satan, fetch," Henry commanded as he tossed the pine knot across the wire grass field.

Satan ran at top speed until he almost reached the knot. Putting on brakes, he slid toward the object grabbing it in his mouth as his rear end slid around. He was back in motion momentarily. He returned the slobber-covered pine knot to Henry.

Jane sat on a stump watching the demonstration. When Satan dropped the knot on Henry's command, she clapped her hands in applause. "Good boy!" She said.

Satan ignored her. His dark eyes looked to Henry for further instructions. Henry reached down to rub him behind the ears. "Good fetch, Satan. Now, let's show Jane some of the other things you've learned."

Henry pulled a morsel of biscuit from his pocket. "Sit, Satan," he commanded.

Satan complied, keeping his gaze fixed on Henry.

Henry held up the piece of bread, "Count, Satan," he commanded.

Satan eyed the bread without barking. Henry held it where he could see it, but kept it in his hand.

"Satan, count," Henry commanded more firmly.

Satan considered the three outstretched fingers before he barked, "Woof, woof, woof."

Henry gave him his reward. Satan gulped the bread and sat waiting for another bite. Henry complied. This time he got the count on the first try. Henry tousled his head and ears before going to sit by Jane.

Jane gave him an appreciative look, "You know something? You're amazing."

"How's that?"

"What you been able to accomplish with that dog."

"He's a smart dog. You just have to keep him practicing. That's all."

"I don't know how you do it. What's the secret?"

Henry pushed his hat back, "There's no secret. You just keep repeating the trick until he's got the hang of it. The more you do it; the better he remembers."

Jane gave the canine another admiring glance, "And to think, Pa was gonna kill him. I'm glad you didn't let him do it."

Henry put his arm around her, tightening his hold, "Yeah, so am I."

Satan came to Henry's side, sat himself on the ground, and hassled, his long tongue hanging several inches from his mouth.

* * *

Satan's education consisted of more than a bag of tricks. Henry was able to train him to help with the stock. The cows were let out of their pen periodically to graze. They often wandered off so far that it became necessary to hunt them up and drive them back to camp. Satan learned to herd the cows. He even learned to control an ornery one.

The control technique consisted of grabbing the errant animal by the nose and flipping it on its back. After one such episode, the cow submitted to Satan's wishes. Henry tried to be sure that Satan didn't harm the cows. Satan heeded the command he was given so he was easily trained to carry out his assignment.

Henry felt more secure with Satan around. He was sure he had been visited by other panthers since the dog had become his constant companion. One night Satan's ears rose as he seemed to listen attentively. He bounded out of the campfire light. A few seconds later, Henry heard a snarl as Satan engaged some unseen enemy. By the sound of the cries, it had to be a cat of some kind. Satan returned a quarter of an hour later with blood on his body. Henry was concerned that he might have been injured, but a search of his body revealed no serious marks.

Satan became a hunter, too--although he wasn't supposed to be bred for it. Henry gave him scraps from the camp kitchen, but these were rather limited. When several working men have to be fed, there aren't many leftovers.

Not only did Satan hunt for himself, he learned to assist Henry. Henry tired of the salt pork that was standard fare for the logging hands, so he went hunting on the weekends. Together he and Satan bagged a rabbit or squirrel. Henry always rewarded Satan with the entrails and other parts of the animal that he wasn't going to use. Satan seemed satisfied with this arrangement.

The bond between the man and dog seemed to have strengthened beyond any possible breakage, but the wildness in the canine came forth eventually.

One night Satan left the camp quietly by himself. Henry didn't mind. He was sure the dog just wanted to roam around on his own for a while. Satan had been gone for some time when Henry heard a disturbance near the stock pens. Henry decided he should investigate. There might be a cat bothering the oxen.

What he found astonished him. Satan was standing near the carcass of a cow. Henry thought the cow had been attacked by a cat until he saw blood on Satan's face. It seemed the dog had attacked the cow.

"Satan, no!" Henry said with emphasis on the 'no.'

Satan bared his teeth in a snarl before he turned and ran into the night.

Henry knelt by the cow and examined it with a lighted match. The throat had been torn open. Blood flowed from the fresh wound which could only have been made by the dog's teeth.

Henry sighed. There would be hell to pay now. Old man Fletcher would surely charge Henry for the cow--not that Henry blamed him. After all, Henry had taken responsibility for the dog and his actions. Oh, well. There went the money he'd been saving.

The first order of business was to find the dog and kill him. It was useless to try and track him in the dark. Maybe he'd be able to find him tomorrow.

Henry returned to the camp feeling a great sense of loss. He had grown fond of Satan. It gave him a sinking feeling in the pit of his stomach when he thought about what had to be done. He wished a thousand times there was some other way, but he couldn't think of one.

Satan stayed away the rest of the night. Henry thought he might come back with the dawn, but he didn't. Later that day, Henry spied him running a circle near the camp, but there was no way to get close enough to shoot him. Henry didn't want the dog to suffer, so he planned to make the death as quick and painless as possible.

Satan returned the next morning, but not the way Henry had hoped. The cows were lowing nervously when Henry went to investigate. There stood the dog over the carcass. His bloody mouth made it clear he had returned to the scene of his kill to eat his fill. Henry moved as close as he dared, the pistol at the ready.

The dog had been too busy eating the flesh of his kill to notice the approach of the man. When Satan caught Henry's scent, Henry was within twenty yards of the dog. In the back of his mind, Henry had hoped he might be able to avoid shooting Satan. But as he approached the dog, Satan raised his hackles, bared his teeth in a snarl, and let Henry know in no uncertain terms that he would not be taken without a fight.

"Easy, boy," Henry said in a soothing voice.

Satan would have none of it. He moved a step or two toward Henry.

"Easy now, Satan. I don't want to hurt you, boy."

Henry's mixed emotions had to be resolved. The dog charged him. Henry stood transfixed. It seemed for a moment that the eighty-pound charging animal might bowl him over. Henry's finger tightened on the trigger. The weapon exploded. The bullet caught the charging animal as he leaped into the air. The dog gave a savage yell of pain and fury. He hit the ground and lay writhing in death's throes.

Henry stood there with tears flooding his eyes. It hurt to destroy the dog even when it was necessary to save his own life. He watched painfully as the life blood flowed from the animal. Life was so unjust. Why hadn't he been able to overcome the wild beast? Why did this animal he had come to love turn on him? Sadly, Henry slowly realized there was no answer to these questions--none that he knew of anyway.

* * *

Months passed. The incident with the dog was beginning to fade. Fletcher had been more than reasonable about the dead cow. He and Henry had buried the carcass of the cow along with that of the dog. They had agreed on a price for the ox, Henry had paid it, and the subject was never brought up again. Fletcher knew what Henry was experiencing, so he didn't make matters worse by belaboring the point.

Life goes on in some form or fashion. The crew finished logging the swamp surrounding camp making a move necessary. Henry was glad to be leaving this campsite. Every time he looked around he saw things that reminded him of Satan. The memories were too painful. He would be glad to get away.

Final preparations had been made for the move. The trucks had been loaded with all the transportable gear. It was a simple matter of pulling the loads to the new camp. Fletcher was walking around the camp making sure they hadn't left anything he needed to move.

He came to the corral where the oxen were feeding contentedly on hay. "Henry," he said, addressing the younger man with a calm voice. "I want you to drive the cows to the next camp. Today's Friday, so you've got 'til Monday to get 'em there. Just take your time. There's no rush."

"Yes, sir. I'll leave with 'em late this evenin', if that's all right with you."

"That'll be fine. I'm leavin' it up to you. Take care of 'em, okay?"

"Yes, sir. I will."

* * *

The Alapaha River meanders along a more or less north-south route though the sandy plains of South Georgia. Millions of years ago an ancient ocean covered the river bed. The land was now a black, sandy loam. People had been living on the land for thousands of years. Many of them managed to grub some kind of existence from it, but most people had given up and the timber was considered the most suitable crop that could be grown.

One testimonial to the effort to farm the land was a house that sat near the sandy three-path road that Henry took to his new campsite. The house had been abandoned several years before. Hannibal Hall had tried to raise a family there with some success. His house had rung with laughter. His children had grown up and moved away to other places as life left them little choice in the matter.

Unknown to Henry, there was a legend that somebody had been killed in the house. The stories weren't clear, but the locals swore that the house was haunted.

Henry had started to the new camp about three o'clock in the afternoon. The sky was threatening as the ox team trudged along the sandy road. The wind came in gusts as the clouds gathered in the west. Progress was okay as long as the road ran north and south. When the course turned west for a brief period, it was difficult to keep the cows moving against the wind.

Cows, as most animals do, have a tendency to turn their backs to the wind. This instinct made it almost impossible to drive them. Finally, a shift in the wind brought the wind directly into the face of the plodding oxen.

The sky was dark now with boiling clouds. An occasional flash of lightning followed by a clap of thunder told Henry he'd better find shelter for himself and the cows if possible. But where was he going to find it in this swamp?

Henry had about given up hope when a flash of lightning revealed the old house just ahead on the left. Henry managed to drive the oxen under what remained of an old boiler shelter. He secured the tie line to a shelter post and made a dash through the driving rain onto the ramshackle porch of the old dwelling.

Henry pushed his way through the weather-beaten door of the house. He found himself in a large room with a fireplace at one end. A piece of board furnished him with fuel for a fire. He whittled shavings from the timber and had a nice fire going in a few minutes. The flickering flames not only warmed him, they mesmerized him so that he began to doze.

The sounds of the pouring rain lingered outside, punctuated with an occasional flash of lightning and its accompanying thunderclap, but the house was as quiet as a tomb. Henry decided he might as well take a nap. With this goal in mind, he lay down before the now roaring fire.

Henry had no way of knowing how long he'd been asleep when he was suddenly awakened by a noise. He sat up with a start, wiping the sleep from his eyes. The sound came again, but it wasn't the sound of the storm. If anything, the storm had subsided. The noise came again. It seemed to be coming from the upper floor of the house. Again the noise was repeated. It sounded as if someone were dragging a log chain across the floor. Maybe they were playing with the chain.

"Well, it seems I'm not alone," Henry whispered to himself.

XII
Cross Ties, Moonshine, and a Song

The noise ceased. Henry listened intently, trying to determine what might have happened. All he could hear was the steady, soft fall of the rain. The wind blew for an instant banging a shutter somewhere on the old house. A cracking sound came from the fireplace. The fire had died to a smoldering bed of hot coals.

Henry reached for more wood, placed it carefully on the red coals, and lay back. He watched as the fire rekindled with the addition of the fat wood. Had he dreamed the noise? It seemed so real, but it had ceased as soon as he had awakened. Or had it? It was difficult to tell what was real and what might have been the product of his imagination. Well, he wasn't going to worry about it now.

Henry sat gazing into the fire. The flames hypnotized him once more, and he fell asleep again. Gusts of wind rattled the old house, but Henry slept on undisturbed. Suddenly the sound of the rattling chain echoed through the ancient structure. Henry came to a sitting position at once. The noise continued. Now, he knew he wasn't dreaming. He was wide awake with the rattle of the chain ringing in his ears.

"How am I supposed to sleep with that racket?" Henry asked himself, out loud.

He reached for the board he'd whittled the shavings from for his fire-starter. Several large, fat lighter'd splinters were easily stripped from the board. Henry used a piece of string he found in his pocket to tie the splinters into a bundle. It made a fairly decent torch.

Henry placed one end of the torch in the fire and waited for the wood to ignite. He soon had a blazing light.

"I'm gonna find out what's in this house," he said to himself.

Slowly and deliberately, Henry walked through the old house. He held his torch high so that the light would penetrate the darkness as far as possible. There was nothing that could have made the noise downstairs. Henry turned to find his way upstairs.

In one corner of the lower floor he found a rickety staircase. Some steps were missing, but there were enough to let him climb to the second floor. Carefully, Henry made his way up the stairs.

Meanwhile, the noise had ceased. Henry found himself at the top of the stairs looking down a narrow hallway. He went from room to room searching each nook and cranny. There was nothing in sight. He was about to turn and descend the stairs when he spied a trap door near the stair case. Reaching up, he managed to pull the door down. The hinges squeaked as the rust came loose. Henry held his torch high enough to see that the opening was clear.

His hand reached into the opening. He felt a ladder laying on the floor of the loft. It was the work of a few seconds to pull the ladder down and place it so that he had access to the loft. Henry climbed the rickety ladder and looked into the loft. It was one big room, but there was nothing there. He was going to descend the ladder when an object caught his eye.

Henry crawled through the trapdoor, pulling himself erect in the loft. The object he had spied was the crown of an old straw hat. Underneath it lay something white. Henry moved the hat crown to reveal a half sheet of newspaper. The name of the paper glared in his torch light. It read: Macon Telegraph. The date line was April 5, 1905. There was absolutely nothing else in the room or the house for that matter.

Henry made his way down the ladder back to his fire. He tossed several pieces of wood on the fire and lay down to rest. As soon as he began to doze, the noise began again. Henry listened. He was trying to determine whether or not the storm was causing the noise. A gust of wind banged a shutter, but the rain continued unabated. The noise continued intermittently. Once, Henry thought he heard the sound of running feet. It sounded as if a child were running barefooted through the second floor of the house.

Henry picked up his torch, lit it at the fire, and made his way to the stairs. As soon as he had climbed halfway up the rickety staircase the noise ceased. He continued up the stairs. Once more he searched every nook and cranny of the upstairs. As he descended the stairs, the noise started again.

Henry turned back to the sound. When he was more than halfway up the steps, the noise ceased once more. Henry did another search of the second floor and attic before descending the stairs for the third time. As soon as he was on the ground floor, the noise resumed.

Henry walked to the fire place, threw what was left of his torch in the fire, and sat down again. The noise rattled through the house for a few seconds, ceased, resumed, and stopped again.

Henry reached for a piece of board and knocked the stack of his fire down. The embers glowed red as the coals began to die. Henry turned toward the door of the house. He stepped outside onto the porch. The rain was still coming down, but the thunder and lightening had ceased. The wind was also calm.

"Good night, mister ghost," Henry said aloud as he made a dash for the boiler shelter. In a matter of minutes he had backed the ox cart and team from under the shed and was headed back toward his old camp.

* * *

Henry raised the broad axe and sliced another four inches of bark from the side of the log he was hewing. When finished, it would be ready for use as a railroad cross tie. Hardwood trees were sawed into appropriate lengths, then they were shaped with an axe. The hewer notched along the side of the log, then cut away the notches leaving a more or less flat surface. Four flat sides gave the cross section of the tie an irregular rectangular shape.

"Boy, finish that 'un up and we'll take a breather for dinner," David Drury called from across the small clearing where they had been working for several days.

"Okay," Henry answered.

David Drury was Henry's uncle by marriage. David and Annie, Eva's sister, had been married for some time. They had three children. Yvonne, the oldest girl, was somewhat younger than Henry, but she idolized him. He was sort of a big brother to her--probably because he would do almost anything she asked.

Henry's work in the Alapaha River swamp had played out, as all such jobs must. When the timber is gone, the laborer is out of work.

He had told old man Fletcher about his experience at the ghost house. The old man had sympathized with his plight, declaring that he wouldn't have spent the night in that house for a million dollars. Henry didn't have any idea how much a million dollars was, but he hadn't stayed there all night for any amount, so he reckoned he wouldn't have either.

It had been hard to leave Jane behind, but Henry had soon placed her memory in a corner of his mind where we put those things we want to remember fondly. They had had great times together. Maybe they would meet again someday.

Back home, Henry found it difficult to get steady work. Eva had urged him to try the new Civilian Conservation Corps, but he had been asked to sign a paper that declared he was unable to find work anywhere else. That would have been a lie--he was never without a job very long when he wanted to work. He had refused to sign. Besides he would have had to give up much of his freedom to a military type atmosphere. That didn't appeal to him. The ability to come and go as he wished was too precious.

That was when David and Annie had come for a visit. David had talked to Henry about his latest enterprise. It seemed David had been able to get a contract with the Southern Railroad to cut cross ties for track repair and new construction. David's only problem was getting someone he could depend on to help him.

Henry had agreed on the spot. He liked David the best of any of Eva's family or in-laws. David wasn't like Eva's family. He didn't come and stay for weeks on end just so he could eat at somebody else's table without making a contribution. Henry resented the burden placed on him and his family by those people that he perceived as able-bodied, but too sorry to work.

The pay wasn't great, ten cents a cross tie, but it was enough to get by. You could make between fifty cents and a dollar a day depending on how many ties you could hew and carry to the truck. Day labor in the turpentine woods averaged fifty cents a day--hardly enough to buy groceries. Besides David was giving him room and board as part of the deal.

David didn't own any timber; he contracted with landowners. The agreement usually called for the property owner to get a percentage of the profits of the sale of the cross ties. This fee was known as "stumpage." David and Henry were working not too far from David and Annie's home on the Nails Ferry road. David had contracted with the Sellers family. They owned a swampy flat, not too far from the road, that was covered in hardwoods-- just what David needed to cut railroad ties.

The swamp was so boggy that it was impossible to use machinery even if David had owned any--he didn't. One old mule was all he had, and he couldn't use it in these woods. The only alternative was to carry the cross ties through a path cut in the rough gall-berry bushes. David's old model-T truck stood parked by the road waiting for a load of ties. It took ten ties to make a full load. That meant David had to make one or two trips a day depending on how many ties he and Henry were able to cut.

Sometimes, Henry went to the railroad yard with David, but many times he would stay in the woods hewing ties while David made the trip by himself. This gave Henry the edge since his tie count went up accordingly while David made the delivery.

Henry finished one side of the tie he was cutting, rolled the log with a cant hook, and started another side. The broad axe made wide cuts as he swung it into the bark of the tree. Chips flew when the axe cut the bark. It had taken Henry a while to get the hang of slicing the wood from the log, but he had mastered it. Now he was hewing a tie almost as quickly as David.

Henry swung his axe one last time, "You want to look at this one?" He asked.

"Naw, you got the hang of it by now. Ain't no need for me wet nursin' you no more," David replied. "Let's take these two to the truck. That'll finish this load. We'll eat dinner, then I'll take the load to town."

"Sounds good to me," Henry said, reaching down for one end of the cross tie. He lifted the end until he could place his shoulder about midway the tie. He stooped slightly and lifted the tie clear of the ground. The weight caused him to bog somewhat in the soft soil, but he was able to maintain his footing as he walked out to the road by way of the rough path.

The truck shook as Henry dropped the tie on top of the pile that lay on its bed. David came up and did the same with his burden. Both men pushed their tie into place, making a neat stack. A piece of chain was thrown over the load and secured to the chassis of the Model-T on each side. David didn't own a set of binders, so he tightened the chain by running a piece of wood under the chain, twisting it until the chain was tight, and tying off the home-made binder with a piece of haywire.

David stepped back and wiped his hands on his dirty pants, "There, that oughta hold it 'til I can get it to Baxley. I keep tellin' myself I'm gonna buy a set of binders one day, but what thu hell, this works just as good, and it don't cost as much."

David mounted the truck while Henry went around to crank it for him. Electric starters were available, but most people didn't bother to add them to these old trucks. The crank handle still hung from the front. Henry reached down and engaged the crank. He gave it an experimental pull. The engine coughed and stalled. Another twist of the crank brought the engine to life.

David adjusted the throttle until the sputtering engine warmed up. Henry swung into the homemade seat on the passenger's side. David released the hand brake, pressed the clutch pedal to the floor, increasing the throttle at the same time, and eased the truck into motion. The entire machine trembled as the power of the engine was transferred to the wheels. Henry thought the four-cylinder engine was going to choke down, but David gave it a little more throttle, keeping the engine alive.

Annie had dinner on the table when they reached the house. It didn't take long for them to wash their hands and seat themselves at the dinner table. The meal was consumed without ceremony. It was nothing fancy, just greens, cornbread and a little side meat. A generous portion of syrup poured over cornbread served as dessert if you wanted dessert.

David pushed his plate back, reached in his shirt pocket, extracted a can of Prince Albert smoking tobacco, and rolled himself a cigarette. He struck a match on his pants leg and lit his weed. A long drag on the cigarette filled his mouth with smoke. He seemed to savor the taste of the smoke before he blew a series of smoke rings. Henry finished his meal and imitated his elder.

"You know," Henry said, "I've been thinking maybe I'd ride in to town with you on this load."

"It's okay by me," David answered. "We're about on schedule with our deliveries. 'Less you want to get a few ties ahead."

"No. I don't think so. I wouldn't want to make too much money at once. I couldn't figure out how to spend it."

Both men laughed at Henry's joke. If there was one thing a man didn't have trouble doing these days, it was spending what little money he could get his hands on.

"Maybe you got some burnin' a hole in your pocket right now," David laughed.

"Nope. But I thought I might go by the five and dime."

"What you need from the five and dime?"

"There's a harmonica in the window. I thought I'd see how much they was askin' for it."

"You takin' up the harmonica?"

"Been thinking I might."

David grinned, "That's the Hester coming out in you. They're always partying. Ain't that right, Annie."

Annie, who was clearing the table, nodded her agreement, "There ain't nothin' like a good time. It helps you ferget what a mess things is in."

David laughed again, "I can't argue with that. Well, I hate to break up the fun, but we got to get going." He picked up his hat from a side table.

Henry got up and moved around the table. He picked up his hat to follow his uncle out the kitchen door.

Annie turned from the cook table where she had just placed the dirty dishes in the dishpan. "Y'all gonna be back in time for supper, er should I wait?"

"We'll be back," David answered.

* * *

Henry had had an interest in music for as long as he could remember. His mother's people taught him the value of music. They celebrated life with music forever, it seemed. Henry didn't particularly like David's comment about his musical interest being from the Hester side of the family, but he couldn't deny the influence. His grandfather, William Hester, was an accomplished banjo picker. His Uncle Brown played the piano rather well, and the whole family was born dancing to the rhythm of some kind of instrument.

Henry hadn't thought of playing an instrument, although he'd sung for sometime, learning most of the songs he knew from the gramophone owned by the George Reynolds family. His interest in instrumental music had been kindled when he met Willy Varnadore. Willy played Guitar. Henry didn't have the money to buy a guitar, but Willy let him practice on his. Henry decided that he could afford to buy a harmonica.

Henry and Willy began to practice together when they could. Both of them worked on the farm so their practice sessions were held on weekends for the most part. They learned several popular songs of the day. Jimmy Rodgers, the singing brakeman, was very popular. His "Blue Yodels" came straining from gramophones in several homes. Cafes almost always had a juke box with some of his records on them.

"Red River Valley" was a perennial favorite as was "Careless Love." "Wabash Cannonball," an old hobo song, was experiencing a revival, and "Wildwood Flower," an old folk tune, was being sung by the Carter Family of Virginia.

Needless to say this repertoire of songs made Willy and Henry quite popular. When a new song came out, they managed to learn it fairly soon. This gave them the opportunity to play at parties and any other gathering where music was considered appropriate. Henry's music even got him into church. He'd never been much to go to church, but folks seemed to like his singing voice well enough to ask him to sing.

Revivals in the brush arbor near Hamilton School attracted huge crowds. The preacher would let groups sing during these meeting, so Henry and Willy found themselves performing for the protracted meetings.

Henry enjoyed the music just for the sake of the music, but it did have a side benefit. It made him popular with the girls. He could take his pick of any one of several for a date at any given party.

Cane grindings were some of Henry's favorites. Willy lived on a farm about a mile and a half through the woods from Henry's home place. Once a year, Will, Willy's dad, held a cane grinding as did most of the local farmers. Anytime the young people got together, it was party time. Henry would pull his harmonica from his pocket and start to blow a tune. Something like "She'll Be Coming 'Round the Mountain" set the dancing feet in motion. If Willy hadn't brought his guitar, somebody would trot to his home and fetch it back in a few minutes. The party would continue until late at night.

Henry's interest in music lead him to an interest in song writing. He didn't have the education or the inclination to write music, but he thought he might try his hand at lyrics. An old folk tune had a haunting melody. Henry had seen the Smoky Mountains of East Tennessee and North Carolina. He thought a song based on the mountains and a lost love might be of interest to somebody else. He had certainly felt the pain of lost love. That qualified him to write the song.

Henry decided to call his song, "On Top of Old Smokey." Others would claim later that the title had already been taken, but Henry was quite unaware of any such title or lyrics. For weeks, Henry worked to fit the words of his composition to the old folk tune. Finally, he had it worked out to his satisfaction.

He sang it for Willy one Saturday afternoon. When he'd finished, Willy nodded with approval, "That sounds like a hit to me."

"Do you really think so?"

"Yeah, you oughta try it out on an audience sometime."

"Okay, I will."

Henry had no idea how to copyright his song. In fact it never really occurred to him that anyone might steal it. He was a bit too trusting in that respect.

One night at a party, Henry had been singing several popular songs. His audience was receptive and repeatedly asked for more. He had about run through his repertoire when Willy urged him to sing his new song.

"Say, folks," Willy announced. "I don't know if you know it or not, but Henry's written a song. How about singing it for us, Henry?"

"Yeah," a chorus of voices cheered.

Henry nodded to Willy to play an introduction. Willy complied, then Henry sang in a clear strong voice:

"On top of old smokey, old smokey so low,
I lost a true lover by courtin' too slow.
Now courtin's a pleasure, and parting is grief,
But a false hearted lover is worse than a thief.
"A thief, he will rob you and take what you save,
But a false hearted lover will lay you in your grave.
The grave will decay you and turn you to dust,
Not a girl in ten thousand a poor boy can trust.
"It's raining, it's hailing, the moon gives no light,
Horses can't travel this dark stormy night.
So put up your horses and feed them some hay,
Come sit down beside me as long as you stay.
"My horses aren't hungry, they won't eat your hay,
So farewell my true love, I'll be on my way.
I'll go back to old smokey, old smokey so high,
Where the wild beast and turtledove can hear myself
cry.
"As sure as the dew drops fall on the green corn,
Last night he was with me, tonight, he is gone."[1]

The audience cheered wildly. They liked it.

"Sing it again," somebody shouted. Henry obliged.

Unknown to Henry, there was a professional singer in the

---

1 This version copyright © 1934 Henry Reynolds

crowd. Two weeks later he heard his song on the radio. Henry had his first taste of professional thievery.

* * *

Henry's uncle, David Drury, had other talents that kept him in the money during hard times. David was an expert maker of whiskey. His product was well known and enjoyed a good reputation among the joints in Appling and Jeff Davis counties. The demand was high, so David found time to distill a few gallons on a regular basis.

There was one problem with this enterprise; it was illegal. That didn't bother David or legions of other small time operators who were in the business. They saw it as just another obstacle to deal with. Some of them got caught, and a few went to jail. Others paid off the local law; who generally looked the other way anyhow.

The nation had just repealed the Eighteenth Amendment which prohibited the sale and manufacture of alcoholic beverages. The great sobriety experiment had been a colossal failure. Gangsters such as Al Capone of Chicago had supplied the speakeasies with illegal liquor, building an empire on crime. Other small time operators had continued to manufacture and sell their product in spite of the new laws.

Finally, during the depression, the government had relented in an effort to stop the traffic in illega alcohol. There was now a tax imposed on the sale of alcohol. It was no longer illegal to make it, but it was illegal to sell it without a tax stamp. Therefore, the moonshine industry thrived all over the nation in spite of the new regulations.

The woods where Henry and David worked gave excellent cover for their still. It was a small operation, one fifty-gallon cooker and a half dozen or so mash barrels. The process was rather simple and inexpensive.

The sugar was the hardest to come by. It had to be bought

in small enough quantities to avoid suspicion. There were lots of stores selling "canning sugar" around the county. Sometimes the sugar was replaced with molasses or some other sweetener.

The basic process consisted of filling a barrel about two-thirds full of corn or some other grain. Sweetener and water were added. This mixture sat until it "worked off." The resulting fluid was known as "cornbuck." Cornbuck was poured into the cooker which had a steam cap on it. The steam was routed through a copper coil of tubing which was suspended in a barrel of water to condense the steam into the finished product. Flavor could be added by placing fruits or artificial flavoring such as lemon extract. Baked apples were one of David's favorites.

One day Henry and David had just put on a cooking. They were having trouble with their fire. Recent rains had wet all their wood in spite of their efforts to cover and keep it dry.

"Damn wet wood," David cursed. "It's gonna take hell with a blower on t' get it t' burn."

Henry stood watching as David tried to get the fire going. "You want me to get some more lighter'd?" Henry asked.

"I reckon so. Don't look like it's gonna start with this."

Henry went to the stump across the clearing, chipped a few splinters from the stump, and came back with a handful of fat wood.

"Here you are. Try this."

David took the splinters and placed them under the sputtering logs. The added fuel caught and the fire leapt up enough to start drying the wet wood. David placed other pieces of wood around the fire so they would be dry when he needed them.

While the men sat gazing into their fire, they heard the drone of an airplane. The sound went by and they thought it was going away, when the plane made a sudden turn. Henry's curiosity got the best of him. He wanted to get a look at the plane. Making his way to the far side of the clearing, he watched as the craft floated slowly over the swamp.

Suddenly, David realized what was happening. He rushed to Henry's side and pulled him into the gallberry bushes flattening him on the ground. Henry struggled for an instant before David spoke.

"Stay down, boy."

"Why?"

"That's a damn spotter plane for the feds. They're likely taking pictures. I hope to hell they didn't get you."

David sat and watched as the plane flew off. "Damn, we're gonna have t' move the still. They've spotted us for sure."

A few days later, Henry was in the court house. There on the bulletin board was a picture. A man in the picture was exposed from the waist down. Henry recognized his belt buckle. A sign under the photograph read, "Can you identify this man?"

XIII
Death on the Highway

Henry rolled the barrel of rosin onto the body of the trailer, set it upright, and twisted it into position. He was loading the trailer for a trip to Savannah. Another four or five barrels would complete the load. He jumped off the trailer and went for another barrel.

Fortunately, no one had recognized him from the photograph in the courthouse. At least they hadn't been willing to identify him. He was thankful for that. A run-in with the law wasn't a pleasant prospect. Henry's experience told him that most law enforcement people were out to line their own pockets at the expense of anybody they could intimidate.

George Reynolds had given him work driving his truck. Henry was glad to be back on the road again. He had enjoyed doing something different, but those jobs had run out, and he needed the work. Truck driving was something he had a bit of experience at.

Actually, George needed Henry. Farmers and turpentiners needed a market for their products. Savannah was the nearest one. Most of them didn't own vehicles that were capable of carrying their products to market, so they had to rely on George and other men like him who were in the trucking business. George was running two trucks and thinking of putting on another. For the first time in five years, things were really looking up.

It was summer in 1934. Henry would turn twenty in a few days. He was sort of looking forward to his birthday. Sometimes he was amazed that he had survived to see this day. The news had come over the radio and newspapers that Bonnie and Clyde had been killed in a shootout near Arcadia, Louisiana. Henry thought how near he'd come to getting involved in one of their robberies and was grateful for his escape.

Henry placed the last barrel of rosin on the trailer, jumped to the ground, and pulled the binding chain across the back of the trailer body. He fastened the chain to a rear stake and pulled it tight with a set of steel binders--no sloppy work for George Reynolds. You did the job the way it was supposed to be done-- at least in George's eyes.

Henry stepped into the cab of the 1932 Chevrolet. A turn of the key and a press of the foot starter button brought the engine to life. Henry let the truck idle until it warmed up. He eased out on the clutch. The truck began to move slowly forward. When the trailer cleared the rosin yard, Henry stopped at the small shed that served as an office for the Tillman Stills.

"How many barrels you got on, driver?" The man at the office inquired.

"A dozen for you," Henry replied.

"Okay, here's the paper work." The man handed him a sheet of paper that served as a "bill of laden."

Henry pocketed the paper without giving it a glance. "See you next trip," he said as he pulled the truck into gear.

"Have a good trip," the man replied.

Henry eased out onto the dirt road that ran by the still. The truck's engine whined, the gears ground slightly, and the exhaust sent up a smoke signal as Henry changed gears. It wasn't easy to get up speed on this road. It was mostly sand and the truck was loaded with twenty-five barrels of rosin--quite a load for the machine.

Henry headed for the Lane's Bridge Road. There was a

bridge over the Altamaha River just five miles or so from the still, but the roads to Savannah weren't that good. He would have to go to Jesup by way of Surrency.

Henry topped the low speed of the axle, flipped the high speed button, and began the shift pattern through the high side of the axle. He had no sooner reached the second gear on the top side when he had to slow down for a creek crossing. This one didn't have a bridge. Even if it had had one, twenty-five barrels of rosin would have likely crushed it.

Henry downshifted to first gear on the low side of the axle. He eased the truck forward, keeping it in motion. That was the secret to making a hard pull through a mud hole--never stop. The truck wheels hit the run of the creek. Water fled before their onslaught. Drive wheels gripped the sandy bottom pulling the heavy load through the creek and up the far bank. The trailer came through without any trouble. Shortly, Henry was on the Lane's Bridge Road headed for the forks where he would turn to Surrency.

The trip to Savannah was uneventful. Henry drove through, Surrency, Odum, Jesup, Ludowici, Hinesville, Midway, and Richmond Hill. U. S. 17 Highway took him into Savannah. He hit West Broad on 17, turned left to Broughton Street, then right down Broughton to his delivery point.

Broughton was his biggest challenge. There were seventeen traffic lights between West Broad and President Street. Ordinarily, that wouldn't have been a problem, except for the fact that the truck had mechanical brakes. Any driver worth his salt could tell you that mechanical brakes were equivalent to no brakes.

The only way to negotiate the traffic lights was to use your gears to slow the truck. Then you had to hope nobody got in your way as you moved down the street. Most automobile drivers respected the size and weight of a truck, but once in a while, some idiot decided to match his small car against the huge vehicle. The result was a crushed car and an unscathed truck.

Fortunately, Henry was able to avoid a collision as he drove through downtown Savannah. He pulled his load to the Savannah Naval Stores dock. Waiting--always part of a trucker's life--took up an hour. Finally, he was able to unload. He watched while the deck hands cleared the trailer. Henry hoped to make it to the Sugar Refinery in time to get loaded before the day shift left. If he could get loaded in time, he could make it back home some time before midnight.

Henry pulled out of the yard and headed his rig downtown again. He had letters authorizing him to cash the bank drafts for the rosin sale. The still owners usually required cash to make their weekend payroll. It was understood that Henry would bring that cash back. Pulling into an empty line of parallel parking spaces across from the Savannah Bank and Trust office, Henry killed the engine to take care of his banking business.

The teller took the drafts and letters, looked at them briefly, and said "I'll have to get one of the vice-presidents to sign for this."

Henry didn't reply. He waited patiently while the teller went for the required signature. In a couple of minutes, the teller returned. He handed a paper across the counter to Henry, "Sign here, please."

Henry scribbled his name on the paper beside the "x" drawn by the teller and shoved the pen and paper back to him.

The teller counted out seven hundred dollars to Henry. Henry placed it in his wallet, folded the receipt, put it in his pocket, and walked out into the sunshine.

Henry was standing on the street corner waiting for the light to change, when a well-dressed man bumped into him.

"Excuse me," the stranger said politely.

Henry was about to cross the street when he reached for his wallet. It was gone. Turning, he sighted the man who had bumped him. He ran down the sidewalk toward the stranger. The man spotted Henry and broke into a run. Henry was on him in another half dozen steps. Grabbing the man's arm, Henry held the man in his grip with the arm pinned behind his back.

"Okay, buddy, let's have it," Henry said quietly.

"Have what?" The stranger demanded.

"My wallet."

The man grimaced with pain, "I don't know what the hell you talking about, mister."

"Yes you do. Now give me the wallet."

A policeman came around the corner. He saw the two men struggling. It took him less than five seconds to close the gap. "Hey, what's going on here?" The cop demanded.

Henry held his grip, "This son-of-a-bitch just picked my pocket."

"That's a damn lie."

"The hell it is. Search him if you don't believe me."

The cop looked at Henry, then the other man. "Let 'im loose."

Henry released his grip, but stood ready in case the pick pocket decided to make another run for it.

The cop looked at Henry, "You say this feller's got your wallet?"

"That's right."

"Mister," the cop said, turning to the pick pocket. "Did you take this man's wallet?"

The pick pocket was an expert at his trade. "No, sir, officer."

"Then you won't mind comin' down to the station with us t' settle this."

"No. I'll go."

Henry and the stranger walked ahead of the policeman. Shortly, they were at the police station. The cop ushered them to a table.

He addressed himself to the accused. "Would you empty your pockets?"

The man took everything from his pants pockets. Henry's

wallet wasn't there, neither was the money.

"Inside coat pocket," Henry said.

"How's that?" The cop asked.

"It's in his inside coat pocket."

"Empty that 'un, too," the cop directed.

The man pulled Henry's wallet from his coat pocket.

"That your wallet?" The cop asked, looking at Henry.

"Yeah, that's mine."

The cop picked up the wallet. He opened it, thumbed through it, and said, "You know how much money you had?"

"Yeah. There's just a little over seven hundred dollars in there."

"That's my money, officer," the pick pocket lied. "I've been saving that money for nearly five years. You ain't gonna let this feller get away with my money, are you?"

I'll be damned, Henry thought. If I don't do something this bastard's gonna get away with that payroll.

The cop looked back at the accused, "What else is in the wallet?"

"Just some papers and such."

The cop rifled through the wallet. He couldn't find any I. D. "Fellows, it's hard t' tell who's lying and who's telling the truth. There's more'n seven hundred dollars here, but that don't tell me who it belongs to." Turning to Henry he asked, "You got any proof this money's yours?"

Henry thought for a moment. He was about to answer in the negative when he remembered the receipt the teller had given him.

"Officer, that money's payroll for folks back home. I've got a receipt for it from the bank. Is that enough proof?"

The cop nodded his head in the affirmative, "It is, if you've got the receipt. Could I see it, please?"

Henry reached in his shirt pocket and handed the receipt to the policeman. The cop looked at the receipt, handed it back, and said, "Looks legit' t' me. Here's your wallet."

The thief looked at Henry with daggers in his eyes.

"You want t' press charges?" The cop asked.

"Damn right," Henry replied.

"You'll have to appear in court."

"When?"

"Don't know. Could be anytime from a week t' a month."

"Oh, well. I ain't got time for that."

The cop thought for a minute, "I reckon I might be able t' come up with another charge where you wouldn't have to testify."

"Anything you say, officer."

* * *

Henry learned a valuable lesson from his encounter with the pick pocket. He never again carried payroll money in his wallet. Long sleeved shirts with the money rolled in the sleeves gave him more protection from thieves. He would learn several lessons while driving the truck.

For the next several months, Henry made numerous trips to Savannah. There were occasional trips to other places, too. He and George would make an occasional journey together. They swapped the driving so that the truck was in constant motion except for food and fuel stops.

Long trips weren't common, but they made a few. One journey took them to Virginia. Henry had good reason to remember that trip. George was a whiskey drinker. Other people drank coffee like George drank whiskey. During a twenty-four hour period, George and Henry consumed twelve half pints of liquor between them. In retrospect, Henry wondered how they managed to drive with that amount of alcohol in their systems.

One trip took them to the mountains of North Georgia to move a family back to South Georgia. Henry looked at the beauty of the mountains and wondered why anyone would want to leave them to return to the sandy flats of the South.

George and Henry hauled all kinds of things. Farm products were the most common, but the truck was loaded with whatever people needed to move. It wasn't uncommon to carry a load of spirits of turpentine to Savannah and return with a load of sugar or other commodities for grocery merchants in Baxley. A typical day saw Henry arise at four or five o'clock in the morning and get back to bed around midnight. He worked long, hard hours. Mostly, because he had no choice.

* * *

One day Henry had a load to go to Brunswick, which lies about seventy miles east of Baxley. He had been through Surrency and Odum. About halfway between Odum and Jesup, he saw a woman standing beside her car. The hood was raised, which usually indicated a distress signal.

As Henry approached, the woman stepped out into the road, waving frantically. Henry geared the truck down, pulled to the side of the road, and stopped the engine. He dismounted from the cab and approached the stalled car.

"Howdy do, ma'am. Something wrong?" He asked.

The woman's face betrayed her anxiety, "My car won't run."

"What seems to be the trouble?"

"I don't know. I was driving along and it just quit."

"Let me have a look."

Henry leaned over the fender of the late model Buick. He checked for loose plug wires. There weren't any. Next he checked the carburetor. He couldn't see anything amiss.

"How about gettin' inside and tryin' to start it?"

The woman climbed into the car and nervously tried the starter. The engine turned, but it didn't fire.

"Just a minute," Henry called.

He reached for the number one plug wire, pulled it off, and held it near the tip of the plug.

"Try it again."

The starter ground as it turned the heavy engine. There should have been a spark of fire across the gap between the plug and the wire. It wasn't there. The smell of gasoline told Henry the fuel pump and carburetor were working.

"You're gettin' gas, but there's no fire."

"Is that bad?"

"I'm not sure. Let me see if I can do something."

Henry pulled the distributor cap. The rotor button seemed okay. He pulled a rag from his pocket and brushed it off. Next he checked the breaker points. They were slightly burned, but they should be working. The condenser connections seemed tight.

"Just a minute. Let me get some tools."

Henry returned, momentarily, with a small screw driver and a point file. He inserted the file into the point gap, carefully filing the points. When he had completed this procedure, he recapped the distributor.

"Okay, give it another spin."

The woman stepped on the starter. The engine gave a cough before it sprang to life. Henry nodded his head with satisfaction, before he closed the hood.

The woman smiled, "Thanks so much. I'll be glad to pay you, but . . . "

Henry, who was never one to take advantage of anyone in trouble, especially a woman, shook his head. "That's okay. You don't owe me a thing."

"Thanks again," she said as she pulled onto the road and drove off.

The Buick was out of sight before Henry got his speed up. He drove on through Jesup. A couple of miles down the road, he spied the Buick sitting beside the road. This time he pulled in behind the car.

"What happened, Ma'am?" He asked as he dismounted from the cab.

"I don't know. I was driving along when it just quit again."

"Okay, I'll have another look," Henry said as he raised the hood.

Henry double checked the plug wires. They were all tight.

A pump or two of the carburetor told him the fuel was still coming to the engine. He opened the distributor cap. He had done everything he could in here. There had to be a bad part. Most likely it's the condenser, he thought to himself. He could probably start the engine by shorting the condenser. This was accomplished with a pinch of the pliers.

"Try it now," Henry said

The woman spun the starter. Excess fuel from the carburetor gave off a pungent smell as the engine came to life. Henry closed the hood.

"Stop at the next service station and get you a condenser, ma'am. It'll cost you about fifty cents. That oughta fix your engine."

The woman smiled, "Thank you." She took off once more.

About three miles east of Gardi, Henry found her beside the road for the third time. Henry stopped, but his patience was growing thin.

The woman didn't say anything as Henry raised the hood again. Henry removed the distributor cap. Maybe he could short the condenser once more and get the engine going.

"Ma'am, you passed a station back there in Gardi. Why didn't you stop and get a condenser like I told you to?"

The woman looked at Henry sheepishly, "Mister, I don't have fifty cents."

"Okay. I don't know if this is gonna work or not. I'm gonna try shortin' this condenser once more. If that don't work, I'll hafta take you somewhere and get you one."

The woman sighed with resignation, "Okay."

Henry pinched the condenser together even tighter. "Try it now."

The engine came to life. Henry closed the hood, stood back, reached in his pocket, and handed the woman a fifty-cent piece.

"Here, stop somewhere and get a new condenser."

"Thanks."

The woman pulled her car onto the road and left again. Henry stood and watched until the Buick was out of sight. He climbed back into his truck and headed for Brunswick. The woman must have made it to her destination. Henry never saw her again.

* * *

The roads of the nineteen thirties were unsafe at any speed. In fact there was no speed limit outside the city limits of certain towns. Some towns didn't have an official speed limit. Baxley had adopted one earlier in the century--really before the common use of the automobile. Five miles per hour was the top municipal speed limit.

The highways were wide open, and people took full advantage of it. Often, they not only killed themselves, but any other unsuspecting driver or pedestrian. Henry found himself at a horrible wreck more often than he could count. Some of them were so terrible, he would leave the scene only to stop and vomit at what he had seen.

The danger to a trucker wasn't as great as that to people in smaller automobiles, but you could never tell when you might be involved. Highway Seventeen, the coastal highway, was a constant source of danger. Henry helped remove the crushed bodies of women and children on many occasions. Sometimes he saw babies die where they had been ripped from their mother's wombs. The sight never failed to turn his stomach.

The highway held other unique dangers for truckers. You had to be careful if you let someone ride with you. There was a popular notion among thieves that truck drivers carried lots of money. More than one driver had been rolled for the loot that he supposedly carried.

Although the depression had relented somewhat with the programs instituted by the Roosevelt Administration, there were still a large number of transits on the highways of the country. Having been a hobo himself, Henry identified with these wanderers. He often gave a man a ride even when it was against his better judgement. Most of the time his kindness was appreciated, however there were exceptions.

Henry had loaded a shipment of rosin the previous day. Leaving before daylight put him near Midway by the middle of the morning. Midway served as a stopover for a Savannah trip. Henry often bought fuel at a service station located within sight of the Old Midway Church where the early settlers had worshiped and buried their dead.

The attendant had filled the truck's tanks while Henry ate a midmorning snack and drank a soft drink. Henry paid for the purchase and was about to leave when a black man approached him.

"Say, mistuh. Could you gives a pore man a ride?"

Henry looked at the stranger. He seemed clean enough. His speech told Henry that he probably belonged to a group of blacks that lived near the Ogeechee River. These people spoke a curious blend of African dialect mixed with English. They were commonly referred to by outsiders as "'Geechees."

"How far you goin'?" Henry asked.

"Sa'ann'h."

"Sure. Hop in."

Henry and his passenger mounted the truck and were soon on their way out of Midway. There wasn't much talk between them. Henry concentrated on his driving while the black man sat staring out the window.

After a long period of silence, the hitchhiker asked, "Whut ya got on dis truck?"

"Rosin."

"Do hit sell fer lots o' money?"

"Sometime. Depends on how good the market is."

"Dis yo truck?"

"No. I'm just drivin' for another fellow."

"How do it pay?"

"Drivin'?"

"Yeah."

"Not much, but it beats the hell out of other jobs I've had."

The conversation lulled. Just before they reached the Ogeechee River beyond Richmond Hill, Henry heard the sound of a tire blowing out.

"Damn," he muttered under his breath, pulling the truck to the side of the road.

When the truck was clear of the traffic, Henry got out to assess the damage. Sure enough, he had a blowout on the trailer. Luckily, it was on the outside.

I've got to get a jack under it quick, he thought, as he went to the truck for his tools. Returning, he crawled under the trailer to position the jack. He had to turn the screw to adjust the jack to the proper height. Having accomplished this task, he began to raise the jack with an extension handle that allowed him to sit out of danger from the load.

Meanwhile, the black man had remained in the cab, or so Henry thought. Henry raised the jack just high enough to keep the inside tire from bursting under the load. He was in the process of fitting the lug wrench to the wheel when he spied his passenger coming around the tailgate of the trailer.

Henry was totally unprepared for what happened next. The hitchhiker charged him, knocking him off his feet. Henry rolled over, eluding the black man's grasp, managing to keep the lug wrench in his grip. The hitchhiker kicked Henry in the ribs with a glancing blow. Henry rolled over once more and came to his feet like a cat.

The black man didn't say a word. He rushed Henry again. Either he didn't see the lug wrench, or he was too intent on his objective. Either way, Henry had a formidable weapon at his disposal, and he wasn't hesitant to use it. Henry had learned long ago that the object in any fight was to win, no matter what it took. He had no illusions of so-called fair-play.

Henry raised the lug wrench as his assailant charged. As the black man came near enough, Henry swung the wrench with all the strength he could muster. The wrench hit the man beside the head, sending him sprawling into the ditch.

Henry stood there breathing hard. The black man lay motionless in the trench. A few inches of water covered the bottom, but it wasn't enough to bury the attacker's face.

Henry saw that he had won the fight. He turned to the task of changing the wheel. When he had finished, he drove off leaving his assailant lying in the ditch.

A few miles down the road, Henry pulled over at a service station. He had to get a replacement for the tire he'd blown.

As he waited for the manager to get his tire he heard an announcement on a local Savannah station: "This just in. The local sheriff's office reports a dead man found just north of Richmond Hill near the Ogeechee River. The black male has not been identified. Anyone with information about this person is asked to contact the Bryan County Sheriff's Office."

The attendant looked at Henry. "Just another dead nigger," he said.

Henry didn't say anything.

XIV
Tug Boats and Railroad Engines

Henry told himself there was no way the law could trace the dead man to him. The killing had been self defense, but there was no way to prove it. There were no witnesses. It would simply be his word against whoever accused him.

The burden of the incident weighed on his mind. No matter how he tried, he couldn't shake the feeling that he would be called to account for something over which he had no control. He decided not to tell anybody, but his load finally had to be shared. He couldn't think of anyone that he could trust more than George. Surely George would back him up if things came to worse.

George listened patiently as Henry told the story. When he had finished, George reassured Henry that he would stand by him no matter what. As they discussed the incident, both of them decided that it might be better if Henry didn't make his regular runs to Savannah. There was an outside chance that a passerby had seen what happened. Until things had a chance to blow over, Henry would work in some other capacity.

* * *

George had an old friend at Brunswick, Captain Sam Smith. Sam, who owned a tugboat, had often transferred cargo from a ship in the harbor directly to George's waiting truck. During these times they often talked about things they would like to do. George had mentioned that he had never been deep sea fishing.

That was all it took to elicit an invitation from Sam. When asked, Sam assured George he could bring members of his family along.

George had made the invitation known one evening at the supper table. There was high excitement as the group of men prepared for the trip. George often took Henry and his sons on fishing trips for days at a time. Sometimes they launched a boat near Lumber City and floated down the Ocmulgee and Altamaha Rivers, fishing as they went. This trip would be a new experience for all of them.

The day came. They left at four o'clock in the morning to make the drive to Brunswick. It should take about three hours to make the trip, barring any bad luck. The truck pulled up to the wharf around seven o'clock. Captain Sam met them with great enthusiasm.

Their gear was soon stowed aboard the boat, and they were under way. Henry had been on a boat a number of times, but that hadn't prepared him for the experience of deep sea fishing. He was okay as long as he could see land, but the moment the boat was out of sight of land, he got seasick.

Sam looked at him from the wheel of the boat. "First time at sea, son?" He queried.

"Yes, sir."

"How ya feelin'?"

"Not too hot."

Sam grinned. It had been a long time ago, but he could almost remember his first time. "Why don't ya have a pull on this bottle?" He said handing it to Henry.

"Don't mind if I do."

Henry turned the bottle up and took a drink of the whiskey. He was accustomed to alcohol, but he'd never tried drinking while seasick. The liquid went down. His stomach churned. He thought he was going to throw it up, but the liquor stayed down. He looked at the water.

"Don't look at thu water, son!" Sam commanded. "It's what

makes ya sick. Look off out there some'ers."

Henry tried not to look at the water, but you might as well have commanded him not to look at a beautiful woman. His eyes kept wandering back to it.

Finally, they were anchored somewhere off the Georgia Coast. Sam assured them they would catch all the fish they wanted that day. Everybody dropped lines in the water. Henry tried to concentrate on his fishing, but it was no use. His eyes kept watching the swells as the boat floated to the top of one, then slid to the bottom of the next trough.

George was having a better time than most of the boys. He was one of those fortunate people who didn't get motion sick so easily. He was worried about Henry though. An occasional glance told him the youngster was having a rough time.

Sam kept his eye on all the landlubbers, passing his bottle around for each one to drink. Henry seemed to be having the worst of it.

"Here, boy, lay in on this likker." Sam commanded once more with authority.

Henry shook his head a time or two without saying anything, but he soon decided he had a choice. He could puke his guts out over the rail, or get so drunk he didn't care whether he was sick or not. He finally decided on the latter. When the day's fishing had ended, Henry barely knew where he was. There was no way he could walk when he finally put his feet back on land.

While the group loaded their fish and equipment for the trip home, George followed Sam to his small office on the wharf. As soon as they were out of earshot, George turned to Sam with a question.

"Sam, I wonder if you'd do me a favor?"

"I will if I can. What is it?"

"My nephew needs a job for a few days. I've been using him on my trucks, but he's kinda got himself in a bit of trouble. I figure it'd be better if he didn't drive for a while."

Sam studied George's face. He wanted to ask what kind of trouble, but decided not to.

"Is he a steady worker?" Sam asked, instead.

"Yeah. It ain't his work that's the matter."

"Okay. Tell you what. I'll give 'im a week's try, then I'll let ya know."

George nodded with satisfaction, "That's fair enough. When can he start?"

"Monday morning, if he wants."

"I'll tell 'im."

That was how Henry came to his job on the tugboat. It was hard work--as hard as he'd ever tackled. The hours reminded him of his trucking. They were up before dawn and didn't quit until well after dark. Sometimes Sam worked his boat around the clock, if there was cargo to be unloaded from a ship. During those times the crew took turns sleeping and working. There was little time for recreation.

Henry enjoyed going out to the big ships. He eventually overcame his sea sickness, enabling him to make trips out of sight of land when necessary. Large ships drew so much water that they could not be towed to an unloading pier. That made it necessary to unload the cargo either piece by piece or at least in small containers.

Shipments of guano from South America were often unloaded by hand one bag at a time. Sam loaded his boat to capacity, then ferried the cargo to the pier for movement to a warehouse. This was hard, backbreaking work, especially since the product was shipped in two hundred pound bags. It took a man with a strong back to handle this cargo for hours on end.

Henry thought it was more fun when they actually gave a ship a tow. Sailors, who spoke in strange tongues, dropped lines to the tug. These lines were secured to the tug. Then the slow process of towing the large vessel began. Henry often compared the sight in his mind's eye to that of a minnow pulling a whale ashore. When two tugs were required, Henry thought it looked as comical as could be.

Always one to enjoy a new adventure, Henry was thoroughly enjoying this experience. What really topped it off for him was the fact that Sam had a daughter just younger than Henry. She was rather tall for a girl, Henry thought. Almost as tall as he was. Her hair, which she wore long and flowing, was blond, giving a hint of Germanic decent. Henry learned that Susie's mother had died some years ago leaving her father to raise her. As a result, she was somewhat tomboyish. Henry didn't mind that much, since it was plain to see she was all woman.

Susie had been given the job of manning the office while her father was on the boat. She took this duty in stride, informing her dad when he had new business and telling his customers when and where to reach her father.

Opportunities for conversation were rare, but that didn't keep the two young people from seeing each other. Susie had a quick smile and the gift of gab much like her father. Henry found it easy to engage her in conversation.

A long, tiring day was over as Henry approached the office. As he stepped onto the porch, he heard a cheerful voice call out, "Hello, sailor. How was your day?"

Henry grinned in response to the winning smile of the blond girl. "Not too bad. Guess I'm gettin' used to my feet rockin' to sleep while the rest of me tries to keep awake."

Susie grinned again, "Just hang in there. You'll get used to it."

Henry returned her smile. She certainly had a way of charming him. He'd considered asking her for a date several times, but he wasn't sure it was such a good idea. He didn't want to get on the wrong side of Captain Sam. The old man had given him work which he needed badly. It wouldn't do to rile him.

As these thoughts ran through his mind for the twelfth time, Susie's smile overpowered Henry's common sense and any remnant of fear he might have retained regarding his relation to Sam. "How 'bout a date?" He asked politely.

Susie flashed him another smile. She had been expecting Henry to make a move, but she didn't want to appear too anxious to respond. "You sure you're up to it. Pa's been working you pretty hard; ain't he?"

"Not that hard."

"I don't know. You look pretty tuckered out to me," she teased.

Henry was sure he'd caught the gleam in her eye. "Not that tuckered. Just give me an hour and I'll be ready and rarin' to go."

"Where'd you have in mind?"

"I don't know. Where would you like to go?"

"There's a nice little beach just a bit south of here."

"That sounds good. What's down there?"

"Oh, there's a little restaurant where you can get seafood, and the beach is white and sandy. Just the place for a stroll."

Henry smiled, "Sounds good to me. When can you be ready?"

"How about an hour?"

"I'll be back for you then, okay."

* * *

Henry eased the Model-A Roadster up to the timber that served as a curb. The little restaurant wasn't too busy. He opened the door for Susie as they strolled into the dimly lit room. A waitress led them to a small table near the back of the dining area. She handed each of them a menu and promised to return.

Henry opened his menu. The light wasn't too good, but that wasn't the worst of the problem. Henry had never learned to read very well. He was functionally illiterate. Gazing at the printed words gave him an almost panicky feeling. He summoned up his courage and decided he could fake his way through this.

Susie was looking through her menu with intense interest. She finished her survey, looked up, smiled at Henry, and said,

"See anything you like?"

Henry held her eyes with his gaze, "I'm not sure. I've never had much seafood. Just fish mostly. How about recommending something?"

Susie looked at him thoughtfully. She wasn't schooled in the tactics of non readers. Ordering for her date was a bit unusual. Oh, well, why not. "I like the shrimp and oysters."

"That sounds good," Henry responded, "I'll try them."

The waitress returned, took her pad from her apron pocket, removed the pencil from behind her ear, and said, "You folks ready to order?"

Susie ordered for both of them. When the waitress had gone, she turned to Henry, "So tell me more about yourself."

* * *

The moon rose as if it were being given birth by the mighty Atlantic Ocean. Waves rolled onto the beach crashing as they crested near the shore. Rays of moonlight shown through the breaking waves giving them a spectral quality.

The spent waters flowed around the feet of the two young people as they strolled barefooted down the beach. Henry and Susie walked hand-in-hand through the young night.

"This is one of my favorite places in the world," Susie said as another wave washed her bare feet.

Henry gazed out over the ocean taking in the serenity of the peaceful scene. "I can see why."

Susie stood still, "Listen," she said almost in a whisper. The roaring of the waves drowned out anything else she might have uttered.

Henry gazed full into her face. The rising moon cast its light on her blond hair giving it a pale glow. Her red lips were slightly parted. Henry leaned over and kissed them firmly. Susie didn't return the gesture, but she didn't resist.

When Henry stood erect, she looked at him. "You sure don't waste any time, do you?"

"I guess not. It seems life's too short to waste. One thing I've discovered, if you don't take advantage of something you might not ever get the chance to do it again."

Susie looked thoughtful, "I . . . I guess I know what you mean."

Henry stood there holding her. She laid her head against his chest. Her mind was in turmoil. She wasn't certain how she felt about this tall, skinny, young man. Should she get involved with him? Maybe she would regret it. On the other hand, she might regret it if she didn't. There was no way to tell. She had often been told to follow her heart, but that could lead to heartbreak as well as happiness. It was like taking a fork in an unfamiliar road; you could never be sure where a turn would lead you.

Henry's mind was filled with thoughts, too, but he didn't give utterance to them. The crash of the surf was all that could be heard as the young couple stood with the spent waves washing their feet.

After a while, Susie pulled back slightly and raised her face toward Henry. When he leaned over to touch her lips with his, she kissed him back. There might not be a tomorrow. Who could tell?

* * *

The engineer sounded the whistle for the yard at Macon. Steam escaped from overload valves as the engine powered down for its approach to the yard. Henry sat in the cab watching the engineer and fireman do their work. The ride from Brunswick to Macon had been interesting. For the first time in his life, Henry was actually riding the train as a passenger and not as a hobo.

The sign at the yard in Brunswick had advertised for firemen on the trains, but when Henry talked to the dispatcher, he learned that he would have to go to Macon to apply. That's how he came to be riding in the engine cab.

As the train slowed, Henry thought about his experience in Brunswick. All-in-all it had been interesting. Captain Sam hadn't been a bad boss as bosses go. He had found Susie a bright and cheerful companion, but despite all this, Henry had felt the need to move on.

Two men had come to the wharf on some business or other. Henry really didn't know what it was, but he suspected they were looking for him. The memory of his encounter with the Negro near Savannah continued to haunt him. He couldn't shake the notion that they had somehow found that he was responsible for the man's death. The specter of the fight continued to haunt him.

Anyhow, he had made a hasty retreat, giving Captain Sam and his daughter the word that he had received news that his mother was sick at home. They had expressed their regret and concern. Certainly they wished him well as he left.

The secretary looked up from the form she was reading as Henry pushed open the office door. She looked up and down the lanky youth before she asked, "What can I do for you?"

Henry cleared his throat, "They told me to see a Mr. Olaphant about the fireman's job."

The secretary seemed interested in some papers on her desk, "Mr. Olaphant isn't here at the moment."

"Do you know when he'll be back?"

"I'm not sure. He . . . "

The door opened behind Henry. A stout man made his way through it, closing it behind him. He ambled up to the desk. "Any calls for me, Trudy?"

The secretary looked at the newcomer, then at Henry. "No calls, but this young man's waiting to see you. Do you have a few minutes?"

The stout man turned to face Henry, "What's it about?"

Henry stood up as straight as he could, "It's about the fireman's job. I saw your sign down at Brunswick. They told me to see you here in Macon."

"Uh, huh. I see. Well, there might be a job and there might not. You had any experience with steam?"

"Yes, sir."

"Trains?"

"No."

"Well, come on in. We might as well find out what you can do. By the way, what's your name?"

"Henry Reynolds."

"Okay, Henry, tell me about your experience."

Henry related his work experience at his uncle's saw mill. Olaphant listened patiently until Henry ran out of information. Sitting with his fingers laced behind his head, Olaphant regarded Henry with a measuring eye. Finally he spoke, "I don't know. Running a sawmill boiler's not quite the same as firing an engine for a train. More responsibility on the train you know."

"Yes, sir. I reckon there is."

Olaphant liked this young man. He might have promise. He had seen a number of young fellows in his time. All they needed was a push; they made good railroad men.

"Tell you what, Slim. I'm gonna give you a chance. What you say?"

"Thank you, sir. I can do it. I know I can."

* * *

The two men approached the cab of the old engine. Henry thought he'd never seen one quite so old. The man in the engineer's cap and overalls motioned Henry up the steps to the cab.

"Get on up there and fire 'er up, Slim. I'll be back directly. Gotta get some paper work afore we take off."

Henry climbed aboard. He found, to his relief, that there was already fire in the box. All he had to do was build a head of steam before they left the yard. Turning to the coal tender, Henry scooped up a shovelful and stepped on the treadle that opened the firebox. He tossed the shovelful of coal spreading it over the smoldering fire. The result was not immediately apparent. Henry had never used coal in George's firebox. They always used slabs from the timber or whatever else might be handy to burn. This was going to be a new experience.

By the time the engineer returned, Henry had a roaring fire and a good head of steam.

Red Halsey, the engineer, climbed aboard heaving his huge bulk up the steps with some extra effort. He was a short, stocky man with a square jaw. His face wasn't unfriendly, but he had the ability to change his demeanor almost at will. His job here was to test a green recruit, and he had no intention of showing any favors. The young man was going to get the third degree.

"All fired up and ready t' go?" Red asked briskly.

"I think so," Henry answered.

Red glanced at all the gauges, checked the water level on the boiler, and sat down in his chair. Looking straight ahead, he said, "We'll be goin' t' Columbus and back. It'll take us about eight hours or so. Think you can handle that, Slim?"

"I can handle it," Henry answered confidently.

Red eased the throttle back. The ancient engine huffed as the steam was released into the compression chamber. Squealing noises indicated that the wheels were attempting to find traction on the slippery rails. The drivers caught; the engine began to move forward.

The train cleared the yard. A signal told them they were clear to the next junction. Red pulled the throttle open. The huffing, puffing engine increased its rhythm. Rails shook beneath the engine as it walked the iron like some giant leviathan.

The terrain from Macon to Columbus is hilly. Ages ago, an ancient ocean washed these hills along what is today known as the fall line. Many of the hills were on the beach of the ancient sea. The residue of sand caused the land to sink in some places and rise in others. Short grades made it difficult to maintain a constant speed. In fact, the pace was sometimes referred to as "dragonfly,"--drag up one hill and fly down the next.

Henry kept a sharp eye on the steam gauge. He was feeling pretty good about his performance until they began to hit the short grades. The steam pressure dropped steadily as they climbed one hill, but it didn't rise as Henry thought it should on the down-grade. He couldn't figure it out.

Red was no help. He cussed and fussed when the engine slowed too much to suit him.

"Dammit, Slim, I got to have more steam on them grades. This ain't no toy railroad we're running. Pour on the coal."

Henry fought to keep the steam up, but it seemed to be a losing battle. Each time it seemed he got a good head of steam, something happened to bring the gauge down.

Henry paused, leaning against the rail of the cab. He sucked huge draughts of air into his lungs. This pace was killing him. For a moment or two, Henry observed Red's manipulation of the controls. It seemed to Henry they were losing too much steam through valves that shouldn't have been open. He's doing that deliberately, Henry thought. No wonder I can't build a head of steam that'll keep this bucket of bolts rolling.

When they stopped to take on water a couple of hours later, Henry was nearly exhausted. The constant battle to keep the fire hot enough to run the engine had worn him down. He took advantage of the break. When they pulled out again, Henry tackled the chore with renewed determination.

Red played with the steam whistle just to aggravate him, Henry thought. The old engine lumbered along, steam leaking from first one valve, then another. Henry watched as his hard built steam pressure dissipated before his eyes.

After four hours of hard, backbreaking work they rolled into Columbus. Red announced that he would be taking care of some business. He advised Henry that they would be leaving as soon as he returned and perhaps, Henry ought to get himself a bite to eat.

Henry took advantage of the break, but he was back on the engine long before Red returned.

Henry found the oil can and went to work. Deliberately and methodically, he lubricated each and every valve he could find on the engine. He had worked around steam enough to know that sticky valves robbed you of a great deal of power.

When his oiling task was complete, Henry went back to the cab to try an experiment with the coal. In another half hour he had a fire going that brought the steam gauge dangerously close to the red mark.

"Uh, huh, you son-of-a-bitch," he said to himself. "I've got you pegged now. Come on, you red-headed bastard. I'll give you all the steam you can blow."

* * *

It took another hour to turn the engine on the turntable, then they were off on the return trip. Henry watched as Red pushed and pulled his levers. Red noticed that the valves didn't leak like they had on the trip out. He glanced at Henry, but held his peace.

When they hit the first grade, the engine held its head of steam, moving faster than it had moved on any hill the entire trip. Henry stepped on the firebox door treadle and tossed another shovelful on the fire. He turned leisurely back to the coal tender and filled his shovel again. After a minute or more, Henry unloaded his shovel in the fiery furnace.

Red did his damndest to kill the head of steam. Henry threw an occasional shovelful of coal on the fire and watched Red. Red knew he was dealing with a new deck. This novice fireman had some how discovered how to make this ancient engine jump through the hoop for him.

Henry had learned a lesson. Initially, he had tried to fire the engine by spreading the fire under the boiler. The result had been a disaster. All he got for his trouble was a semi-hot boiler. The secret, he found, was to bank the coal near the center of the firebox. This created a hot spot, but the heat dissipated across the boiler bottom resulting in a rolling boil that gave off more steam. By keeping his coal bank replenished, Henry could rest from his shoveling more than half the time.

Red was strangely quiet when they rolled into the Macon

station. Henry had held his tongue during the entire trip. He really wanted this job, but he didn't feel like he'd been given a fair shake.

As soon as the train came to a full stop, Henry dismounted from the cab. As he walked away, Red called out, "Hey, Slim. Where you goin'?"

Henry stopped, turned deliberately, and said, "Just as far as I can from this damn railroad. You give me a piece of junk to work with. Then you do your damndest to work me to death. You and ever' son-of-a-bitch on this railroad can go to hell."

Red seemed taken aback. "Don't go, Slim. You passed the test."

"The hell, I did. Your can take this job and shove it up your butt hole, you hear me!"

XV
A Death in the Family

"Gee!" Henry commanded the mule. The slow-moving creature took his time turning at the end of the row. Henry followed with the "grasshopper" plow. Clucking to the mule, he set the plow in the ground. After a few steps, Henry called, "Whoa."

The sun was bearing down on this warm spring day. Henry looked across the field and considered how much work there was still to be done. He might be able to finish it by nightfall if he worked late. Pulling a bandanna from his pocket, he wiped his face. There was no shade in this field, only wide open space. That made it seem as if the glaring ball of fire in the sky was hotter than ever.

Clint Crosby had given Henry work for a few days. Trucking of farm products was rather slow during the spring of the year, so George didn't need him right now. Besides there was the matter of the law. Henry could never quite shake the notion that they were still looking for him. He wasn't exactly afraid, but he was very suspicious of any stranger who came around. There was no reason to take unnecessary risk.

Henry spoke to the mule. The plodding animal strained against the trace chains pulling the plow forward. Up and down, up and down the rows they went. The monotony was only exceeded by the heat.

Finally, Henry halted the mule at the end of a row, looked at the sun, and decided it was time to go to the house for dinner--the midday meal.

As Henry opened the lot gate, he could be the hearing the buzz of voices coming from the back porch of the Crosby house. He relieved the mule of the burden of harness, threw a few ears of corn in a trough, dumped a bat of hay in the opposite end, and made his way toward the porch.

"Mist uh Henry. You wash up now. Dinner'll be on in jest a mini'," Mattie, the Crosby's maid called. She had spied Henry through the open door of the kitchen.

Without a word, Henry walked to the wash shelf. He poured three or four dippers of water from the bucket into the wash pan. Rubbing his hands generously with lye soap, he proceeded to wash the grime from his hands. He finished washing his hands, flung the water from the pan into the yard, and wiped his hands on the towel.

"Don't you git no dirt on that clean towel," Mattie called.

Henry grinned to himself, holding his peace. You would have thought Mattie was his mother the way she fussed over him. Henry inspected the towel. He couldn't see any dirt. It really wasn't that big of a deal, but he didn't want to get on Mattie's bad side. After all, she was the cook, too.

The Crosby family had already eaten, so Henry found himself at the table alone except for Craig, the youngest boy. Mattie bustled around as she set warm dishes on the table.

"You eat up now, ya hear. Need t' keep up yore strength. That plowin's hard work," she said.

"Thanks," Henry replied.

Henry dug into the meal with satisfaction. The Crosby's set a good table. They weren't rich necessarily, but as Henry would say, "They were good livers." Clint carried the mail locally. In fact, he timed his route so that he'd be home for dinner each day about noon. Henry would have been asked to sit down with the family if he had been at the house early enough.

The fact that you were hired help didn't keep you from eating with the family unless you were black. For instance, Mattie would not have been asked to join the family for a meal under any circumstances, even though she had been a faithful employee for years. Such behavior was not restricted to the Crosby family; it was practiced area wide.

Henry ate in silence. Mattie went to the stove, picked up a hot smoothing iron, and proceeded to the other end of the kitchen where she had set up her ironing board. She hummed to herself as she smoothed the wrinkles from Clint's white shirt. That shirt had to be spotless; he'd want to wear it come Sunday.

Craig had been quiet for sometime. In fact he'd been quiet too long for him. If you knew him, you understood there was some devilment going on in his head when he was quiet. He also had a personal conviction that one of his reasons for living was to aggravate Mattie.

"Mattie," Craig said solemnly.

"Yas suh," Mattie responded somewhat absent-mindedly. A black person didn't dare address even a child without respect.

"They're movin' thu river."

Mattie's hand paused as she responded, "Dey is?"

Craig sat there with a poker face. Mattie seemed lost in thought for a moment. The absurdity of Craig's words sank in.

"Aw! Ain't studin'," Mattie said calmly. She went back to her work. Craig grinned with satisfaction. Henry smiled to himself and continued his meal.

* * *

Henry pulled his pistol from his belt, aimed carefully, and shot the hog between the eyes. The shoat fell over squealing in agony. Reaching for his knife, Henry slit the animal's throat allowing the blood to drain. The meat wouldn't be fit to eat if the animal wasn't bled properly.

Thus, began the slaughter of most of the family's hogs. It wasn't unusual for them to kill enough for meat, but this wasn't usual. Expenses had to be trimmed. Drought had hit hard this past summer. There wasn't enough feed to keep the hogs through the winter. Slaughtering the animals and smoking and salting the meat was the only choice.

Friends and family had gathered from miles around. They would help with the work. Their pay would consist of fresh meat from the hog killing.

George and Gussie were there. Eva, Henry's mother, seemed to be everywhere at once giving instructions. The job would go on as long as it took, even midnight if necessary.

Henry enjoyed these times. It gave him a chance to visit with other folks without feeling he was wasting his time.

The conversations turned to all sorts of subjects, not the least of which was the weather. Everybody had an opinion about that. It hadn't rained a measurable amount in so long most of them had forgotten the last shower.

The whole country was suffering from dry weather. News reports out of the Midwest told of areas where whole farms were being blown away by the wind as the earth parched under a relentless, blazing sun. Fields that had been turned for spring planting were slowly, but surely, relieved of their topsoil as northerly winds blew the earth across the country. The area, including Oklahoma, had been dubbed "The Dust Bowl."

Thousands of people were being displaced. Their familiar surroundings were abandoned in an attempt to find sustenance for survival. Every so often, Henry would hear reports of the Okies and their plight in California. He vaguely realized how fortunate he was to have his home. At least he had a place to come when all other possibilities had been exhausted. The trick now would be to hang onto it.

Eva had instructed him to kill all the hogs, except those she thought she could feed through the coming winter. That meant a lot of work, and it all had to be done in the shortest possible time. Refrigeration was unknown on most farms. There were icehouses in town, but farmers couldn't afford to pay to have their meat kept there. What's more, they needed their food close at hand. The solution was the same as it had been for hundreds of years. The meat had to be smoked or salted so that it could be preserved on the farm.

"Lo-Lordy I ain't never seen so much meat in one pile," Joe, Henry's brother stuttered.

His hands were covered with blood from removing the entrails of a hog. He started to wipe his dripping nose, thought better of it, and reached for a towel to wipe his hands. The smell of raw meat was pungent, but a stuffy nose didn't help.

Henry looked at Joe, "Yeah. It's a pile of meat all right, but we've got a long way to go. All this has got to be finished before we sleep tonight."

"We wo-won't ne-ever make it," Joe observed.

"We'll make it or know the reason why not."

Joe hesitated. He always felt a little intimidated by his older brother. Henry was always bossing him around. This occasion was no exception. Why did he have to put up with that kind of talk from Henry?

"Better get back to work," Henry said. "If Ma catches you goofing off, there'll be hell to pay."

Joe grumbled under his breath, picked up the pan of hog guts and made his way to the cleaning table.

The work continued. George came to the scalding pot to help Henry with an exceptionally large hog.

"Here, boy. Let me give you a hand," George offered.

Henry took one hind-leg of the hog while George grabbed the other. Together they slid the huge hog into the hot, steaming water.

George and Henry had a special relation. They'd been close for a lot of years now. Henry thought of George as a father, and George loved Henry as much as any of his children. Although it was never said, each of them seemed to understand this arrangement in his own way.

"I don't know what folks are gonna do if this drought don't break," George said as he and Henry rolled the hog over to scald the other side. "Seems like it ain't rained in a coon's age, an old coon at that."

Henry reached for his knife. He scraped some of the scalded hair experimentally. It came off to his satisfaction. "I know what you mean. We'll be lucky if there's any corn to feed the hogs this winter. I walked through the field yesterday. Nothing but nubbins everywhere I looked."

George changed hands to rest his tiring arm, "You know, I was at the feed store in Baxley the other day. Old man Silas says there's a new plant that might help us make it through the winter. It's called Chufas. He says folks have had lots of luck with it in some parts of the country."

"Chufas?" Henry asked. "I ain't never heard of it. Where'd it come from?"

"Old man Silas said somebody brought it over from Europe. Italy, I think."

"How'll it help us?" Henry asked.

George turned his head and spat on the ground before he replied. "It's supposed to grow in dry weather."

"That's good."

"Yeah, I was thinkin'; I might plant some in the firebreaks on my place. That way I could just turn my hogs loose in the woods."

Henry moved the hog so that a portion of the hair that had not been wet was submerged in the hot water. "That sounds like a good idea. If you put it close to the branches, the water might flow down and help it grow."

"That's how I figure it, too. Lord knows when we'll get another rain of any useful amount. I don't think I've ever seen it this dry. Least ways, I don't remember it."

Henry pulled the hog up, scraped more hair, experimentally,

and said, "That's about enough for this one. Want to help me hang him up on the rack?"

"Sure," George answered.

Henry sliced the skin between the bone and hamstring in each of the hog's hind legs. He slid the "hanging stick" through the cuts and turned to George.

"Ready when you are," He said.

George grasped the opposite end of the stick and the two men struggled to hang the hog on the post that stood near the steaming boiler.

George grunted with the effort. When the hog was suspended, he said, "That one's heavy enough. Ought to get a ton of lard outa him."

Henry began scraping the hair, "Yeah, at least that much."

George stood watching as Henry cleaned the animal inch by inch. His roving eyes explored the work his nephew did. A gleam of satisfaction showed in his eyes. He was proud of this boy. Henry could do most anything that came to hand, and George congratulated himself that he was, in part, responsible for his nephew's ability to do many chores well.

"The preacher over at Spring Branch is trying to get folks to come over for a prayer meetin'. Seems like he thinks we can ask the Lord to send us some rain," George ventured as he watched.

"I don't reckon it'd hurt nothin'," Henry answered.

"I guess not, but I've noticed that the Lord takes his own good time answering prayers, sometimes."

"I know what you mean. I reckon his schedule ain't the same as ours."

The conversation continued as the two men worked steadily to complete the task before them. Evening shadows began to lengthen, prematurely it seemed, in the November afternoon. It soon became clear that the work would last well into the night.

* * *

"Henry, you and Alvin come here," George called as the two young men entered the front porch.

George stood near a rocking chair. A stack of papers in his hand, implied that he'd been busy working on some project or other. Henry and Alvin waited for George to speak.

"Boys, I want you to make a run to Savannah. The Mills brothers have a load of rosin to take to the port. Here's the papers," George said, handing the stack to Henry.

"Don't dawdle now. It'll take you awhile to load the truck. When you get to Savannah, go by the sugar refinery and pickup a load of sugar for the Toliver warehouse. Is that clear?"

Henry took the papers, folded them, and stuffed them in his shirt pocket. "Yessir," he answered. "Is that all?"

"That's all 'till you get back. I'll give you another job when you finish this one. Okay?"

George studied Henry and Alvin's faces for another instant before he said, "Here's a problem for you, Alvin."

George often gave his children problems to solve while they were on a trip. He believed it helped them to stay sharp as well as learn some valuable problem-solving lesson. This exercise wasn't rhetorical. George expected the problem to be solved, and Alvin and Henry knew he required an answer in a reasonable time.

Alvin listened as his father spoke.

"If eggs are twelve cents a dozen, how much would one hundred eggs cost?" George asked.

"Is that it, Pa?" Alvin asked.

"That's it. I'll be looking for you to have the answer when you get back."

Alvin scratched his head and looked at Henry. "You gonna give Henry a problem, too."

"Sure am," George replied. "Henry, here's yours. A man met a lady with a flock of geese. 'Good morning, Mam, with your hundred head of geese,' he said.

"'I'm sorry, good sir, but I don't have a hundred head. If I had twice as many as I have, half as many more, and two and a half, I'd have a hundred head,' she told him.

"Now, here's the question; how many does she have?'"

Henry repeated the question to be sure he had understood all the information. George prompted him when he faltered. Finally, Henry seemed satisfied that he had everything straight.

"How long have I got to find the answer?" Henry asked.

George considered for a moment before he said, "That one's a little harder than Alvin's. I'll give you a little more time if you need it."

Henry and Alvin left a few minutes later.

* * *

Henry struggled with his problem all through the loading of the truck. Alvin did likewise. Neither of the young men was adept at solving problems, but they were both inspired by George. It was something like competing for grades in school. If you made a favorable impression, you were raised in standing, at least as far as you were concerned, personally.

Henry and Alvin spoke to each other infrequently. They never discussed their individual problems between them. The competition caused each of them to keep any solution to himself.

They had been on the road for two or three hours before they had exchanged more then a few sentences between them. Henry had tried several ways to solve his problem, all to no avail. Alvin sat on his side of the truck mumbling to himself. Henry paid no attention.

Finally, Alvin broke the silence. "I don't understand why Pa give you the hardest problem. Everybody knows you're so dumb you won't find the answer by the middle of next week."

It was true that Henry was slow when it came to academics. That had been obvious to even himself since he was a child. Many of his peers had said so more than once, but that didn't make Henry any less sensitive about his handicap. Alvin, frustrated with his own inability to reach a conclusion, had decided to rankle Henry with this unpleasant reminder.

"Who says I'm dumb?" Henry demanded.

"Everybody says it. Ain't you been listening all your life?"

"Look here. Just because I have a hard time with some things don't mean I'm dumb."

"Yeah, you just ain't smart enough to figure out how dumb you are. That's the biggest problem."

"Okay, Mr. Smarty Pants, if you're so smart, what's the answer to your problem?"

Alvin smirked, "I'll tell you the answer to mine if you'll tell me the answer to yours."

"You know I don't have the answer yet."

"That's right. And you won't have the answer no time soon. You're too dumb."

Henry decided to let the argument ride for the time being. But that didn't keep him from fuming over the slight Alvin had cast on his mental abilities. As long as he could remember, Alvin had teased him about his slowness. The more he thought about it, the more his anger grew. He knew he wasn't as fast as a lot of other people, but they had no cause to aggravate him with the fact. He'd be damned if he was going to take it anymore.

Henry and Alvin stopped for fuel at Midway. Henry busied himself while Alvin supervised the filling of the tank, paid for the fuel, and prepared for his turn to drive.

When Henry returned to the truck, he had a lit cigarette in his lips and a cup of liquid in his hand. Alvin sat under the steering wheel looking straight ahead. Before he could put the truck in gear, Henry accosted him.

"Wait just a damn minute!" Henry said emphatically.

Alvin looked at Henry with some bit of alarm. It was clear that Henry was angry about something.

"What is it, now?" Alvin asked, quietly.

"We've got something to settle here and now."

"What's that?"

"This business about me being dumb."

"Oh!"

"That's right. We're gonna put a lid on this thing right now."

Alvin glanced at the can of liquid in Henry's hand. "What's that?" He asked nervously.

"Gasoline," Henry replied.

"What you gonna do with gasoline?"

Henry puffed his cigarette deliberately. "I'm gonna pour it on you and set your ass on fire!"

"You're crazy as hell!"

"Damn right, I am."

Alvin looked at Henry's eyes, attempting to see if he was serious. They sometimes played jokes on one another, but one glance told Alvin this was no joking matter. He swallowed hard.

"Look, Henry, you wouldn't do that, would you?"

"Try me."

Alvin could see he'd backed himself into a jam. It didn't set right with him to apologize, but he knew he was between a rock and a hard place. If he couldn't persuade Henry to change his course of action, he was going to end up injured or maybe even dead. It hadn't once occurred to him that Henry would take anything he said so seriously. He had to wriggle his way out of this, or he was going to be sorry.

Alvin told himself to calm down. Taking a deep breath or two, he decided he'd have to apologize. When he started to speak, the words almost hung in his throat. Finally, they came out.

"Henry, I'm sorry. I was wrong."

"Damn right, you were."

Alvin paused before he continued. "I had no right to say what I said. It was stupid of me."

"You've got that right."

Alvin considered his next words carefully. "I don't know

what else to say."

"How about 'I won't do it again?'"

"Okay, I won't do it again."

Henry stared at Alvin. His voice measured each word as he spoke. The delivery was cold and deliberate.

"Listen to me. From now on, keep your damn opinions to yourself. If I so much as hear another word out of you about me being dumb, I'm gonna whip your ass 'till you can't set for a week. That clear?"

Alvin swallowed hard. He didn't say anything.

"I asked you a question, dammit!"

"Sure. Anything you say."

Henry watched Alvin's face for some hint that he meant what he said. Henry had found he could tell quite a bit about a man's word by watching his eyes. The eyes were the windows of the soul, Henry believed, though he might never have heard the expression.

Alvin hoped Henry's anger was subsiding, but he didn't take any chances. He looked straight ahead, trying not to give Henry the impression that he wasn't listening.

"If that's clear, we can go," Henry said deliberately.

"It's clear."

"Okay, you just remember what I said."

Alvin pushed the shift lever into first gear and eased out on the clutch. The truck moved forward slowly. Alvin glanced at the mirror before he pulled out onto the main road. Henry watched as Alvin shifted out. When they had reached perhaps twenty miles per hour, Henry poured the cup of gasoline out the window. A moment later he flipped the butt of his cigarette out, too.

* * *

Henry heard the sound of the car before it was visible. That wasn't unusual. The rough wash-boarded road by the house always announced the presence of an automobile long before you could see it, but this one sounded different. There wasn't as much rattle as usual. There was a standing joke about Fords and baling wire. Everybody agreed that you could fix them with haywire. Since almost everybody in Appling County owned a Ford, nobody minded the joke.

The car pulled up in the front yard. George stepped out, shut the door, and admired his new car.

"What you think of her?" He asked Henry.

"Looks good. What kind is it?"

"Brand spanking new Chevrolet."

"Nineteen thirty-seven?"

"Yep."

Henry walked around the car admiring it. He'd seen lots of new cars, but this one was different. His Uncle George was driving it.

"Mind if I sit in the driver's seat for a minute?" He asked.

"Help yourself," George replied, motioning Henry to the driver's side door.

Henry slid into the soft cloth seat and enjoyed the feel of the material as it embraced him. He looked over the dash, placed his hands on the steering wheel, and admired the hood ornament.

"She's a beauty all right. Must have set you back a bundle?"

"That's a fact. More'n I wanted to pay, but hell, I ain't never owned a car. All my life I been spending money on trucks. This time I decided I was gonna buy something I wanted, just because I wanted it."

Henry looked around. The interior was as luxurious as he'd ever seen. It was almost, but not quite, a dream.

"Can I drive her?"

"Sure."

George went to the passenger side, opened the door, and settled in as Henry started the engine. Henry eased out on the clutch and the car went into motion as smoothly as a flowing stream.

The test drive was a success. Henry admired the new car and

was as happy for George as if he, himself, was the owner of the automobile.

A few days later, Henry returned from a trip to Savannah. He hadn't been in the yard more than five minutes when Cap Branch drove into the yard.

Henry spied him and went to meet him. "Good evenin', Mr. Branch. How're you?"

"I'm fine, son."

"If you're lookin' for Uncle George, he ain't here."

Cap looked at Henry soberly. "I know, son. That's why I'm here."

"How's that?"

"Henry," Cap said carefully, "I'm afraid I've got bad news."

"What's that?"

"Your Uncle George has been in a wreck."

Henry paused before he asked, "How bad is it?"

"Real bad, son."

"Is he all right?"

"No, son. He's dead."

XVI
Slashing the Pines

The news upset Henry more than he let on. He had been raised with the macho attitude that men don't cry, but that admonition didn't mean much at the moment. If he had given into his instincts, he would have cried openly, but he controlled his outward emotions.

"Mr. Branch, what happened?" Henry said, struggling not to choke on the words.

Cap could see the emotion on Henry's face. It was plain to him that this young man might need more support than he pretended. I'd better go slow with this, thought Cap.

"George was driving his new Chevrolet, you know."

"Yes, he bought it just the other day. Go on."

"Well, it seems he backed out in the road near Red Dot when somebody came flying down the road and hit him from behind. Tore the car up pretty bad.

"When they got to George, he was barely breathing. The impact had crushed him between the seat and the steering wheel. He died before they could get him out of the wreck. The doctor said it could have been a heart attack, but it was probably brought on by the impact."

Henry swallowed hard before he said, "Where's his body?"

"They took him to the undertaker. Thomas', I think."

"Thank you. I'll need to tell Aunt Gussie."

"Would you like for me to come with you?"

"If you don't mind."

Gussie took the news with a grit of her teeth. She had been through a lot with George over the years. It hurt to lose him, but there was little she could do. She was just thankful he'd lived until most of their children were grown. God knew she didn't know what she would have done with a family of small children. Eva's tragedy when Gus, George's brother, died had been an example of the trouble that could bring.

The funeral stood out in Henry's memory like none had ever done before. Henry had been less than six years old when his father died, so he really didn't remember that much about it. Even the loss of three of his grandparents hadn't hurt like losing his Uncle George.

The whole affair of the funeral seemed like some kind of weird nightmare. Henry stood by as the preacher spoke words over George in an attempt to comfort the family. Those words, in spite of the good intentions behind them, failed to give Henry the comfort he sought. He couldn't comprehend the loss he had sustained.

When the graveside service was concluded, Henry waited until the grave diggers filled the grave. Everyone slowly went away, except Henry. He stood there for what seemed like a long time. When he found himself alone at the grave, he lost the composure he had kept so bravely in front of the others. Tears streamed down his face as he poured his heart out to the only man he had ever truly loved and trusted.

Henry had no way of knowing how much he had lost. Only time would tell. Each day he found that he had problems that would have been much easier to bear, if only he had someone to share them with. George had provided that someone as long as he'd lived. Now, Henry had no one he could confide in. Even the pain in his mind and body seemed a heavier burden because he couldn't share it with another living soul. The image, he felt obliged to project, and the way he felt, were opposed to each other.

After George's death, Henry didn't have a road job for a while. George's business went to his sons, and it took time for people to trust them with the things George had handled with such expertise. Besides, Henry couldn't very well work for Alvin after the run-in they had had. There was nothing left to do but look for another job.

There were other truck owners around. Henry tried working for some of them, but he found himself at a disadvantage simply because most of these men demanded things of him that George hadn't. For instance, Henry didn't read very well. In fact, he was functionally illiterate. So reading a bill-of-laden was practically impossible. As soon as his employer discovered this, Henry was out of a job.

George had always handled things in such a way that Henry's reading ability hadn't been much of a factor. For one thing, George and Henry usually went to the destination together at least once. Furthermore, George had always been careful to give explicit verbal instructions. Henry was gifted with an extremely good memory, but he found symbols on paper difficult to deal with. This problem always interfered with any attempt to better himself on a job.

Henry found himself at odds with bosses, too. They often demanded things he found unreasonable. He'd had numerous encounters that caused him to think more and more about being his own boss. That way, he wouldn't have to put up with any-body's bull.

The big problem, Henry found, was you had to have money to start your own business--the one commodity he was sorely lacking.

This set of circumstances brought Henry to the conclusion that he would have to fall back on a job that didn't require him to read. The turpentine woods met that criteria for the moment. Even here, though, he still had to put up with a boss or sometimes bosses.

In those times, most of the turpentine work was carried on as a landowner operation. These people hired day-laborers to work for them. That way, they managed to keep most of the profits for themselves. Several large landowners worked a crew of men in their woods at what amounted to little more than slave wages. Daily wages of fifty-cents to a dollar were common.

Many operators had their own distillery where they processed the raw gum into its component parts, rosin and turpentine. This operation led to the establishment of what were commonly called "still quarters."

Men moved their families into these housing groups where they paid little or no rent at the discretion of the landlord. In those instances where the rent was not a direct transaction, it was considered part of the compensation for the work rendered by the day-laborer.

Conditions were far from ideal in these communities. Families found themselves crowded into cramped living quarters. As in many such places, tempers flared. Fights between wives were common. Children found themselves in conflict with other children. Life was a mess, to put it kindly.

When possible, Henry avoided crew-work. He liked being in the woods with as few people as possible. In fact, working alone was preferable to being part of a crew.

Henry found work with the Mills brothers, Sam and Lee. It wasn't the most favorable situation, but a man had to take what he could find. Even in the late thirties, the depression still held the working man in its grip. The country would not see any appreciable increase in working class employment until manufacturers geared up for World War II.

The work was hard and the pay was less than desirable, but Henry was able to make an agreement whereby he worked certain "Crops of Boxes" by himself. But this arrangement wasn't without its pains in the butt.

Woods riders were hired to check behind crews who chipped the boxes or dipped the gum. Some of them were fairly reasonable; others were a pain in the ass.

Basically these men checked to make sure that each tree had been chipped or dipped. If they found that the worker was missing a certain tree, they flagged it as a reminder that it had been missed.

Henry tried to make sure he was getting all the boxes, but he sometimes missed one without being lax in his work. On such occasions, he didn't mind the flagging, but Sam Mills had hired an especially aggravating woods-rider by the name of Oren Sapp.

Henry was working a crop of boxes near Piney Bluff on the Altamaha River. The crop consisted of about fifteen thousand faces. Henry had no means of transportation unless Sam or Lee picked him up and took him to his work. Since they often took longer to take him to the job than Henry thought they should, he walked, or more exactly, ran the twelve miles from his home to the woods. By this means he was able to finish the job in less time.

When possible, Henry tried to arrange his pay by piece work, that is, he was paid by the thousand for each thousand boxes he chipped. If he finished the job in less time, he still received the same amount of pay he would have for more time. This arrangement made it possible to work at your own pace. Such a provision wasn't possible in crew-work. There you were paid according to the time you worked rather than by production as in the piecework situation. Henry thought the piecework agreement was fairer than the time pay.

That was where the worker became suspect in the eyes of the employer. Many landowners felt they were being cheated under piecework, so they sent their woods riders to check on their pieceworker regularly.

Henry was hot and tired. He'd run the twelve miles to the river that morning and chipped two thousand or so faces when he saw Oren come riding through the woods. He stood and watched as the woods rider slowly rode his grey horse in a zigzag pattern over the trails Henry had covered.

Oren stopped, leaned down in the saddle, scrutinized the face on a tree, and broke a tip from a gallberry bush. Placing the "flag" on the tree, he continued to follow Henry's trail.

Henry knew he'd chipped the tree, so there was no reason for the flag. He figured Oren was just being his usual hard-boiled woods rider.

Henry had concealed himself in a gallberry patch while he watched, so Oren was somewhat surprised when Henry stepped out in front of his horse.

"Lookin' for me, Oren?" Henry asked quietly.

Oren sat his saddle in silence for a moment. "Not particularly. Just checkin' boxes like I'm paid to do."

"I saw you flag that tree a minute ago."

Oren sat as silently as the Sphinx. He seemed to study Henry's face, trying to determine whether he should confront him. "So!" He said sarcastically.

"So, I chipped that tree."

"Who says you did?"

"I do."

"And I say you're a damn lie."

Henry stood braced for trouble. If there was one thing he'd learned in his life time, it was to be ready to fight when you confronted a man like Oren. Oren was a bully, pure and simple, but you had to show him where to get off. If you didn't, he never ceased harassing you.

"Let's go take another look at it." Henry suggested, quietly.

"There ain't no need to look. I say it ain't been chipped, so it ain't been chipped."

"What's got your back up, Oren?"

"You, dammit."

"Why me?"

"You think you're too damn good to work with the regular crew. Think you're somebody special. Think you're gonna get away with sloppy work."

"That's a lie, and you know it. I've never cheated anybody on a job."

Oren spat on the ground at Henry's feet. "The hell you ain't. You sons-a-bitches are always goofing off. If you was worth a damn, you'd be doing something 'sides chippin' boxes."

Henry wanted to reach out and grab Oren's foot, throw him from the saddle, and stomp hell out of him, but he resisted the urge.

Henry eyed Oren calmly. "It's none of your damn business what I do. If you weren't a meddling son-of-a-bitch, you wouldn't be flaggin' trees that I've already chipped."

"I call 'em like I see 'em," Oren spat.

"You're blind as a bat this time."

"I'm gonna report you to Sam."

"Go ahead. Spill your guts. See if I give a damn."

Oren had about had a bellyful. He was ready to clip Henry. He reached for a club that he always carried.

Henry saw the attack coming. He stepped back as Oren swung. Oren lost his balance and fell from the saddle. His momentum carried him to the ground, knocking the breath from him.

Henry didn't give him a second chance. Lifting his foot, he slammed Oren in the butt with the heel of his boot. Oren rolled over cussing, climbed to his feet, and rushed Henry.

Sidestepping the rush, Henry clipped Oren behind his left ear. Oren landed like a ton of brick. His breath came in short, deep gasps. He stood up, shaking his head to clear it. Henry stood by, waiting for his next move. Oren swung at Henry with the club. A glancing blow on the shoulder caused Henry to flinch, but he grabbed the club arm and sent Oren sprawling into a gallberry patch.

Oren scrambled to his feet and struggled through the gallberry bushes. His face was scratched from contact with the rough bark of the bushes.

"Damn you. I'm gonna kill you, you son-of-a-bitch," Oren shouted as he rushed Henry again.

Henry swung his two-clasped fists under Oren's chin as he charged. The impact sent him sprawling on his back. Oren rolled over, spat a mouthful of blood, and tried to engage Henry in a clench as he rose from the ground.

Henry eluded his grasp and kicked Oren on the shin. Oren cursed, grabbed his leg, and hopped on one leg until he was out of Henry's reach.

Henry stood his ground. There was no need to take the fight to Oren. He was getting all he could take on his own.

Oren stood breathing hard, holding his leg, and grimacing with pain. He glared at Henry. Oren hated to admit defeat, but he'd had about all he could take for one round.

Henry held Oren in his gaze. He fully expected Oren to rush him again. His eyes fell on a lighter'd knot at the base of a nearby tree. Henry stepped over, scooped up the knot, and faced Oren.

"You had enough?" Henry said through clenched teeth.

Oren continued to glare at Henry, "This ain't finished!" He said.

"No, I don't reckon it is. You're so damn bullheaded, looks like I'm gonna have to kill you."

"There's more ways than one to skin a cat," Oren breathed.

"Yeah, I reckon, but you come at me one more time; I'm gonna do my damndest to knock your block off."

"That's okay. I'm gonna report you to Mr. Sam. He'll take care of you."

Henry watched as Oren hobbled over to his horse, gathered the reins in his hand, pulled himself into the saddle, and rode away slumped over the saddle-horn. Henry watched him until the gallberry bushes hid Oren from sight. He dropped the lighter'd knot and sat down to rest.

* * *

Sam Mills never said a word about Henry's encounter with Oren. Henry couldn't quite figure that out. Either Sam was deliberately keeping quiet or Oren hadn't said anything to Sam. The latter was more likely. Oren would have been humiliated by the obvious marks of conflict. It's hard to save face when you're wearing the brand of defeat on your face.

Although Henry preferred to work alone, there were times when he found himself in the crew. Turpentining was hard work, so finding men willing to do it wasn't easy. Employers often found themselves hiring people that would have been left out, if they'd had a choice.

Several Negroes were among the crews hired by the Mills brothers. Henry had been brought up with prejudices that were common among southern whites, so he found it difficult to work with some of these people. However, he also found some of them quite friendly and entertaining.

Buddy Mims lived on the Mills farm in a little house by the highway. He and his fellow blacks often spent their break time on the job discussing current events among their people.

One Monday morning, the crew had been working hard in a particular piece of woods. Everybody flopped down to catch a few breaths of fresh air and rest. After a short bantering session among the men, the conversation turned to other matters.

"Y'all hear 'bout Oscar?" Somebody asked.

"Whut 'bout 'em?" Another responded.

"He be back."

"Back frum where?"

"Africa."

"No."

"Shore nuff."

"Yeah. Ya knows he left 'n' went over dare."

"Hadn't heard uh word 'bout it. When'd he go?"

"Oh, musta been more'n uh year."

"Dat long?"

"Yeah."

"How come he went over dare?" A third party chimed in.

"Said he wuz goin' back t' his native country."

"He said dat?"

"Shore did."

"How come he come back?"

"Said it wuz turrible over dare."

"How dat?"

"He said all dey had t' eat was rice."

"Rice?"

"Yeah, rice."

"Huh. Ain't dat peculiar."

"It shore wuz. He sayed dey'd talk 'bout killin' and eatin' ya, too."

"No foolin'."

"Dat's whut he sayed."

"Lord, how come dey talks lack dat."

"'Cause dey's can-ables I reckon."

"Ya don't say."

"Yeah, dem people been killin' 'n' eatin' one 'nother fer uh long time."

The conversation about Oscar continued in the same vein for a while. By and by, the subject changed.

Buddy looked at Henry with an inquiring eye. "How ya t'day, Mistuh Henry?"

"I'm fine, Buddy. How're you?"

"Ain't never felt better in muh life as I recollect. Ya have a good week'n'?"

"Yeah. You?"

"Lord, yeah, Mistuh Henry. I allus has good week'n's. Whut you do dis week'n'?"

Henry grinned, "Oh, the usual. You know, the movies and

such."

"Git any likker?"

"Oh, a nip or two."

"Play cards?"

"Nope."

"Man, ya don't knows whut youse missin'. Me an' muh frens had de bes' time 'n' de worl' playin' cards and drinkin' likker."

"Is that right?"

"Yassuh, Mistuh Henry. Dey ain't nothin' lack be'n' a nigger. Why, if'n you wuz t' be a nigger one week'n', you wouldn't wanta be no white man ever uhgin."

Henry laughed while the crowd of black men nodded in agreement with Buddy. It was plain to see these men enjoyed themselves despite their poverty and, what seemed to Henry, their backward ways.

Most of the men in the crew were ready, willing, and able to pull a joke on anybody that came handy. The Negroes were no exception.

One morning, the crew was on the body of Sam's 1915 Model-T truck. They were on their way to a job. The usual laughing and joking had consumed most of their time together.

Suddenly, Sam pulled the truck to the side of the road and stopped. There was no cabin on the truck, so there was little chance of anyone missing anything they wanted to see. Sam stepped off the running board with a grunt.

"Eh, boys," he said. "Got to stop and draw my beer."

Sam strolled over to the roadside where he proceeded to urinate.

The situation was made-to-order for a practical joke, and Buddy couldn't resist the temptation.

As soon as Sam's water was flowing freely, Buddy cleared his throat and said in a strong, firm voice, "Good mawin', Mam."

Sam reacted just as Buddy had anticipated. He looked around with a jerk and wet his pants as he tried to put his penis back in his clothes.

Everybody on the truck howled with laughter.

"Which one of you sons-a-bitches done that?"

Nobody said anything. They were all too busy laughing.

Buddy was doubled over in almost hysteric laughter. He could hardly breathe, he was so convulsed.

"Buddy, damn your black hide, you said that, didn't you?" Sam demanded.

Buddy caught his breath long enough to say, "Nawsuh, hit twern't me, Mistuh Sam."

"You're a liar!"

Buddy burst into another gale of laughter. Finally, he came up for air, caught his breath and said, "Yassuh, I 'spect I is."

Sam wasn't without the ability to appreciate the joke. What got him the most was the fact that the joker had been Buddy.

"Damn your black ass, I'll get you for this."

Buddy held his lips together, trying to avoid bursting out in another laughing fit. "Yassuh, I 'spect ya will, Mistuh Sam, but hit wuz too good t' pass up."

Henry never knew whether Sam kept his word or not, but Buddy told the story every chance he got, laughing all the while.

* * *

A sense of humor helped the men make the best of a bad situation, but there were times when even this couldn't keep them from conflict. Tempers ran short often. Fights between workers sometimes broke out. When they did, the best policy was to let the men settle it themselves. Stepping in could earn you the animosity of both parties.

Not only were there conflicts among the men, sometimes one or the other of the crew found themselves at odds with the boss. Sam had some common sense about dealing with men. On the other hand, Lee, Sam's brother, was sorely lacking in this quality. Lee had been raised to believe he ought to be obeyed without question. Such obedience was not common among men who, for one reason or another, believed they should question those in authority.

Lee also had a problem dealing with men because most of them perceived him as stupid. He was the butt of more jokes than Sam, simply because he acted so foolish.

Sam had to pull his brother out of more than one scrape when he'd gotten himself in over his head. Sam tried to divide work responsibilities with Lee, which led to more trouble than it was worth.

One cold morning in January, Sam sent Lee with the crew. A crop of boxes needed raising, that is, the drain tins and cup were being moved up the tree so that the gum could reach the cup with less accumulation on the tar face. The men had been doing similar work during the winter since the fall scraping and dipping had been completed.

Everybody was bundled in at least two pair of pants, or a pair of long johns and pants, with a matching set of shirts and jackets. Even then, the cold bit their skin through their clothes.

The freezing January cold had left a skim of ice on top of the local ponds. A man was courting pneumonia if he set foot in those icy waters.

Lee pulled the truck to a stop near the end of a pond. The men dismounted and began building a fire. Warmth, in limited amounts, began to help them bear the cold when Lee stepped up to give orders.

"Okay, men. We've got to finish this crop today. We're gonna start in the pond."

The men looked at one another. "Did he say the pond?" Somebody asked.

"That's what he said," another answered.

A general grumble went through the crew.

"Why the pond?" Somebody wanted to know.

"'Cause I say so," Lee answered.

Henry was in no mood to enter the freezing water any sooner

than necessary. "Look, Lee," he said. "Why can't we work out here on the hill 'till the pond warms up some? At least let the ice melt."

Lee looked at Henry with daggers in his eyes. "Who put you in charge?" He asked.

"Nobody, but it makes more sense to work the hill first. That way the ice'll have time to thaw before we do the pond."

It was like waving a red flag in front of a bull, when Henry challenged Lee. Lee stood on one foot, then the other. He stuttered and stammered, then said:

"By damn I said we was gonna do the pond first, and we gonna do it."

Henry turned to the rest of the men, "How about it men? Are we going to wade that freezing water when we've got a good dry hill to work?"

Nobody said anything.

Henry looked at Lee, "The rest of you can follow this fool if you want to. I'm working the hill until the water warms up."

Lee reached for Henry's clothes. That was a mistake. Henry thought the gesture was a blow. He turned and hit Lee under the chin. Lee fell backwards over a box of nails. Most of the crew laughed.

Henry picked up his tools, turned toward the hill, and walked off. The crew looked after him for a moment before they followed his example.

"Henry! You're fired!" Lee shouted.

Henry stopped, turned to face Lee, and said, "That's fine with me. You can take this job and go to hell with it!"

XVII
A Wife and a Son

Henry cussed as the wrench slipped. His knuckles bled from the scrape they received from the slipping tool. The 1929 Model-A Roadster was on the blink again. It seemed there was never enough time to keep it running. Henry got mad enough to set fire to it sometimes, but it was the very first car he'd ever been able to call his own. Joe had helped him buy a car earlier, but that one had been shared so that Henry seldom used it for personal reasons.

Henry wiped the blood from his hand, reached for the wrench, and resumed his task. It looked like he was going to have to rebuild the starter. He could push the car and crank the engine, but that method was a nuisance. Besides, if something was supposed to work, it should work.

"Henry!" Eva called from the back steps of the house. "You gonna work on that old car all day?"

Henry pulled himself from beneath the car before he responded. "What you need, Mama?"

"Nothin' special I reckon. You've just been working on that car all day. Since today's Sunday, I thought you might want to rest awhile."

"I'd like to, Mama, but I've got to see if I can get this wreck runnin'. If I don't, I'll have to walk to work again next week."

Eva paused before she said, "Okay, I'd like to go see Ma when you can take me."

"I'll take you when I get the car goin', okay?"

"That'll be fine."

Henry turned back to the task at hand. The starter was jammed in so that there was barely room to remove it between the frame and exhaust. He finally twisted it until he could slide it through the small opening. Damn, Henry thought to himself, the son-of-a-bitch that built this didn't build it to work on.

The bolts on the starter came loose with a pull. Henry looked at the armature. There was a purple looking burn on the surface. That probably meant the field coils were bad. Something sure as hell made that burn. The whole starter would likely have to be replaced--more damned expense. Where's the money coming from, Henry thought? It seemed every cent he could rake and scrape went to keep the old car running. Well, that was life. If you had a car, you spent money. If you had money, you didn't have a car.

Working on the Model-A became a regular Sunday affair. It seemed there was no way around it. Come Sunday, the car had to be repaired so Henry could drive to work next week. Eva often accused him of tearing it up so he could work on it all day Sunday. At least, she claimed, it kept him from taking her anywhere on the weekends.

* * *

The car had given Henry a new advantage, however, when it came to dating. For years now, he'd had to walk most everywhere he went. That made it hard for him to actually take a girl on a date. Sometimes he would ride with the Wise brothers, but he really didn't like to have other boys around when he was courting a girl. He didn't feel comfortable saying the things he thought she wanted to hear in the company of other boys.

Now he could go to a girl's home, pick her up, and take her to town for a hamburger and a movie. The car helped interest the girls, too. It was more exciting to be able to leave the house. Sitting around under the watchful eye of your Ma and Pa wasn't always comfortable. Besides, if you wanted to smooch, it was better to be alone.

Henry had known lots of girls in his time, but he'd never--at least since Avis--considered marriage. In fact, marriage was one of the farthest things from his mind. I'll marry someday if I can find the right girl, he told himself.

Henry had been playing the field so long that he was completely unprepared for what happened when he met Lois. One of his neighbors told him about her. He decided he'd like to get to know her.

She was the daughter of Zeb Johnson, a Baptist preacher. Her mother had been killed in an accident some seven or eight years earlier, and she'd lived with her widowed father all that time. Faithfully, she had stayed with her father until the end. Suddenly, at the age of eighteen, she was alone in the world except for her sisters and brothers. Her sisters had married, leaving her with her father. Now he was gone.

Okella, her sister, had taken her in, but living with Okella and her husband wasn't Lois' idea of how things should be. Lois' life had revolved around her father so long that she felt as if there was little or no purpose for her life. Living with her sister made her feel like she was a burden. She was ready for a change.

Henry's and Lois' first meeting was a bit awkward. Lois hadn't had many beaus, and she found it hard to talk to a man--a total stranger anyhow.

Henry's greater experience gave him the ability to set her at ease, however. Their conversation began to smooth some as Henry asked:

"Do you like movies?"

Lois wasn't quite sure how to answer. Her father, with his strict interpretation of what was and wasn't proper, had forbidden her to see motion pictures.

"I don't really know," Lois answered. "I haven't seen any."

"Would you like to?"

"I...I'm not sure," Lois said uncertainly. It was hard to break a lifetime of behavior at once. The thought caused her some consternation, but after a moment she agreed hesitantly. "Yes, I think that might be fun."

"What about Saturday? I could pick you up. We could get something to eat and go to the movies."

"Okay."

* * *

Henry Fonda spat a stream of tobacco juice before he said, "You heard, Jesse. Git off'n our land."

The next moment the screen was filled with action of a fight between the James brothers and the railroad men. When the choreographed fracas was over, Fonda (a.k.a. Frank James) spat a second time and said, "Next."

Lois watched the moving shadows on the screen in fascination. The vivid colors and sounds were a new sensation for her. Screen images seemed to loom over her larger than life. This type of entertainment held her spell bound. It was, indeed, an intriguing new experience.

The scene where Pinky talked to Jesse about his newborn son was a little embarrassing to Lois. She wasn't accustomed to hearing people talk about babies like that--at least, not in public. The darkened theater helped hide Lois' blush. She was grateful for that.

During the next few months, Lois and Henry saw several movies, but the date they most often enjoyed was Sunday night at church. Henry sang solo hymns frequently. Lois enjoyed that immensely. This was something she could identify with and participate in.

As Henry saw more of Lois, he realized that this relationship was quite different from those he'd known with other women. He began to think of her as a possible lifelong companion.

When Henry mentioned his feeling to his mother, Eva, she cautioned him about his wild and carefree ways. This admonition caused Henry to think more seriously about marriage. Would he be able to put aside the life he'd lived for the past many years?

How could he provide for a wife and family?

Finally, Henry decided to pop the question.

He and Lois had been to Spring Branch Church one Sunday night. They were returning to Okella's home. Henry parked the Model-A Roadster in the driveway, turned off the engine, and sat silently for a moment. He cleared his throat.

"There's something I've been meanin' to talk to you about," he said.

"What's that?" Lois responded.

"Well," Henry hesitated. "We've been seeing one another for sometime now, and I was wondering . . . "

The words trailed off into another silence.

"You were wondering what?" Lois asked with a note of bewilderment in her voice.

"I was wondering if you felt the same way about me that I feel about you?"

Lois studied Henry's face for a moment. "I don't know. How do you feel about me?"

"Well, I-I think I'm in love with you."

"Oh!"

"Yes, in fact, I was thinking of asking you something."

"You were?"

"Yes."

"What's that?"

"I was thinking of asking you to marry me."

Lois sat silently for a moment. The proposal wasn't totally unexpected. In fact, she'd hoped Henry might do just what he'd done, but she wasn't really prepared to give him an answer. She felt apprehensive--not quite sure of herself.

"I-I'll need sometime to think it over," she said.

"That's all right. Take all the time you need," Henry answered.

"I-I'd better go in. Okella will wonder what happened to me."

"Okay. When can I see you again?"

"Why don't you come back on Wednesday?"

"I'll be here." Henry reached for her, pulled her against him, and kissed her soundly. "Good night."

* * *

Henry waited patiently for Lois' answer. He waited more patiently than he'd ever waited for anything in his life. The answer would come all in good time. Maybe it would be the answer he wanted to hear.

On Wednesday, Henry was at Lois' house before the agreed time. It was unusual for him to see her during the week--what with the work schedule he followed--but he'd made a special effort to be there.

Henry and Lois exchanged greetings. They lingered as pleasantries were exchanged among the family members. Finally, they were alone. Neither of them mentioned the subject that was uppermost in their minds.

Henry pulled the car into a driveway at a local service station. "Would you like something to drink?" He asked.

"Yes. Thank you, I would."

"Co-Cola okay?"

"Yes. That'll be fine."

Henry disappeared into the little country store. Lois could see him as he went to the drink box, opened it, and took out two bottles of Coca-Cola. Paying for the drinks, Henry returned to the car, handed Lois her drink through the car window, and seated himself behind the steering wheel.

They both sat in silence, sipping from their drinks. Henry decided he'd give them both time to finish the drinks. That way he could return the bottles without having to pay a deposit.

Lois had almost drained her bottle when she decided to restart the conversation. "You know what you asked me on Sunday?"

Henry decided not to be too eager. The answer might, after

all, not be what he hoped for. "Yes. I remember."

"Well, I've thought it over, and I've decided to say 'yes.'"

Henry almost sighed with relief. "Yes?"

"That's right. Yes."

"That's good."

Henry hesitated before he said, "Would you like to set the date?"

Lois thought for a long moment. She didn't want to rush into something, but it would be nice to move out of Okella's house as soon as possible.

"How about a week from Sunday?" She asked.

"That'd be fine." Henry replied. "That'll give me time to get the license and make some arrangements."

"It's settled." She said.

"I reckon it is. What would you like to do tonight?"

"I'd like to just ride around for a while, if you don't mind."

Henry pumped the accelerator, stepped on the starter, and the engine sprang to life. That rebuilt starter was working all right.

* * *

Henry spent the next ten days busily preparing for the coming wedding. It seemed there was no end to the things that needed to be done. He and Lois went to the Clerk of Courts Office to get the license. That was three dollars. It seemed a high price, but Henry wanted to marry, so he paid the fee without comment.

Then there was the question of where they would live. Henry had never had to provide shelter for anyone but himself. When he thought of it, Eva had done that for the most part. There were exceptions--when he was working away from home--but those had been rare. I'll ask Mama if we can live with her for a while, he thought.

"Mama, I've decided to marry Lois," Henry announced one morning.

"I thought as much," Eva replied.

"I was wonderin' if we could live with you 'till we found a place of our own?"

Eva seemed to think the question over before she said, "I reckon you can, but it'll be kinda crowded. How long do you think it'll take for you to find a place of your own?"

"I'm not sure. I was thinking I might see if I could rent a house with the Mills. It would be convenient to my work, too."

"When's the wedding?"

"Next Sunday."

"That soon?"

"Yeah, we thought there wasn't much reason to wait."

"I see, well, you're welcome to stay here, but keep in mind, I won't be waitin' on your new bride. She'll have to learn to do for herself."

Henry grinned, "Knowing you, Mama, it couldn't be any other way."

* * *

Henry knocked at the door and stood back nervously. Beside him, Lois stood waiting quietly. An eternity seemed to pass before the door opened to reveal a middle-aged man dressed in white shirt and black pants--the accepted garb of a preacher. He stood there looking for a minute.

"What can I do for you?" He asked politely.

Henry's tongue almost stuck to the roof of his mouth.

"We . . . we wanta get married," he managed to say.

"Um . . . I see. Well, don't just stand there. Come on in."

The preacher led the way into the living room. He motioned Henry and Lois to a seat on the couch. "Have a seat. I'll be with you in a minute."

Preacher Fenell strode out of the room. Henry and Lois sat smiling at one another nervously.

"Frances, would you come here, please. We've got company. It's Henry and Lois. They want to get married."

Frances Fenell came from the kitchen wiping her hands on her apron. "I'll declare, so you two have decided to tie the knot? Isn't that wonderful?"

The couple acknowledged Mrs. Fenell's words with a nod of their heads. Words weren't easy for them just now.

Reverend Fenell came back with his Bible and a book of some kind.

"I was just saying to Reverend Fenell the other day. One of the most enjoyable parts of being a preacher's wife is being able to see young couples get started out on the right foot. Isn't that right, dear?"

"That's right. That's exactly what she said," Fenell said with a wide smile. "You know what we say, 'Preachers hatch 'em, match 'em, and dispatch 'em.'"

Directing himself to Henry, he asked, "Do you have the license, young man? You know it ain't legal 'till I sign the license."

"Yes . . . sir. I've got it here somewhere," Henry said, fumbling in his pocket for the paper. He finally pulled it from his pocket, handed it to Fenell, and waited expectantly.

The preacher looked at the paper, mumbling to himself, as he read the contents. "Looks like everything's in order here. Y'all ready to get on with it?"

Henry and Lois both nodded. Their voices seemed to be out of working order.

"Very well. Y'all stand up now."

Henry and Lois complied.

"Frances, are you ready to witness this ceremony?"

"Ready, dear," she replied.

"Let's get on with it then. Dearly beloved," Fenell intoned in his most serious voice. "We are gathered here in the presence of this company to witness the joining of this man and this woman in holy matrimony. . . ."

Henry stumbled through his vows. Lois was a bit more coherent. Finally, the ceremony was over.

"I now pronounce you man and wife," Fenell said with a note of finality. He paused. "Well, son, kiss your bride!"

Henry gave Lois a peck. Fenell grinned.

"Frances, don't we have something we could give this young couple for refreshment?"

"Coming right up," she answered.

Henry reached for his wallet. "How much I owe you?" He asked.

"Oh, most anything. How much you think she's worth?" Fenell grinned.

Henry handed him a five-dollar bill.

"Brides is worth more 'n they used to be," Fenell said with a chuckle.

* * *

Lois paused between strokes of her broom. It seemed she had swept the house a hundred times that week. Still, the dust found its way through the cracks in the weather-boarding. The tenant house she and Henry had gotten as part of his deal with the Mills brothers wasn't much to look at, and it was even less than it should have been to live in.

You just couldn't keep the inside clean. What with the wind blowing off the open fields, it was like living in a desert sandstorm. The freshly plowed fields gave up their topsoil to the ceaseless March winds. The result was grit in and on everything in the house. Cleaning house had never been Lois' long suit. Now, this place was slowly driving her nuts.

She and Henry had married last fall. Living with Eva, her mother-in-law, hadn't been too bad, but she could hardly wait to get a house of her own. She wasn't too sure that had been a good idea. At least, this dirt trap.

The sun stood in the sky about an hour high. Lois looked at it and decided she'd better start supper. Henry would be home soon--hungry as a bear. Working turpentine did that to men. It seemed you could never cook enough to fill them.

The kindling caught as Lois stuck a match to the fat wood. Smoke made her grimace as she stood waiting to be sure the fire was burning. Shortly, the flue began to draw and the stove began to warm. She busied herself at food preparation while the fire brought a pot of water to a boil.

The sun had hidden itself in the west when Lois heard the familiar sound of the Model-A. Henry pulled up in front of the house, switched off the lights, and cut the engine. Lois could hear him climbing the short steps to the front door. She wiped her hands on a dish cloth before going through the house to meet him.

Henry stood there covered with sweat-stained clothes. Tar covered his hands and arms to the elbows. This certainly didn't look like the young man who had come courting her. She thought, this will take some getting used to.

Henry greeted her with a smile, "How's my best girl?"

"I'm okay."

"Is there something wrong?"

"No."

"You don't sound very convincing. What is it?"

"It's the house."

"What about it?"

"I can't seem to keep it clean."

"It looks fine to me. What's happenin'."

"It's the dust. There's no end to it."

"Oh, I see. Well, don't worry about it. When the crops are put in, the wind won't blow the dust so bad. We always had to put up with the dust at Mama's. Believe me, there was plenty of it between the two fields on each side of the house.

Lois gave in. Henry reached for her, hugged her, and planted a kiss full on her mouth.

"Oh! You stink!" Lois said, wrinkling her nose.

"I don't smell as good as you, but a bath'll help some. Do I have time for one before supper?"

"If you want, but you can eat first. Supper's on the stove if you'd like to eat first."

"That sounds mighty good. I could eat a horse."

* * *

Lois didn't tell Henry about her morning sickness for two or three days. In fact, he learned about it on Sunday morning after it had begun the previous week. Lois was cooking a late breakfast when she suddenly had to leave the stove, bolt to the door, and throw up in the backyard.

Henry was at her side almost immediately. "You all right, Honey?" He asked with great concern.

Lois caught her breath. "I'm not sure."

"Was it something you ate?"

"I don't think so."

"Have you been feelin' sick before today?"

"Some. I threw up Friday."

"Why didn't you tell me?"

"I didn't want to worry you."

Henry looked at her with compassion. "You'd better see the doctor tomorrow."

"I don't want to see the doctor. I'll be fine. I don't trust doctors."

* * *

Doctor Branch walked into the room where Henry sat waiting. He laid his stethoscope on the table beside a chair, sat, and drew a long breath.

"How is she, Doc?" Henry said.

Doc sniffed, "Oh, she's fine."

"If she's fine, why's she throwing up?"

Doc grimaced. It was always a chore to explain to young people why something he found so routine happened.

"She's pregnant, son."

"Pregnant?" Henry almost shouted.

"Yeah, pregnant."

"When?. . .I mean . . . the baby?"

"Oh, I'd say it was about seven, maybe eight months. It's kind uh hard to tell, but it can't be much more'n that."

Henry was ecstatic, but he restrained himself in the presence of the doctor. A baby, he thought. This is wonderful! A son of my own!

"Can I see her?" He asked more calmly than he felt.

"She'll be here in a moment. Nellie's helping her get dressed."

"Can you deliver the baby, Doc?"

"Um . . . I don't see why not. After all, I've helped bring quite a few of 'em into this world."

"How much?"

"Huh?"

"How much for treating my wife and delivering the baby?"

Doctor Branch scratched his head before he responded, "Oh, I reckon twenty-five'll be about right."

"I'll get you the money."

"There's no rush. Baby won't be born for a while."

Henry looked up as Lois came from the examining room. She looked rosy-cheeked. He thought she was beautiful.

* * *

Lois might have looked rosy, but she didn't feel that way. Maybe that's what's known as: 'Beauty is in the eye of the beholder.'

The bouts with morning sickness continued. Lois found herself fighting depression. She thought of herself as ugly. The baby inside her continued to grow and do well according to the doctor, but she was constantly having problems.

Henry's concern grew for his wife and child. He tried to reassure Lois, but sometimes it seemed a losing battle. Finally, he made arrangements for her to stay with his mother.

Fall came early that year. October was colder than usual. Frost covered the land several times. Winds made the temperature feel as though the bottom had dropped out of the thermometer. The contrast with the hot summer had everybody shivering in their shoes.

November had promised to be just as tough, but people were adjusting to the weather by this time. Henry was scraping and dipping for the Mills brothers when the time came.

On the morning of November twelfth, Lois lay in bed longer than ususal. Her belly was so big she could hardly see her feet when she stood. Surely, she thought, this baby has to be born soon.

As soon as she was up and moving about, she began to feel the first labor pains. Henry went to fetch Doc right away. The pains continued with varying intensity throughout the day and into the next morning.

At five o'clock in the morning, Lois delivered a son. Henry was ecstatic. Lois was thankful the ordeal was over.

As Henry held this new bundle of life, his thoughts could not have touched on the world and what the actions of a madman would do to him and his family in the near future. In his mind, the future was bright.

XVIII
The Woes of War

Henry handed his son to Eva. She held him close to her and examined him throughly.

"He looks a little like you," she said.

Dr. Branch stood nearby packing his bag. He was weary from the vigil he'd been through, as they all were. He snapped his bag shut.

"I don't know," Henry said. "It's hard to tell."

Henry turned to Doc. "Ain't he powerful ugly, Doc."

Dr. Branch cleared his throat, reached for his coat, and grinned. "Why no! He's an exceptionally fine looking baby."

The morning progressed. Henry stayed close to Lois for much of the time. They were both excited. Lois was trying to rest, but the excitement had been too much for her. Finally, she drifted off to sleep from sheer exhaustion. Henry took the opportunity to check on Van, his newborn son.

He found Van in the arms of his grandmother. She held him in one crooked arm while feeding him something with a spoon.

"Mama, what's that you're giving him?" Henry wanted to know. It appeared to be coffee.

"It's just a little coffee with milk in it," Eva replied.

"But, Mama! Coffee?"

"Sure. He's got to have something to settle his nerves."

* * *

Henry enjoyed being a father. He spent as much time as possible holding his son and talking to him. No matter what time of day or night, Henry managed to find time to be there when he could.

Life was quite different now. A family gave Henry new responsibilities he'd never known before. He had done a good deal of raising of his brothers and sisters, especially Willie and Marie, but that was different. There had always been Eva to make the hard decisions. Now those choices were his and Lois'. Things had to be done right. Henry wanted a better life for his young son than he'd had. He was determined that Van would have it.

These thoughts were foremost in Henry's mind as he looked to the future. The one thing he could not have foreseen was those events that shaped his life from without.

The very month that Henry and Lois had married in 1939, Hitler had invaded Poland setting off World War II. Hitler had been agitating Europe for some time, but United States citizens were opposed to U. S. intervention. The popular notion was that the U. S. shouldn't interfere in the affairs of other countries. War in Europe was a remote thing for most Americans. Besides, there was the Atlantic and Pacific Oceans to protect the U. S. No one could attack across those formidable bodies of water.

On the other hand, there were many who remembered World War I. That conflict hadn't accomplished anything as far as they could tell. European countries, far from settling their problems, were squabbling again. Let them have their wars.

Congress passed acts in 1934 and again in 1937 to prohibit U. S. ships from carrying arms to warring nations. They further required cash payment for goods sold to warring countries. Even U. S. citizens were barred from taking passage on the ships of those nations. Many felt these measures would keep the U. S. out of any conflict now in progress. The United States had declared its neutrality.

However, the events of September 1939 caused others to

take a second look at the U.S. stance. President Roosevelt urged Congress to enact the first peacetime draft in the history of the country. In the summer of 1940, Congress passed legislation requiring all males between the ages of 21 and 35 to register for the draft. The law required one year of military service.

Henry did his duty, registering with his local draft board. He and others were assured that it was highly unlikely they would have to serve. Thus, Henry's new family had formed under the threat of worldwide conflict.

* * *

Spring of 1941 came. The war in Europe was in the news almost every day. William L. Shirer reported from Berlin regularly. Radio and newspapers carried headlines warning of the consequences of each battle. Still, the U. S. did not intervene. The mentality of the country was reflected among the local population.

One evening as Henry and Lois visited with the Varnadores, the subject of the war came up:

"You registered for the draft, yet?" Willy Varnadore asked.

He and Henry had been practicing their music. Will, Willy's father, was sitting in the porch swing while Henry and Willy sat on each side of the doorsteps, each with his back against a post.

"Yeah," Henry answered. "I took care of that a while back."

"I was gonna register, too, except Pa didn't want me to."

Old man Will spat a stream of chewing tobacco juice into the yard and harrumphed. "Ain't no son o' mine gonna fight no damn war in U'rope. I went off over there more'n twenty years ago. It didn't do no damn good. Them sons-a-bitches been fightin' ever since I was knee-high to a toady-frog. I say it's a waste o' time and money. This country better stay the hell outa it."

Henry wasn't much of a debater, but he felt compelled to say, "What if we can't stay out of it, Mr. Will?"

Old man Will spat again, "We can stay outa it, if we're amind to. There's two big oceans a separatin' this here land from the rest o' the world. I reckon, by thunder, there ain't nobody gonna come over them."

"What about ships and such?"

"Ain't no problem near as I can see. Boats is too slow. We'd know they was comin' way afore they got here. Just blow 'em outa the water. That's all it'd take."

"How about planes?"

"Aw hell, them toys can't fly over no ocean."

"Lindbergh flew to Paris from New York, didn't he?"

"Yeah, but that's different."

"How?"

"That plane o' his was a damn flying gas tank the way I heard it. Warplanes'd have t' hold too much gas."

Henry thought for moment before posing his next question. "What about planes on boats? They say they've got boats that planes can take off and land on."

"That's a bunch a bull. You ever seen a plane git off the ground on anything like the length of a boat. It just ain't possible, I tell you."

Henry had one more question. "How about submarines? Could they sneak up and attack us without us knowin' it?"

"Tain't likely. We got 'em, too, you know. We'd know they was comin' a thousand miles."

The old man had an answer for everything, but Henry wasn't convinced. If half of what he'd heard about weapons of war was true, anybody who wanted could attack at most anytime. It was best to be prepared.

Willy did register for the draft, despite old man Will's objections. There was a penalty for not registering, so he decided he didn't want to go to jail to please his father.

* * *

Shortly after noon on Sunday, December seventh, the illusion of U. S. security was shattered. News came by radio that the

Japanese had bombed Pearl Harbor. Most Americans had no idea where Pearl Harbor was. They just knew it was U. S. territory.

People scrambled for their maps in an effort to decide where the attack had occurred. Even the most rabid isolationists were disturbed to find that the Imperial Japanese Air Force had spanned more than half the width of the Pacific Ocean.

Not only the attack frightened Americans, its magnitude was staggering. More than 2,000 were killed and most of the Pacific Fleet was destroyed. The mood of the country changed almost overnight as people realized their dreams of isolation had been shattered forever.

Henry and Lois were at Eva's when the news came. Joe's radio had been playing on a music station when the newsflash interrupted it.

The announcer stopped the recorded music. Silence ruled the airwave for a brief time. Then a voice came through the static:

"Today, at noon Eastern time, in a daring surprise attack, the Japanese bombed Pearl Harbor, a United States possession in Hawaii. Details are incomplete at this time, but it appears there have been extensive casualties and untold destruction in the American Pacific fleet. We will keep you informed as we receive more news from Honolulu. Now back to our program."

"There goes our war," Henry said to no one in particular.

"Yeah. Sure sounds like it," someone answered.

"I might get that call from the draft board before I know it," Henry added.

"Lord, I hope not," Lois said.

"Me neither," Eva seconded.

* * *

On December 8, 1941, President Roosevelt appealed to Congress for a declaration of war. His speech was carried by radio, thus many in the nation heard him say:

"Yesterday, December 7, 1941, a date which will live in

infamy, the United States of America was suddenly and deliberately attacked by naval and air forces of the Empire of Japan . . .
I ask that the Congress declare that since the unprovoked and
dastardly attack by Japan on Sunday, December 7, 1941, a state
of war has existed between the United States and the Japanese
Empire."

By January 1, 1942, twenty-six nations had joined in a pledge
to accept no separate peace until victory over the Axis Powers.

Americans rallied to the war effort. Local draft-boards called
up their boys to go show them sons-a-bitches they couldn't fool
with the U. S. A. If you weren't competing to see how many men
you could muster, you were considered unpatriotic.

Henry's call came in the spring of 1942. Willy Varnadore
was called in the same draft. Swiftly they were caught up in the
rush to get Americans in the various theaters of war.

Henry packed his bag for a trip to Atlanta. He had been
instructed, along with two dozen or so other men, to be on a train
heading for Atlanta on Monday morning.

Lois sat on the side of the bed as Henry put a changing of
clothes in the new cardboard suitcase he had bought for the trip.
As far as he could remember, it was the first store-bought suitcase
he'd ever owned.

"How long will you be gone?" Lois asked. There was a tear
in her voice although she tried to hide it.

"I don't know. They said we might be shipped out to a
training camp directly from our examination. There'll likely be six
or eight weeks of basic. After that, I think they might give us a
week or two at home before they send us overseas. I oughta be
back in six to eight weeks."

"I wish you didn't have to go."

Henry turned to her, put his arms around her, and held her
close. "I wish I didn't either, but we've got to do our part. The
Japs have hit us, and it looks like the whole world's against us.
We've got to fight, Honey. There's no other way. Now buck up.

We'll get through this somehow."

Lois gave a weak ghost of a smile. Her lips quivered as she spoke. "Okay."

"That's my girl. Now dry your eyes and don't let everybody see that you've been crying."

* * *

The train whistle sounded as the engine approached the Baxley depot. Henry, Willy, and several other men stood on the platform waiting to board. There was an air of expectancy in the crowd. Some were laughing and joking; others were quiet and reflective. Willy looked over the town. It wasn't much to look at, he thought, but this could be the last time he would see it for a long time. On the other hand, it could be the last time he saw it, period. Life was uncertain at best, but a man going to war could never be sure he was coming home.

The train stopped opposite the platform. A conductor stepped off, strode to the main ticket window, handed the station-master some papers, and turned to the group of men.

"This the new recruits that's goin' to Atlanta?" He asked.

"That's right, sir," a short, fuzzy-faced, young man answered.

"You in charge of these men?" The conductor asked.

"Yes, sir. I've been instructed by the draft-board to see that they all report to the army examination facility in Atlanta."

"I take it you've got something to show me then."

"Yes, sir, right here, sir," the young man said handing the conductor a sheaf of papers.

The conductor looked at the papers for a moment. "Every-thing seems to be in order. Now, listen up you men! You'll all be traveling in the same car. There's other recruits on this train, too. I don't want any unnecessary fussing or fighting going on. Is that clear?"

Most of the men nodded their assent.

"That's good. Now I want you to go to the third car down the line there. That'll be your assigned car. You're free to move about once we're in motion. As long as you don't give me any problem, that is."

The men filed onto the indicated car and took their seats. A screech of air-brakes suggested the train was about to move. Sound bursts from the whistle preceded the train going into motion.

Henry and Willy sat beside each other looking out the window. Baxley passed in review as the train picked up speed. Soon, the buildings had disappeared. Woods and fields could be seen moving past the window.

Henry laughed out loud.

Willy looked at him. "What's so funny?" He asked.

"I was just thinkin'. Just a few years ago, I'd have been riding a freight for free."

Willy smiled. "Yeah, you would have, wouldn't you. Times sure have changed."

"You can say that again."

Both men rode in silence for a few minutes.

Willy spoke. "How did Lois take your leaving?"

Henry's look sobered. "She took it pretty hard. I hated to leave her and Van. I hope I'll be comin' back before too long."

"I know what you mean," Willy said with a sigh in his voice.

* * *

Henry stood in line with, it seemed, five-hundred other men as the army doctors poked and prodded them in places they never imagined anyone would want to look. None of the recruits had a stitch on. Their clothes had been dumped in lockers for the duration of the examination. It was a totally humiliating experience.

One doctor would poke a tongue depressor in your mouth, demand that you say 'ah', and then ask you a question while the wooden instrument rested on your tongue. Anything you said came out garbled.

The next doctor demanded that you bend over while he

looked up your behind. If he couldn't see what he wanted to, he'd poke you there, too.

Modesty was totally absent from the proceeding. Henry couldn't remember being in a more degrading situation. He was totally exposed.

But modesty didn't seem to be a problem for some of the men. One burly fellow seemed to enjoy the experience. Henry couldn't help seeing as the man played with his penis and talked too loud.

"Boys, it's good to have a big'un. Comes in mighty handy sometimes."

Nobody answered, but that didn't discourage the talker. He was obviously an exhibitionist, and this was a prime moment for him.

"Yessir. Lots o' gals like'em big."

After listening to this for a while, another fellow challenged him. "You married?" He asked.

Noisy looked at him with a grin a yard wide. "Hell yes, mister. What's it to ya?"

"I just wondered. If I was married, I'd be ashamed of havin' one like that."

"Ashamed! Why?"

"I'd be ashamed to let folks know my wife's behind was that big."

Noisy laughed and continued his show. He was soon pulled out of the line. Henry never saw him again.

The examination continued. Eventually, Henry found himself answering all kinds of personal questions. Questions he thought would have been better left alone.

As the interrogator paused, a Sergeant stepped up to the desk. "What is it, Sergeant?" The Captain demanded.

"I've got them reports you asked for, sir."

"Sergeant, why did you interrupt me? Can't you see I'm busy with this man?"

"Yes, sir. But I thought you wanted them right away."

The Captain looked annoyed. "Sergeant, you're not paid to think. Is that clear? You're paid to obey orders."

"Yes, sir," the Sergeant said as he gave a somewhat sloppy salute, did an about-face, and left the scene.

Henry considered the Captain for an instant. "I don't know about that," he said. "When it comes to my ass, I'm gonna do some thinkin' for myself."

The Captain looked at Henry, started to utter a reply, thought better of it, and went on to the next question.

Willy and Henry found one another when the examination was over. They both headed for the cafeteria where they ordered a sandwich and a cup of coffee.

"How'd it go?" Willy asked as they seated themselves near a window.

"I didn't pass," Henry said. "You?"

"Yeah, they passed me. What's the matter? Did they say?"

"Yeah. They said my nerves was shot."

"Your nerves?"

"Uh, huh."

"What's wrong with 'em?"

"Don't know. The doctor just said he couldn't pass me on account of I might go berserk and get a whole platoon killed."

"He said that?"

"That's what he said."

Willy sipped his coffee. "Reckon you'll be goin' back to your wife and family then."

"Yeah. Looks like. You?"

"I'm shippin' out with the next group."

"That soon?"

"Yeah. Looks like I'm gonna be gone longer than a day or two."

Henry considered his friend's face for a moment. "I wish I was goin' with you, hoss."

"Yeah. Me, too."

Henry left for the train an hour later. He and Willy shook hands as they parted.

"Be seein' you, pard," Willy said with restrained emotion.

"Okay. You take it easy, hoss. Don't do nothin' I wouldn't do, you hear?"

"You bet," Willy smiled.

The two men parted with heavy hearts. Neither of them had any assurance they would ever see the other again.

* * *

Henry considered the road in front of him. It was wet and boggy. In fact he'd spent more time digging his truck out of bogs than hauling pulpwood lately. The Florida sun caused a steam of heat to rise from the swampy ground, wrapping you with heat on heat. Palatka, Florida was a hot place in the early summer of 1942.

Coming home from Atlanta, Henry found he couldn't rent a crop of boxes. He hadn't tried earlier because he was certain he would be called up for the draft, and just as sure he'd be on his way overseas in a few weeks. When his business with the army was settled, all the work he wanted was taken. That was when Jack, his cousin, offered him a job in Florida. Henry had accepted, although it meant moving Lois and Van, too. Things weren't quite as simple as they had been when he could pack his grip in a flour sack and hit the road anywhere he pleased.

Henry started the truck. He let the engine idle until it warmed. It was better not to try and pull a rough stretch of road with a cold engine. It was likely to stall, and you didn't want that in this sandy, swampy soil. Henry reached for his pipe, packed it with Prince Albert smoking tobacco, lit it, and clenched it between his teeth.

Shifting the truck into "Grandma," first gear, he let out on the clutch. Slowly, the heavily loaded machine began to compress the mud as it moved through the slush. As soon as he had enough rpms on the engine, Henry shifted to second gear in order to avoid excessive spinning of the drive wheels. The engine gave a cough as the strain on the transmission changed, but it stayed alive under the tremendous pull Henry was demanding of it.

The truck fish tailed slightly as the rear wheels slipped into first one and then the other side of the ruts. Muddy water rushed out from the plowing front wheels like the tide of the Atlantic Ocean. Henry gripped the steering wheel with both hands. His teeth clenched the pipe tighter as the pull continued.

Slowly, the truck made it to the far side of the bog. As soon as it hit solid ground, Henry relaxed a bit. When the truck came to a full stop, he reached for his pipe. The bowl didn't seem to be in the right place. In fact all he had in his mouth was the stump of the pipe stem. The bowl had fallen to the floor of the truck cab. It lay there smouldering.

"Damn!" Henry said to himself.

"That was some kind uh pull!" Olan Mock said with short gasps of breath.

"Yeah. Damn near set myself afire with my pipe." Henry held up the two pieces.

"I'll be damned. Ain't that somethin'? You musta been pulling as hard as the truck."

"I reckon I was. Get in here. We got to unload this wood before Jack has a fit."

Henry backed the truck down the ramp to a dock where a barge had been tied waiting to receive the pulpwood. It felt a little shaky to back a loaded truck onto a floating dock. In fact, there had been instances where men had lost their truck when they got too close to the edge. This barge work was tricky. Henry had about decided he'd had enough of this Florida weather and these damn floating parking lots.

* * *

The rains came to Florida. It rains in Florida during all

seasons, but the hurricane season can be a soggy experience. Work had come to a standstill. The woods were so wet a man could hardly stand in them without bogging, let alone, drive a truck through them.

Men without work tend to find something to occupy their time. On this particular day, they had gathered at the equipment shop. Not to work, although Jack had decided to make some repairs while he had the opportunity, but to shoot the breeze.

Outside, the rain came down in buckets. The metal roof of the shop made it difficult to hear. Men raised their voices to compensate for the din. One Dobb Carter, who was a transplant from Baxley, stood in the crowd watching the falling rain. His chinless face was a study in perplexity. He shifted his weight between his feet as if he were doing some kind of ritual dance.

"What is it, Dobb?" Somebody asked loudly.

"This damn rain!" Dobb replied.

"Yeah. What about it?"

"It's Florida rain."

"So?"

"You Floridians call Florida the state of sunshine and flowers. It's rained ever day since I got here, and I ain't even seen a damn water-lily."

The crowd laughed. It seemed to help relieve the tension.

Rain, along with Jack's growing bitchiness, caused Henry to rethink his decision to move to Florida. Besides, Verde, Jack's wife, had picked a fight with Lois. That was one of the hazzards of living in a quarters community. Being too close to one another physically, made it hard to avoid fights.

Lois held her own though. She'd told Verde to stop bothering her or she was going to whip Verde's ass. The trouble between the women naturally spilled over to their husbands. Jack, knowing Henry's reputation for fighting, decided he wanted no part of the fuss.

"Henry," Jack said the next day. "Don't let us get mad with

each other. Just let the women settle it."

Henry had agreed, but the incident was just another aggravation he could do without. This wasn't working out. He had to do something. But what? Work at home was scarce. He had no idea if he'd be able to make a dollar. Times were bad for most folks. The war was beginning to get on everybody's nerves. Uncertainty was the order of the day. It was a hard decision.

XIX
The Death of a Child

Henry had made up his mind. He was going to Georgia. Enough was enough. The problem lay in the fact that he'd been without work so long in Florida that he had almost spent his last dime. A tank of gas was more than he could afford. He figured he'd need that much to get home. Where was he going to get it?

Lois sat with him to make plans. Together, with a few coins she'd put away, they had three dollars. That might buy enough gas to get home, but what if they had a flat on the road. It was good to have some pocket change for an emergency. Besides, the baby's milk was low. He'd need special food. They couldn't afford to let their money get any lower.

Henry hit on a plan. His Model-A would run on almost anything that was combustible. He'd borrow some fuel from Jack to supplement what he could buy. The nearest gas station sold him three gallons of gas. He would get the rest from Jack.

Henry took his five-gallon gas can to Jack's equipment garage. The only fuel available was kerosene. Jack had a fifty-five-gallon drum of it. He used it to lubricate crosscut saws in the pulpwoods. Henry set his can near the drum, found a piece of siphoning-hose, and started the kerosene flowing.

It was important to keep Jack from finding out what was going on, so Henry went to the house for a minute. He figured he could return in plenty of time to stop the flow before the can was full.

Jack was in a more than usual talkative mood. The two of them rambled on about one thing and another. All the while, Henry tried to get away.

"I'll be seein' you, Jack," he would say.

But Jack would come back with another question.

Henry could just see his can running over, the kerosene flowing over the floor and out the door. He had to get away. Finally, he walked off with Jack still talking.

As soon as Henry was out of Jack's sight, he hurried to the shop. Sure enough, the can had over flowed. Kerosene made a wet spot over a wide area. Henry snatched the siphoning hose from the drum, threw it in a corner, and prepared his retreat. Jack could figure the spill out later.

Three gallons of gas and five gallons of kerosene gave Henry eight gallons of fuel to go from Palatka to Baxley. Maybe it was enough? It had to be enough. The problem lay in the fact that once the mixture was burning, the engine couldn't be stopped for any reason. Henry figured that he might not be able to start it on the mixture.

Accordingly, Henry and Lois packed what little they could carry. The next morning they were up early. Sunrise was still more than an hour away. Olan had secretly planned to go to Georgia with them. He was waiting when they stepped out the door.

"Here," Henry said as he placed the pillowcases containing most of their clothes in the back seat. Lois handed him the box she held under one arm while she cradled Van in the other.

"Is there anything else we should carry?" Henry asked.

"I don't think so," Lois answered. "The way I feel right now, the devil can have anything we leave behind."

Henry started the engine. He let it warm for a minute or two before adding his can of kerosene. When the can was empty, Henry tossed it across the yard, stepped to the driver's seat, and accelerated the engine slightly. He waited to see if his mixture was going to burn. There would be hell to pay if Jack found that spilled kerosene and connected it to him.

Henry, Lois, and Olan pulled out in the dawning of what turned out to be a fairly decent day. At least, it didn't rain on them.

Chugging through St. Augustine, they made their way to Jacksonville. The Model-A was running fine. A working fuel gauge was a luxury Henry couldn't afford. He had no idea how far he was traveling on a gallon of fuel. Getting home was foremost on his mind. If he ran out of fuel, he'd cross that bridge when he got there.

Following U. S. 1, they made their way through Callahan. By midday they were near the St. Mary's River. So far so good, Henry thought. They were almost halfway there.

They stopped in Folkston to get something to drink and use the restroom. Van complained of hunger, so Lois fed him on the road. The Model-A chugged along on its fuel mixture like a sewing machine, as Henry would have said.

Waycross was in sight in another couple of hours. The day was hot and sticky. Even the wind from the ride didn't cool them much. Once Henry noticed the oil pressure dropping. He was almost sure the oil pump had gone, but somehow it started working again.

Sunset found them near Alma. The car had run hot a few miles back, but water from a nearby ditch had saved the day. With a little luck they would be home before midnight.

The lights on the old car were just slightly better than striking a match. Henry strained his eyes attempting to see the road ahead. An occasional pothole would send the car bouncing back and forth. He always managed to keep it between the ditches though.

Lois didn't say much. She was so glad to be rid of Florida that she would have suffered almost anything she could imagine to get home. After all, she'd never been out of Appling County until a few months ago. Florida had been like a living hell for her. She was glad to be rid of it.

Baxley's street lights caused fleeting shadows to flow as the Model-A chugged through.

"We're almost there, girl," Henry said, glancing at Lois.

"I never thought I'd see Baxley like I see it now," Lois replied.

"How's that?"

"Let's just say I'm glad to be back."

Clint Crosby's farmhouse was visible when the car started sputtering. Henry petted the car as if it had been a beloved horse.

"Come on old fliver. Don't let us down now," he coaxed.

But the faithful machine had gone as far as it could. The fuel mix had burned until the last minute. Now the moisture in the tank was too much for the firing system. The engine would die.

Henry gave up. He let the car roll to a stop.

"Well, old gal, I reckon you've done good by us. Can't fault you a bit," he said as he stepped out.

It was just half a mile to Eva's place. They walked the rest of the way.

* * *

The face on the pine was as long as Henry had ever seen. It took a ten-foot handle to reach the top. Working this timber wasn't going to be easy, but he couldn't see where he had a choice. This had been the only crop of boxes he could find after returning from Florida. It was a small crop, only three thousand faces, but it would have to do. Jobs weren't very plentiful in Appling County. Especially jobs that paid a living wage. A man with a family had to do the best he could. Sometimes Henry thought back to the days when he would have gone anywhere to work, but those days were gone. He couldn't do that now.

In the midst of summer, the heat was almost unbearable. The shade of the trees and bushes gave some relief from the blazing sun, but sweat still flowed freely from Henry's pores as he walked from tree to tree.

Turpentine work wasn't as monotonous as factory work, but it certainly ran a close second. You reached up with your puller, hooked on the side of the face, gave it a yank, and cut a slice of bark and wood from the tree. Then you turned and repeated the procedure on the opposite side of the tar face. The resulting gashes caused resins to flow from the wood and sap until the tree healed. In a week or so it was necessary to repeat the work to keep the gum flowing.

Some trees yielded more than others, but you could harvest a quart or more per month from each tree during the warmer months of the year. The problem with these trees was the length of the face. So much area had to be covered before the gum reached the cup that most of your tar collected on the face as scrape. It was far from an ideal situation.

Henry had to sell the Model-A soon after he returned from Florida. That was a blow, since he was again without transportation. Hard times had forced the separation. The old car had been a good one; it was hard to part with it.

Lois and Henry struggled through the summer of 1942. They managed with little, and, on some occasions, nothing. Turpentine didn't sell very well despite the war. Hand to mouth living had become a way of life once more.

There were fewer pleasures. Once they had been able to take in a movie on Saturday, but the lack of transportation made it nearly impossible to travel the thirty-mile round trip to Baxley on a regular basis. Henry walked everywhere he went, except when he could catch a ride with one of his neighbors.

When he had gum to sell, he rode the truck to town, collected his pay, and shopped for a few groceries. Meanwhile, Lois stayed home. The isolation would have been devastating to a less secure person.

It was during this time that Henry and Lois developed a habit that they cultivated for years to come. Henry had always loved western movies. Since movies were an unaffordable luxury, he started buying pulp western magazines. They didn't cost very much, and unlike movies you could pick them up and lay them down when you pleased. Henry could barely read, so he had never bought magazines before. Now Lois, who was quite a good reader, was willing to read to him. They spent many an enjoyable Sunday afternoon reading the works of such notables as Max Brand. Wild West Weekly became a staple in their home.

Fall of 1942 found Henry and Lois in a little better financial condition. Henry had a good harvest of scrape to gather. The gathering was so large that he decided to hire his half-brother, Willie, to help him. Willie, who was seventeen at the time, stayed until the work was complete, but he was restless. He found the routine boring and hard. However, there was one memorable occasion during that sojourn.

Willie had worked hard all week scraping the tar from the faces and dipping the gum. The work was bad enough, but the falling scrape hit you in the face and covered your clothing. You had to use kerosene to dissolve the tar from your body. Your clothes had to be washed in hot, boiling water to melt the tar residue from the fabric. As far as Willie could see, this was no way to make a living.

Saturday came. Willie thought it was about time he and Henry reaped the reward of their labors. They loaded the gum on the Tillman's truck and rode to Baxley for the sale. Henry did his usual grocery shopping, and they caught the truck back to the farm.

When they got back, the house seemed empty. Lois and Van had gone to spend the week with Eva. They sat around for a few minutes before the boredom got to both of them.

"Runt, what's on your mind?" Henry asked Willie.

Willie looked at Henry, "What's on yours?"

"I'm thinkin' I don't want to spend the night in this house. What about you?"

Willie grinned, "I thought you'd never ask."

Henry thought for a moment. "What do you say? Let's go to town and take in a movie. We'll go to Mama's afterward."

"That sounds good to me, but how do we get there?"

"Your bicycle."

"You mean ride my bicycle?"

"Sure. Why not?"

"I think it's crazy for two grown man to ride a bicycle fifteen miles to see a movie, but I'm game if you are."

"It's settled then. Let's go."

The two men mounted the bicycle and made their way up the hill toward the Eason graveyard. In those days there was precious little paving and none of it was wasted on country roads. With one of them on the seat and the other on the rear fender, the two men pedaled the sandy road from the farm to Baxley. They saw their movie and went to Eva's for the night. Their muscles healed, but their memories stored the event for the rest of their lives.

* * *

Lois learned that she was pregnant with their second child in the fall of 1942. Henry was caring, but not quite as solicitous as he had been when she was carrying Van. He carried Lois to the doctor, but he wasn't too concerned. After all, this fathering business was becoming old-hat. Things would work out.

Something, however, had to be done about his work. He certainly didn't want to work those high boxes another season. They were already too high. Another year would be impossible.

With this in mind, Henry sought another crop for next year. In those days, turnover wasn't great--a man who had a crop usually stuck with it--but an opportunity often presented itself.

Henry met his friend, Olan, in town one afternoon. Olan shared the news that Red Carter had a crop and so did his sister Myra. Olan had contracted to work one crop, but they needed somebody for the second. Finally, Henry and Olan agreed to work both crops together. They would form a partnership and split the profits down the middle.

Shortly Henry and Lois moved into an old house on Myra's place. The house consisted of one large room with a shed-room for a kitchen. A porch and small room on the opposite side of the house completed the living arrangements. A fairly large fireplace at one end of the great room provided what heat they had.

Henry managed to get enough money to give his family a nice Christmas. He'd been very young when his father died, but it seemed to him his father had made Christmas special for them. Henry wanted to do the same for his family.

Lois got a new dress that year, and Van, who had just turned two, got a tricycle. The house became the two-year-old's racetrack as he rode the tricycle from one end to the other, often riding it to the kitchen door and throwing it to the ground through the open door. You would have thought it should have been his prize possession. It was, but he was a typical two-year-old.

The war news in early 1943 was encouraging. General Eisenhower, Commander-in-Chief of the Allied forces in the North African Theater of Operations, had begun the campaign to oust the enemy from that portion of the continent. About the same time U. S. Marines and Army infantry forces captured Guadalcanal in the Solomon Islands.

Henry tried to keep up with the war. He now had renewed interest. His half-brother Willie had volunteered and was somewhere in the Pacific. It was no easy task for a man who could hardly read, but Henry felt he needed to be informed. All this time, draft laws were changing. He never knew when he might be called a second time. The army might ignore his nerves next time.

March came. Henry had steady work now. He was grateful for that. Lois was due any day now, so he checked on her regularly, since his work was within easy walking distance of the house.

As far as they knew, everything was all right with the baby. Then on the tenth of the month, Lois went into labor. Henry fetched Dr. Branch, right away.

Doc came to their home and examined Lois.

"Everything looks normal," Doc said as he finished the examination. He lay aside his stethoscope. "We'll just have to wait and see."

Lois spent a restless night. Eva had come to help her during the delivery. She stayed up all night with Lois. The next morning the baby was born.

Henry waited anxiously while the birth took place. This one didn't work on his nerves like Van's had a couple of years ago. He tried to assure himself that everything was going to be fine.

But something was wrong. The thin walls of the house carried sound so well that you couldn't have missed a noise if you'd wanted to. Henry could hear Doc working with Lois and Eva. When the baby was delivered, there was no cry.

Henry resisted the urge to dash into the room. Doc came out a few minutes later. His face was grim.

"What is it, Doc?" Henry asked. "Something's wrong? I can tell."

Doc sighed, "I'm afraid so Mr. Reynolds . . . "

Henry waited. "Is my wife okay?"

"Your wife's fine."

"The baby?"

"The baby was stillborn."

"Plain talk, Doc, please."

Dr. Branch gathered his courage. "The baby's dead."

"Dead?"

"I'm sorry."

"Dead? Why? What happened?"

"She, it was a girl, had a condition we call hydrocephalus."

"Hydro . . . what?"

"Hydrocephalus. It's a medical term."

"What's it mean?"

"Well, most folks call it water-headed."

"Water? I don't understand."

"You see, spinal fluids collect in the head. The head doesn't develop as it should. More to the point, the brain doesn't develop."

"The brain? You mean she didn't have a brain?"

"That's a crude way to put it, but, basically, that's right."

"How's that possible?"

"I don't know. Most of us won't admit it, but there are lots of things we don't understand. It's just one of many things we don't know the reason for. A birth defect, if you will."

"Was it something we did?"

"No. There's nothing you could have done to prevent it."

Henry had trouble accepting that. In the pit of his stomach, a pain began. It progressed until he thought he might vomit. There must have been something.

Doc must have sensed what was happening.

"Look. These things happen. It's not something we do or don't do. It just happens. God knows why."

"Can I see my wife?" Henry said with a tear in his voice.

"In just a minute or two. Your mother's helping her right now."

It seemed as if an eternity had passed before Eva appeared at the kitchen door. She stood there quietly with a look of compassion on her face. She'd never lost a child, but right now, it seemed the dead child might have been her own. Her heart went out to Henry. She would have been perfectly content to take him in her arms and comfort him, but she knew his manly pride would not allow it.

"You can come in, son," she said, instead.

Henry rose, walked to the door, and disappeared into the large room. Lois lay on their bed. A sheet over a dresser covered what could only have been the body of their baby. Kneeling beside the bed, Henry grasped Lois' hand. He held it momentarily before she burst into tears. Henry soothed her with his hand rubbing her hair.

"I...I'm so sorry," Lois managed to say between sobs.

"It's all right," Henry whispered. "It's not your fault."

Tears streamed down Henry's face. He'd always been told that men don't cry, but the people who said that had never felt what he felt at this moment. Emotionally, he was torn asunder. Drawn two different directions at once, he wanted to comfort his wife; at the same time, he wanted to pour out his grief. The thought even flickered across his mind that God was punishing him for some sin he'd committed.

Lois remained unable to express herself. She clung to Henry, while her mind tried to deal with the tragedy. Gradually, she passed into sleep from sheer exhaustion.

Henry felt Eva's hand on his shoulder. He looked up.

"Son, why don't you go get some rest?" She asked.

"I...I couldn't, Mama. I'll just stay here."

"It'd be better if you did. Lois is resting. She's gonna need you more when she wakes up."

Henry stood up. "Okay. You'll stay with her?"

"Sure. Now go on."

Henry walked from the room. As he stepped into the kitchen, the walls seemed to close in on him. It was as if he'd been confined to a prison. A prison from which he had to escape. Making his way to the outside door, he descended the steps and walked off into the woods.

All around him, the promise of an early spring blossomed. It seemed nature, herself, mocked him, but then the quiet began to penetrate his consciousness. As if a still small voice was saying, "Be still and listen."

But Henry had no desire to listen. His soul was filled with rage, rage at his own impotence. This wasn't like facing an enemy you could see. You could confront that enemy. You could pound it with your fist, smash it with a weapon, or pursue it until it was lost in the distance.

Death wasn't like that. A man had absolutely no power over this enemy. He might as well stand naked before a foe and allow himself to be whipped with the cat-of-nine-tails. Henry had lost fights in his life, but none of them had been as great as this loss. Death, it seemed, was always the victor. He had no weapon against it.

A fallen log near a bubbling brook gave Henry a place to rest his weary body. He sat there and listened to the quiet noise as the flowing water meandered over the tree roots. For just an instant, a thought flickered across the consciousness of the grieving man.

That flowing stream wound its way to nearby Caney Creek, which in turn flowed into Ten-Mile Creek. Then the Altamaha River carried the tiny droplets to the mighty Atlantic. Eventually, the water came back again in the form of rain. Was life like that? Did life really die, or was there hope after all?

Henry didn't know the answer. He doubted anybody really knew. Oh, some preachers told you they knew, but Henry wasn't sure they knew what they were talking about. How could a man understand such things? It simply wasn't possible.

Henry must have sat for an hour or more. One wisp of thought after another seemed to flit through his head. A million questions, each of them more perplexing than the one before, kept bothering him. Finally, he reached a decision. There were things that had to be done. Life had to continue. He couldn't let this incident control him forever. His life had continued without his Uncle George; it must go on now.

* * *

Henry fitted the pine boards together to form a small coffin. Red had loaned him some lumber to fashion the tiny box. It had to serve as Annie's casket. He and Lois had decided they couldn't bury the baby without giving her a name. Somehow it didn't seem right to just bury her as the infant daughter of Henry and Lois. They had chosen Annie Elizabeth from Henry's grandmother

Hester. Both of them thought it was a beautiful name.

With all the loving care that goes into doing something for someone you love, Henry finished planing the top of the coffin. He rubbed his hand over the wood. It was smooth. A good piece of work, he thought. There was just one problem. The box would soon rot in the damp soil. Henry tried to put that out of his mind. Better not to think of such things, he told himself.

Eva picked up the child from the dresser where she had been laid and placed the small body in the casket--Lois would keep the dresser as long as she lived. It was wrapped in a blanket that someone had given Lois. Pulling the blanket back, Eva gazed on the face of innocence for the last time. She's beautiful, Eva thought. She stood back while Henry and Lois took one last look at the child they would never know.

After a few silent moments, Henry covered the casket and nailed the lid shut. He and Joe were to take the child to the cemetery. Henry and Lois didn't own a burial plot, so they had requested a grave site in the Hester Cemetery. Henry's grandmother had granted it graciously.

Henry placed the small casket in the back seat of Joe's 1934 Chevrolet. Eva and Lois were left alone as the car disappeared down the winding three-path road.

At the cemetery, Henry dug the small grave himself. As he finished the task, Annie, his grandmother, came, together with some of the family, to be there for the burial. Among this last group was a minister. Lois had insisted that the Bible be read over Annie. Brother Black opened with prayer, read some verses, and closed with a prayer.

The grave was filled. Henry looked to his left as he stood at the foot of the grave. There lay his father just a few feet away. His grandfather was also buried nearby. This seemed an appropriate place for his baby.

* * *

News came from the war front, but it didn't mean a lot to

Henry and Lois. They were still grieving for their lost child. Lois, especially, had a hard time dealing with the loss. To her friends and family, it seemed she would never complete her grief.

Then, one day, news came that made Henry take notice. He was shaken from his grief for Annie by another shocking bit of news.

"Son, did you hear the news?" Eva asked when Henry stopped by her home.

"What news, Mama?"

"About Willy Varnadore."

"No. I don't think I've heard any news about Willy for more than a month. What's wrong?"

"Will said he got a telegram two days ago."

"What did it say? Is Willy dead?"

"He didn't know. All the telegram said was 'missing in action.'"

XX
Listening to the Call

"Missing in action" was considered by some to mean the person was dead, but there were other possibilities. Maybe Willy had been captured. At least he would still be alive. No one could imagine what that might mean. Germans were suspected of atrocities on their prisoners, but nobody had any cold, hard facts. There were simply rumors.

Henry hoped against hope that his friend was not dead, but as more bodies or at least coffins came home, the hope faded. One father had insisted that his son's coffin be opened. A pair of dog tags with some soil was all they found. Many people began to suspect they had buried coffins with dirt in them. The government offered no explanation to the families.

The home front was feeling the effects of the war more as rationing took its toll on the American people. At first, gasoline had been in short supply because more was required to power the machines of war. Most people bore this burden with a minimum of complaint. They took necessary measures to compensate for the inconvenience.

Then food began to be rationed. Such commodities as sugar were held in reserve for the war effort. Meat became harder to get. Shortening was hard to find. These rationing actions put many Americans in a bind, especially those who were dependent on grocery stores for their supplies. Even farm families found it tough to supply their tables with the usual commodities.

Gasoline was one thing. Food was something else. Black markets sprang up almost over night. Those people who were smart enough or stupid enough, depending on your point of view, made a killing in the food black market.

Henry and Lois found themselves without enough sugar to sweeten a cup of coffee. Sugar was available, but it was difficult to find enough rationing coupons to buy it. People began trading coupons, sometimes at inflated exchange rates, to get the food they needed. Hoarding became common. When Henry finally got his rationing coupons for sugar, he and Lois stored away as much sugar as they could in a dresser drawer.

They were able to raise hogs, so they had meat most of the time. There were occasions when they couldn't buy lard, but a hog killing of their own or one of a neighbor helped remedy that shortage.

Nineteen forty-four came with a change in the war. The Allies began to bring the war home to the Axis powers. Long-range Super Fortress planes (B29s) made bombing raids on Japan. The invasion of Italy commenced in January of that year, and, in May, Allied forces began a push that took them to Rome. In the early morning hours of June 6, an invasion fleet of some 7,000 ships landed American and British divisions on Normandy beaches. Airborne divisions dropped behind the German lines. The invasion of Europe was well under way.

At home, the news was received with renewed hope that the boys would soon be coming back. Some families still held out, hoping for the safe return of their loved ones. Others grieved or worried when they couldn't find out whether their sons or fathers were dead or alive. Many Americans were willing to do their share, but some gave more than others.

* * *

John, Henry's and Lois' third child, was born in August. Henry changed doctors this time. In the back of his mind, he wondered if the doctor hadn't been partially responsible for the death of his daughter. He also made different arrangements for the birth. Van and Annie had both been born at home. This baby would be delivered at a hospital.

Doctor Holt had converted an old dwelling into a makeshift hospital. Lois had nurses and attendants working with her during this birth. Everything went fine. The baby was healthy and normal as far as anyone could tell.

Henry worked and waited for news of his friend Willy. It was a long time coming, but finally word came that Willy had been captured by the Germans. Thank God, Henry thought, maybe he can survive at least. All sorts of images flashed through Henry's mind. It was hard to imagine what life might be like in a German prison, but Willy was tough.

Periodically, news came that the Allied forces were making their way toward Germany every day. In September, Allied forces crossed the German border. The Battle of the Bulge followed in December. Each word helped renew Henry's hope that Willy would make it home.

The hurricane came that fall. Huge storms seldom came as far inland as this one, but this one made a swing and found its way across South Georgia. Henry had some warning. Radio reports told of the hurricane as it tracked up the East coast of Florida. Few people made any serious preparations; most of them thought there was nothing they could do.

Henry stopped at Eva's the day before the storm hit.

"Mama, there's a storm headed this way. It's on the radio."

"How bad is it, son?" She asked.

"Pretty bad from what they say. South Florida's takin' quite a pounding."

"What makes you think it'll come here?"

"The way they said it was traveling. 'Northwest,' they said."

"Well, there ain't much we can do is there?"

"How about your roof? Is it okay?"

"I think so, but there's some loose shingles on the crib. I saw'em the other day. Looked like the wind had blowed'em off earlier."

"Okay, I'll take a look. Where's your hammer?"

"Out in the wagon shed. There's nails, too."

Henry looked at the gathering night. "I'm gonna need some help. Coot, how about getting your flashlight. You can hold a light for me while I tack shingles."

Coot, Eva's grandson, ran to his hiding place, retrieved his prize possession, and followed Henry to the wagon shed. Henry found the hammer and nails.

"Where's the ladder, Coot?"

"Gracky told me to put it behind the shed."

They found the ladder, carried it to the crib, and climbed to the roof. Several shingles were loose. Henry began pounding nails into the roof. Some shingles had to be retrieved from the ground where they had fallen. It's a good thing I'm getting this done, otherwise Mama could lose most of her corn, Henry thought.

At home, Henry found Lois and the babies huddled near the fireplace. The damp in the air was just enough to cause a chill to seep through to your bones. A single oil lamp gave off a flickering light. Country folks didn't have electricity in those days.

"Everything all right at your Mama's?" Lois asked as Henry came in the large room that served as both living room and bedroom.

"Yeah. I think so. There wasn't much I could do. Me and Coot managed to repair the crib a little."

"Did you hear any more about the hurricane?"

"Just that it's coming our way. You?"

"Mr. Carter come by late this evenin'. He wanted to see if we was all right. He said there wasn't nothin' new."

Henry stood by the fire warming himself. Van was playing with a small toy truck. Lois held John in her lap. Outside the wind could be heard as it blew around the corner of the house. The sound reminded Lois of stories she'd heard of ghosts haunting places. Rattling shutters added to the din of racket.

"I'd better go see about the animals," Henry said. "That piece of tin in the hog pen might blow away in this wind."

Lois nodded as he went on the errand.

The winds came more viciously as the hurricane approached. An old house with holes in the weatherboarding and a tin roof is not much comfort in a storm. The rain may not wet you, but the noise can keep you awake forever.

Somewhere a shutter came loose. The banging drove Henry from the bed. He found the noise. One of the windows near the fireplace had blown open. Henry was drenched as he reached for the banging shutter. When he pulled it closed, he found the latch had been ripped off. Leaving the shutter swinging in the wind, he struck a match to look for something to fasten the window. A puff of wind caused the match to go out.

Henry cursed under his breath, reached for a second match, struck it on the mantle board, and lit the lamp. The light flickered in the relentless onslaught of the wind. Finally the chimney settled the flame. Picking up the lamp, he went in search of a substitute latch. In the kitchen he found some small hemp rope, but he didn't think it was strong enough to hold. What would do the job? He couldn't think of anything for a moment. Finally he decided to see if he could find a nail.

The tool box near the kitchen door held his hammer and several small nails. Finding one large enough to hold against the wind was another matter. Holding the lamp as close as he could to the box, Henry found a twenty-penny nail. That ought to do the trick, he thought.

Returning to the fireplace, he set his light on the mantle next to the flapping shutter. The wind swung the shutter as Henry tried to grab it. He cursed again as the wood slammed against his hand. For some unknown reason the wind seemed to slack. It was as if the fury had abated for the moment. Henry grasped the shutter, pulled it closed, and held it while he drove the nail through the brace and the side of the window jam. As soon as the job was complete, the wind roared again with all its fury.

Lois had remained in bed. She had John in her arms. Van sat beside her wide-eyed and wondering at the sound of the storm. He'd never heard or seen anything like it. John was asleep, oblivious to what was happening. A gust of wind caused the tin roof to rattle as if it were a tablecloth being shaken out after clearing the dishes.

Off in the distance, Lois thought she could hear a loud noise. "What's that sound?" She called to Henry.

Henry paused, drying his body with a towel, and listened.

"Sounds like a freight train, but it can't be," he answered.

The noise grew louder. Henry couldn't figure it out. Then a thought crossed his mind. He's heard his grandpa Hester talk about being near a tornado once. That was how he'd described it--sounds like a freight train.

"It's a tornado," Henry shouted above the sound.

"Wh . . . What can we do?" Lois shouted in reply.

Henry tried to think. It wasn't easy. Sometimes in an emergency, one finds that time seems to slow. Henry felt that sensation now.

"Quick!" He shouted. "Get the boys and come with me."

Lois did as she was told. Henry went to the glass window that separated the large room from the shed on the porch. He pulled the bottom window up with a slam and helped Lois and the boys through the small opening. This room had no outside window--not even a shutter. They would be safer in here if the tornado hit. Henry joined his family in the small room.

Gusts of wind seemed to shake the old house off its foundation. Henry could have sworn he felt the house shift, but it held together. The roaring sound came nearer, rising to a crescendo. A gust of wind spun the top of the huge oak near the chimney.

Henry could hear as the tree hit the side of the house. It was hard to tell, but he thought it might have hit the chimney.

While they waited an eternity, the noise passed on to the east. Then the rain came with renewed vigor. It was as if the sky had fallen with all the fury of an ocean washing over the house. A drip started over Henry's head. He decided it was time to return to the main room.

Dawn revealed how close the tornado had come. Through the open shutter, Henry could see the huge oak laying across the yard fence. A crack in the side of the chimney showed where the tree had knocked the structure apart as it fell. Fortunately, the side of the house was undamaged.

The eye of the hurricane hovered over the house for some hour or so, then the storm renewed its onslaught. No further damage was done as the winds found their way to the northeast. Late that afternoon, the sun came out. The world lay washed and clean. Scattered debris was the only reminder that the storm had passed that way.

* * *

The Allies were closing the gap in Germany. In late March of 1945, they had slashed halfway across Germany. A month later Hitler committed suicide to escape capture by Soviet troops. German troops began surrendering all over Europe. On May seventh, the German high command surrendered unconditionally. The war in Europe was over.

Henry received the news with joy. That meant his friend Willy might be coming home soon. However, there was still fighting in the Pacific. His brother was there. It remained to be seen whether he would make it home alive.

News reports began to filter in that thousands of prisoners were being liberated from the Nazi camps. The stories carried accounts of the brutality Americans had received at the hand of their captors. Many people found these accounts hard to believe, but they also began to hear about the Nazi death camps. "How could this be?" They asked themselves. Surely civilized people wouldn't do such things.

Henry began to think the Germans might have tortured Willy or put him to death on a whim. These thoughts troubled him until he couldn't sleep at times. He had to know the fate of his friend.

On August sixth, the United States dropped an atomic bomb on Japan. Three days later a larger bomb hit Nagasaki leaving it in ruins. The war had come home to the Japanese. Six days later the Japanese surrendered unconditionally. World War II was over.

Men were returning from the war. It seemed every day brought news of the homecoming of somebody, but Henry still did not know Willy's fate. Finally, Willy's father let it be known he'd heard from his son. He was on board ship headed for the United States. That was good news indeed.

It was hard to wait. Henry wanted to shake his friend's hand and welcome him home. In late October, Willy came home on the train. Henry joined the Varnadore family as they met Willy.

Everybody waited expectantly. The train came to a halt. A conductor stepped down, unfolded the step, and stood back as passengers descended from the train. Henry spotted Willy through the window before he reached the door. He was thin as a rail, but he seemed all right.

Willy stopped at the top step, looked over the crowd and made a dash for his mother. Henry watched the reunion with tears brimming in his eyes. After hugging his mother, Willy turned to his father. They exchanged a warm handshake--hugging was considered unmanly. Will looked him up and down.

"You all right, boy?" He asked with genuine concern in his voice.

"Yeah, Pa. I'm fine."

Willy turned to Henry, "Pard, it's good to see you," he said, extending his hand.

"Same here, Hoss," Henry said quietly.

Willy looked around. "It's good to be home. There was times when I thought I wouldn't ever see this place again. The old town don't look bad from here."

"Look," Henry said. "I'll just let you be with your folks for now, but how about us gettin' together later?"

"Sounds good to me, Pard. I'll see you later."

The next Saturday, Henry met Willy on Main Street. They exchanged greetings, chatted about one thing and another, and were running out of chat when Henry said:

"How long since you've seen a movie?"

Willy thought for a minute. "I saw some on the ship coming over, but it's been a coon's age since I took one in here in town."

"Would you like to go? I think Charles Starret's playin'."

"Sure. To tell you the truth, I don't much care what's playin'."

"Come on. I'm treating."

When the movie was over, Henry and Willy headed for the Busy Bee Cafe. It was their favorite place to hangout and chat.

They ordered hamburgers and coffee. While they waited for their order, a small group of men came in and seated themselves at a nearby table. One of them turned and looked at Willy with a scrutinizing glance.

"Hey, boys, it's Willy Varnadore," he said. "When'd you get back?" He asked.

"Few days ago."

"Tell us about the war," the man said.

"I'd rather not talk about it," Willy replied.

"You kill any Japs?"

Willy sighed. This old boy didn't seem to know his geography, he thought. "I was in Europe."

"Oh, then you was fightin' Germans."

"That's right."

"You kill any of 'em?"

"I don't know. I don't want to talk about it."

The man grinned. "Some war hero. Can't even tell us what happened."

Willy ignored the barb. He considered getting up, but thought better of it. Might as well get this thing settled here and now.

"Look, I don't like to talk about it. I'm not sure whether I killed anybody or not. War ain't like you see it in the movies. It's hell. You're trying to stay alive. That's all you give a damn about."

The waitress brought their food. Willy tasted his gingerly. It needed a little flavoring.

"Pass the salt, please."

Henry handed the shaker to Willy. Willy's eyes had grown hard--a look Henry had rarely seen before.

The man at the next table wouldn't let it rest. "What'd you have to eat?"

Willy ignored him. Biting into his sandwich once more, he chewed thoughtfully. The meat tasted all right.

"Come on, soldier," the inquisitor demanded. "Tell us something about what happened. Most of us didn't get that much news."

"Why didn't you join the army?"

"My Pa put in for a deferment for me. Said it was a hardship case."

"If you'd been there, you wouldn't ask."

"It was that bad?"

"It was that bad and worse."

"Say, you was a German prisoner, weren't you?"

"Uh, huh."

"What was it like?"

Willy was about to get up and walk out when Mr. Solomon who owned the local grocery warehouse came through the cafe door.

"Come 'ere," one of the men at the table said to Solomon.

"This here's Willy Varnadore. He's just back from the war."

Solomon sidled over to the table. "Do I know you?" He asked Willy.

"I'm not sure. I've seen you around, but I can't recollect us meeting."

Solomon scratched his head. "Now, I know. It was my boy, Sammy. He said there was another boy from Baxley in the camp with him. Did you know Sammy?"

Willy hesitated. He didn't want to answer.

"Please," Solomon begged. "My boy died over there. I want to know what happened."

Willy studied the old man's face. "I don't think you want to hear this, Mr. Solomon."

"Yes, I do. Tell me."

Willy decided to evade the question. After all, he didn't want the man to hear the truth from him.

"Mr. Solomon, we had it hard in that camp. Men were dying every day from something or other. It could have been the food. God knows it was bad enough."

"Food? What kind of food?"

Willy sighed, "Liver. They fed us lots of liver."

"Liver?"

"That's right. Why?"

"My boy didn't eat nothing that weren't kosher. He was raised that way."

That was his problem, Willy thought, but he didn't say it.

"Why liver?" Solomon demanded.

"I reckon it was what they had the most of."

"Where did they get it? Was it tainted?"

Willy didn't want to say what he was about to say, but the old man stood there demanding to know the circumstances under which his son had died.

"We weren't quite sure where the liver came from, but we suspected it was human liver."

"They fed my boy human liver?"

"That's right."

"How do you know it was human?"

"I don't."

"Well?"

"Look, Mr. Solomon, the Germans were killing people all the time. When a man died they took him to this building in the compound. We never saw him again, but an awful lot of meat was taken from that same building. That's why we think we were eating human liver."

The old man snorted. "Human liver! I can't believe it! Why would they do such a thing?"

Willy didn't try to answer this time. He figured the old man had enough to deal with as it was. It was just as well; he didn't want to talk about it anyway.

"How did my boy die?" Solomon asked.

Willy stood up, laid a dime on the table for the waitress, and turned to Henry. "You ready?" He asked.

Henry nodded his assent.

Willy started for the door.

Solomon interrupted him again. "You were there. I want to know how my boy died."

Willy turned, looked Solomon in the eye, and said, "As near as I can tell, he starved himself to death."

"No! He wouldn't do that! Not my Sammy!"

"Like you said, Mr. Solomon, I was there. But if you already knew the answer why the hell did you ask me the question?"

* * *

Henry was winding his way through the woods. It was a pleasant day. The sun shown brightly. There was hardly a hint of a breeze. Olan had taken the day off, so Henry was alone with his thoughts. Such times helped him reason through things.

He often dwelt on the things Willy had said. War and its

horrors were hard to understand, but he understood taking a stand for your independence. He'd been doing that since he was a small boy. People would take advantage of you if they could. You had to be on your guard all the time. That was one reason he'd found it so hard to get along with bosses. They tried to intimidate you. If they had some power over you, it was harder for you. Henry had had more than a bellyful of that. That was why he was chipping boxes now.

Henry came out of the brushy trail. A grove of trees stood on the hill not more than a hundred feet away. I'll chip these before I go back to the branch, he thought. Walking over to the grove, Henry decided to hang his hack and rest for a spell. He sat under a large pine and rested with his back braced against the tree.

As he sat there, his gaze lifted to the pine's needles. If there was any wind, it didn't show. He couldn't imagine a more peaceful setting. Slowly, Henry became aware of a sound. He turned his head. The sound seemed to be coming from the tree or maybe the grove.

It sounded as if the trees were breathing. They are breathing, he thought. For several minutes, Henry sat still listening to the quiet sound. Strangely enough, he'd never noticed this phenomenon before. It was as if he was communing with the trees. A strange sense of peace passed over Henry as he sat there. Where else could a man find such solitude? Certainly not in a crowd or a city! Such things were impossible.

This is where I belong, he thought. Here I'm my own man. I don't have to answer to anyone. Peace is worth more than money. You can't buy peace.

Henry stood, reached for his hack, and chipped the face on the tree he'd been leaning against. He checked his work, nodded with satisfaction, and walked to the next tree.

Epilogue

Forty years later, Van stood over his father's grave. As he gazed about, the shade of a row of pines cast a long evening shadow over him and the grave. These pines were all that remained of a spring head that had once flowed through what was now known as Omega Cemetery. The neatly trimmed grass beneath them belied the fact that those same trees had once been surrounded by gallberry bushes.

A sigh of wind came through the trees--then silence. "Daddy," Van said to his father. "You're certainly buried in an appropriate place. Those trees cast their shadow just right this time of day."

Van stood listening to the quiet afternoon. On the highway, a truck disturbed the stillness, but after it passed Van thought he heard the slightest sound coming from the trees.

On any given day you can stand by Henry's grave and hear the "call of the pines."

River Pilot

By William V. Reynolds

In 1908 the waterways were still the best way to ship timber to market. A time-honored tradition was the rafting of timber down the Ocmulgee-Oconee-Altamaha River system. The men who did this were a hardy lot. It took a special breed of men to survive the challenges of this life.

River Pilot is the story of one of these men, William Augustus Reynolds (Gus). According to his father, Gus has river mud in his veins. Together with other men of his time, Gus struggles to make a living as they cut trees from the river swamp, build rafts, and float them down river.

Eva Hester meets Gus at a family reunion, and they are eventually married. Together they work to raise a family. Eva struggles with loneliness and anxiety as she waits for Gus to return from the river.

With the strong support of Gus and his family, she is able to build a good life until the day tragedy intervenes. For the first time in her life, Eva must face the facts of life and deal with them the best that she can.

Hard Times
The Sequel to River Pilot

In the 1920s, there was no Social Security, no aid to dependent children, and no welfare. A widow with children was either dependent on her family or friends for support. In some instances, this wasn't a great handicap, but for the laboring class, it was especially burdensome.

This was the world, as Eva Hester Reynolds knew it, when she was left alone by the death of her husband. There was little she could do to earn a living. Women were commonly discriminated against in business matters and other areas of everyday life. An unmarried woman, widowed or single, was considered a threat to those women who still had the security of a husband, and they were determined that those "available" women be married.

Eva, thinking that this might be the better way, decides to remarry, but it may have been a mistake. Where she had found peace and contentment with her first husband, there was now a battle of the wills. To further complicate matters, the nation was caught in the worst economic crunch in its history.

Hard Times is the story of a family's survival during one of the darkest eras of the 20th century, *The Great Depression.*

Meet the Author

Biography

William V. Reynolds was born the son of a sharecropper in South Georgia. His early years were spent in a transition period -- not quite primitive, not quite modern. As a result, he has firsthand knowledge of farming with a mule, picking corn by hand, harvesting cotton and tobacco, killing and dressing meat, and a host of other things that one learns growing up in a rural community.

He graduated from high school at age 17 and began his college education at a small South Georgia college. He later graduated with a bachelor's degree in mathematics education. During his teaching career, he also earned a masters and education specialist degree.

Since retiring he has been writing historical fiction as well as other works. He finds historical fiction to be his favorite area, because he gets to speculate on what life might have been like for the people of a given era. Even in college, he developed an interest in history, but he didn't feel that he could make a living teaching it. He enjoys reading history, not as dry facts, but about the people who made it happen. A friend of his used to say: "History is not dates and places. It's people. If you want to study history, study the people who made it."

Although teaching has been his profession, he has had a variety of experiences. Besides growing up on the farm, he has worked as a movie projectionist, theater manager, shipping clerk, and truck driver. He is also an ordained minister although he does not hold a seminary degree.

He has traveled extensively throughout the United States. One of his books is a travelogue based on a trip that he and his wife took through the western U.S. Other than traveling, his favorite sport is fishing. He says, "There's nothing more relaxing than drifting down a lazy river while flipping a bug under the bushes. Large bream and red-breast lay there waiting to play tug-of-war with the angler who has the patience to wait."

Honors

Double Eagle Enterprises proudly announces that William V. Reynolds, the author of *River Pilot* and *Hard Times*, has recently been recognized in **Who's Who in U.S. Writers, Editors & Poets**. It is a Biographical Dictionary of the most influential writers, authors, and poets of the 20th Century and promising, noteworthy writers of the 21st century who through a combined goal have influenced thought through words. Major libraries, researchers, journalists, educators, employers, businesses, publishers, magazines, public relations agencies, and other literary institutions rely on this prestigious publication as the primary source of information on writers of vision, diplomacy, aptitude, investigative journalism, poetic passion, and scholarly wisdom. Those who have been nominated for this honor have come to the attention of the media, publishers, agents, and readers throughout the country because of their contributions to literacy, literature, creative visions, and imagination through the written word.